ADVANCE PRAISE FOR
A NEW LEAF

"With great clarity, A *New Leaf* offers a sweeping and important view of today's changing attitudes toward marijuana."

—Amy Wilentz, author of *The Rainy Season*
and *Farewell, Fred Voodoo*

"A comprehensive look at the political and social revolution taking place that is leading to the day when marijuana will inevitably be legal in all fifty states. The authors take us on a journey to meet the people on the front lines of this transformation."

—Dale Maharidge, co-author of the Pulitzer Prize–
winning *And Their Children After Them* and
author of *Bringing Mulligan Home*

"Martin and Rashidian have crafted a superb, lucid look at why cannabis prohibition has hurt the world in ways many of us would have never guessed. They put a human face on sterile laws and policies and provide the most up-to-date information on today's controversies about the plant. They treat readers to an accessible and well-documented explanation of the backhanded and thoughtless way we have arrived at our current predicament and emphasize that thorough and considerate approaches are our only way out."

—Mitch Earleywine, author of
Understanding Marijuana

"A *New Leaf* is a wonderful read for anyone who wishes to have a better idea of how dastardly this prohibition has been, particularly in its last years. Fortunately, it is now virtually over and what we are seeing is a culture desperately trying to find accommodations to this 'new leaf' on the block."

—Dr. Lester Grinspoon, associate professor emeritus
of psychiatry at Harvard Medical School and author
of *Marihuana Reconsidered* and *Marihuana: The
Forbidden Medicine*

"I thought I knew everything about cannabis and its journey toward legalization. Well, A *New Leaf* proved me wrong. I emphatically recommend this eye-opening book to everyone, especially those who believe they know the entire story. A must-read."

—Neill Franklin, executive director of Law
Enforcement Against Prohibition

A NEW LEAF

The End of Cannabis Prohibition

Alyson Martin and Nushin Rashidian

THE NEW PRESS

NEW YORK
LONDON

Requests for permission to reproduce selections from this book should be mailed to:
Permissions Department, The New Press, 120 Wall Street, 31st floor, New York, NY
10005.

Published in the United States by The New Press, New York, 2014
Distributed by Perseus Distribution

LIBRARY OF CONGRESS CATALOGING-IN-PUBLICATION DATA

Martin, Alyson.
    A new leaf : the end of cannabis prohibition / Alyson Martin and Nushin Rashidian.
    pages cm
    Includes bibliographical references.
    ISBN 978-1-59558-920-0 (pbk.) -- ISBN 978-1-59558-929-3 (e-book) 1. Marijuana
--Government policy--United States. 2. Drug control--History--United States. 3.
Marijuana--Therapeutic use--United States. 4. Drug legalization--United States.
I. Rashidian, Nushin. II. Title.
HV5822.M3M376 2014
363.450973--dc23
                                                      2013034220

The New Press publishes books that promote and enrich public discussion and understanding of the issues vital to our democracy and to a more equitable world. These
books are made possible by the enthusiasm of our readers; the support of a committed
group of donors, large and small; the collaboration of our many partners in the independent media and the not-for-profit sector; booksellers, who often hand-sell New
Press books; librarians; and above all by our authors.

www.thenewpress.com

Book design and composition by Bookbright Media
This book was set in Goudy Oldstyle

Printed in the United States of America

10 9 8 7 6 5 4 3 2 1

For our parents

CONTENTS

INTRODUCTION

Along Came Mary

A nother prohibition is ending. On November 6, 2012, voters in Colorado and Washington were the first in the world to successfully challenge nearly a century of bad policy and misconceptions about cannabis.

In downtown Seattle, the Hotel Ändra was dressed white and blue, the team colors of Washington State's Initiative 502 campaign. Supporters hoping for a victory, cannabis legalization, walked into a smartly decorated ballroom and picked up bumper stickers and pins. Activists and politicians anxiously buzzed about to pass the hours. Alison Holcomb, then drug policy director for the ACLU of Washington State and the woman leading the state's legalization push, wore a black blazer and fuchsia shirt. She paced and whispered to her colleagues, scouring tablet screens for clues long before votes had been counted. At this early point in the night, the expressions on the brunette's angular face moved so fluidly between nervousness, confusion, and excitement that it was difficult for photographers to capture a representative portrait.

Around 7 P.M., the owner of one of the largest and most successful medical cannabis dispensaries in the country arrived. Steve DeAngelo was unmistakable even in a crowd, with his signature long, tight pigtail braids and dark fedora. He listened as a woman stood closely and told her story. DeAngelo got that a lot. Earlier that year, he was the star of his own Discovery Channel show, *Weed Wars*. His two Harborside Health Centers are in the Bay Area, but he had a soft spot for Seattle. Just a few months before, he had spoken at Seattle's well-known Hempfest, attended by tens of thousands each year. "I've been working on this issue for my entire life. . . . And I know tonight, when 502 passes, that there's going to be a whole lot of angels dancing in heaven," DeAngelo said, his eyes flooding. "It's not very often that I find myself at a loss for words, but I'm grasping to describe the magnitude of the emotion that I'm dealing with right now."

Meanwhile, 1,330 miles away at Denver's Casselman's Bar and Venue, hundreds of Amendment 64 supporters squeezed shoulder-to-shoulder, increasingly unable to remain composed in front of the many live cameras.[1] It could have been a St. Patrick's Day gathering; many people wore green, in one way or another. A man in an emerald dress shirt held a green and white YES ON 64 sign. He walked up to Mason Tvert, a face of the Amendment 64 campaign, and extended the sign. The stout millennial scrawled his signature, handed back the memento, and smiled sheepishly before walking away to fix his red tie.

In the previous five years, the Rocky Mountain state's medical cannabis industry had grown faster and more sophisticated than any other, earning a feature on *60 Minutes* and its own National Geographic show, *American Weed*. The state's nearly seven hundred dispensaries had grossed $186 million in sales and paid the state $5.4 million in sales taxes from mid-2011 to mid-2012.[2] Dispensary owners had combined typical American ingenuity and science to propel cannabis into the future. Using a process similar to coffee decaffeination, they had created a cannabis extract and stuffed it into a simple and smokeless e-cigarette-like contraption; it looked like the intersection of Venice Beach and Apple. Colorado was serious about cannabis.

Nearby, a woman and man embraced and smiled calmly. By the time 9 percent of precincts had reported and people saw the numbers from KDVR Fox31 Denver, there was loud whistling, clapping, and yelling: Amendment 64 was ahead 52 percent to 48. As the imminent reality of cannabis legalization swept the room, the racket swelled to a roar. A man repeatedly cheered and pumped his arms as if trying to lasso something.

When it appeared a final call might soon be made, people took photographs and videos; hugs abounded. A man who sported a tie-dyed shirt and a balding crown with long hair dangling past his nape walked around aimlessly. Near the cameras, a lady with a foam cannabis leaf over her hand joined a guy who smiled, mouth agape, and made the "hang loose" sign to whoever tuned in to watch the revelry. This man with impressive sideburns held a YES ON 64 sign above his head and beamed. The rounds of high fives were never-ending.

It was a celebration to remember. The crowd began to chant "Sixty-four! Sixty-four! Sixty-four!" They punched the air with clenched fists and clapped along to "Co-lor-a-do."

Finally, Tvert took the stage. The room quieted.

"I'm so proud to be up here saying that we are standing in the first state in our nation—" The crowd noise drowned out his speech. Tvert tried again. "For a lot of people, it's always been very difficult to talk about this issue. And hopefully tonight, after this initiative has passed and demonstrated that a majority of Coloradans think it's time to end marijuana prohibition, people will not be scared anymore. . . . To know that, come this time next year, there will not be ten thousand arrests for marijuana is a good, good feeling." The whooping and merriment continued.

For the first time, in the state of Colorado, ten thousand people would not be handcuffed, taken to a police station, and charged for simple cannabis possession. Ten thousand people would not have their permanent records tarnished by a misdemeanor drug charge. Ten thousand people would not have to explain that possession charge to a potential employer or landlord.

Brian Vicente, a lawyer who advocated for medical cannabis in Colorado for nearly a decade and helped draft Amendment 64, took the stage. "Tonight we made history. This is something you're going to tell your kids about," Vicente said. "Marijuana prohibition started in 1937. The first person arrested was in Colorado." The crowd booed. "Colorado fucking turned this thing around tonight." And with the f-word came gaiety.

Back in Seattle, Holcomb stood at a podium. Voters in Colorado had decided in favor of cannabis: Amendment 64 had passed. Holcomb looked stunned, but happy. She rallied the people before her. "I don't know how you guys feel about being number two, but I would be okay with that," she joked.

Until that moment, the question was whether one of these initiatives would pass. Now there was potential for two. Still, there was no relief from the tension. An initial report from King County showed that, with approximately 250,000 ballots returned, Initiative 502 was trailing slightly at 49.23 percent to 50.77. Several people groaned. The mood dampened. "It's all right," someone yelled. "Oh, wait a second, they also have Mitt Romney winning at this point," Holcomb laughed. "So these obviously are early ballots. . . . I think, hopefully, we're going to see these numbers improve as the night goes on."

Many key supporters of cannabis legalization—some expected, some, including Seattle city attorney Pete Holmes, perhaps atypical—surrounded Holcomb in anticipation.

"There are? There are numbers? Let's see, let's see, let's see," Holcomb said, away from the microphone. "Make way for the screen! We're going to get some results. Oh, you guys are killing me. It's killing me." The vote percentages popped up on the screen. Holcomb struggled to make an announcement while everyone in the room swiped at their smartphones and tablets.

"All right, I'm looking at something on a phone right here that's for King County that says Initiative 502 in King County has earned 63.82 percent of the vote." The cheering and applause doubled. The most populous county in Washington had voted yes, and the rest of the state would likely follow.

"Thank you, thank you all. Thank you. All right, I'm going to go ahead and just give my victory speech right now because I can't—" Holcomb said, her speech broken by an ovation. "I am so proud and so humbled to stand among the voters of the great state of Washington who have this day taken an historic vote. I am so proud of the very careful consideration, the very thoughtful reflection, and the very robust and animated conversation that has gone on around this groundbreaking decision. And ultimately, I'm most proud that, despite controversy and uncertainty, Washington State exhibited tremendous leadership in reexamining a failed policy and being willing to examine promising alternatives.

"Today, the state of Washington looked at seventy-five years of a national marijuana prohibition and said it is time for a new approach," she continued. The state of Colorado felt the same way. And for the first time in history, so did 50 percent of Americans.[3]

Roger Roffman, professor emeritus at the University of Washington, cannabis-dependence treatment professional, and co-sponsor of Initiative 502, took the podium and said, "Finally, we are about to harness what we've learned through science. New marijuana tax dollars will flow to communities throughout our state for drug prevention programs that work. We'll also see new revenues for education about marijuana that is based on science, not on ideology. . . . We will begin using data rather than wishful thinking to measure how well our efforts to prevent marijuana harm actually work . . . because marijuana tax revenues will be allocated to evaluation and research."

Washington's Initiative 502 campaign was known for the diverse group it brought together in support of cannabis reform, uniting everyone from hippies to politicians to travel guide Rick Steves. At the podium that night, Steves was as dynamic as when he hosts his television series *Rick Steves' Europe*. Steves tells his mostly middle-aged American audience to be "temporary locals," and they listen, because he's charming and seems like a peer. Steves hosted a series of roundtable discussions with Holcomb called "Marijuana: It's Time for a Conversation," which no doubt helped pass the initiative.

"I'll tell you one thing, the whole country is going to wake up tomorrow and look at Washington State and Colorado," Steves said, "and recognize that this is the beginning of taking apart prohibition one state at a time."

Just before 9 P.M., the *Seattle Times* finally made the call that Initiative 502 passed. When it all became certain, Holcomb simply added, "Ladies and gentlemen, I don't know if you're aware of what's just happened, but effective December 6, 2012, if you are an adult twenty-one or older in the great state of Washington, you can no longer be arrested for possessing up to one ounce of marijuana." General mayhem ensued. "May I remind you, however, that I said December 6. Proceed at your own risk," she laughed and stepped away from the microphone.

When voters in Washington and Colorado closed the curtain, considered their choices, and punched the ballot on Election Day 2012, why did most choose cannabis legalization?

Over the past two decades, more Americans have been exposed to cannabis than at any other time in recent history. According to *The Path Forward*, a report co-authored by Colorado representative Jared Polis and Oregon representative Earl Blumenauer and released in February 2013, more than 106 million people now live where cannabis is legal for medical or general use.[4] As of April 2013, according to Pew Research, 77 percent of Americans believe cannabis can legitimately be medicine and a landmark majority, 52 percent, support legalization for general use.[5] Yet the federal government refuses to accept these broader societal shifts. Americans are, for the first time, truly weighing the harms of cannabis prohibition against the harms of cannabis. For example, prohibition has led to more than 8 million cannabis-related arrests in the last decade—of those, 88 percent were for mere possession.[6]

One reason for the change in public opinion is the education Americans have received from over twenty years of access to medical cannabis. The more often people saw the cannabis plant on TV screens, in newspapers, and, sometimes, down the street, the more comfortable they grew with the notion of legalization. When he led the reefer madness crusade to banish cannabis in 1937, Harry J. Anslinger, first commissioner of the U.S. Treasury Department's Federal Bureau of Narcotics, warned, "This drug is entirely the monster Hyde, the harmful effect of which cannot be measured."[7] But if cannabis now legally replaces or supplements conventional pharmaceuticals for an estimated 1 million Americans in twenty states and Washington, D.C., it's increasingly clear that it must not be as dangerous as we were—and, in some cases, continue to be—told.[8]

More Americans feel comfortable coming out about their cannabis use, too. Forty-eight percent of adults eighteen or older admit they tried cannabis at some point in their lives.[9] Popular culture has accurately reflected shifting views about the plant. Increased use and acceptance of cannabis for medical (and "medical") reasons might be why even Meryl Streep and Steve Martin could light a joint, party with the kids, and feast on chocolate croissants in the movie *It's Complicated* without controversy.

On top of that, numerous influential types have spoken in favor of reforming drug policy, including Arianna Huffington, founder of *Huffington Post*; Deepak Chopra, the man who made millions by making people feel better holistically; and Richard Branson, founder of the Virgin Group. All three sit on the honorary boards of the nation's foremost drug policy reform organization, the Drug Policy Alliance.[10] Year after year, cannabis continues to make the strangest bedfellows, uniting liberal Barney Frank and Tea Partier Ron Paul in Congress, for instance; they worked on two cannabis law reform bills and co-authored a letter to President Barack Obama to insist the federal government not intervene in states with cannabis laws.[11]

The economic and social implications of cannabis legalization, both domestic and international, have also become more apparent in recent years. As Americans clawed their way out of a recession, more and more states passed medical cannabis laws and, slowly, more brick-and-mortar storefronts emerged. It soon became obvious that there is money to be made. When budgets started to feel the recession pinch, voters wanted to harness the economic power of cannabis to mitigate the impact. Colorado earned $5.4 million from medical cannabis sales taxes between 2011 and 2012; California estimates annual sales tax revenues between $58 million and $105 million.[12] Now, with the passage of Initiative 502, voters in Washington have opened the door to over half a billion dollars in annual tax and fee revenue for their state, money that can be directed toward cannabis education, research, and dependence treatment, among other public health initiatives.[13] Voters in Colorado know that, beginning in 2014,

$40 million in tax dollars from general-use cannabis each year will be earmarked for schools.[14]

At the same time, the financial costs to curb this momentum and fight the domestic drug war are staggering. The White House National Drug Control Budget for 2014 noted that $9.6 billion of its total $25.4 billion is allocated to domestic law enforcement.[15] These resources are intended to stem the availability of drugs—but the money has not been wisely invested if nearly half of those law enforcement efforts result in the arrest of cannabis users, as has been the trend for years. Of the 1.53 million nonviolent nationwide drug arrests in 2011, 49.5 percent were for violations involving cannabis and an overwhelming 87 percent (or about 663,000) of those arrests were for minor charges involving possession.[16] Typically, nine cannabis possessors are arrested for every one dealer. In the meantime, cannabis use and availability have increased; the money has been tossed into the wind.

Voters have also started to connect the American appetite for cannabis to conflict beyond our borders. The United States spends over $5 billion each year to fight the international drug war, with an emphasis on Latin America.[17] Over the last decade, drug trafficking organizations in Mexico have become more violent, and an estimated sixty thousand people have been killed as the result of drug-related conflict.[18] If passed nationally, cannabis legalization in the United States would remove—and these are conservative estimates—roughly 30 percent of the at least $7 billion total profits these organizations receive from the illegal sale of drugs accross the border.[19] (Estimates on total profits and the share of cannabis vary; this isn't exactly an industry that files earnings reports.)

Americans also increasingly recognize the social costs of the domestic drug war on our fellow citizens. These millions of arrests, and the subsequent criminal record, often lead to loss of income, housing, child custody, and student financial aid. When voters in Colorado and Washington pulled the yes lever, they also spoke out against a system of entrenched racial inequity that is manifested and propagated through cannabis law enforcement. Across the country, blacks are nearly four times more likely than whites to be arrested for cannabis possession, even though they use cannabis at comparable rates.[20] Arrest statistics vary from city to city, but New York City provides an illuminating example because its law enforcement tactics have earned national attention and contribute to the state's having the highest number of cannabis possession arrests in the country. Between 2002 and 2013, the New York Police Department made 5 million stop-and-frisks, or unannounced police pat-downs, on the street with the stated intent of finding guns. Of all of those stopped, 86 percent were black or Latino—and 88 percent were innocent.[21] If police were looking for guns, they didn't find many: fewer than two-tenths of a percent (0.2 percent) of all stops resulted in guns found.[22] Due to these tactics, however, there has been an increase in cannabis possession arrests. In 2011, at the peak of stop-and-frisks in New York City, arrests for cannabis possession also peaked at 50,484.[23]

Forty years and $1 trillion later, only 4 percent of Americans support the war on drugs.[24]

With each new piece of information about potential tax revenue, skyrocketing arrests, and the racist nature of cannabis law enforcement, it was as if voters saw the color panels begin to match on the side of a Rubik's Cube. When cannabis legalization made it to the ballots in Washington State and Colorado, voters in those states essentially decided whether they wanted to spend billions of dollars to arrest millions of men and women while sending a massive check to drug cartels during an American economic crisis—all over a nontoxic substance that is less harmful and addictive than alcohol. On that election night, more than

3 million voters in those two states definitively said enough is enough.[25]

———∿∿∿———

Most people today cannot recall the tumultuous process by which Americans returned alcohol to the table after our first prohibition, but we are witnessing the similarly dramatic reintegration of cannabis into society. It seems that nothing can kill the cannabis plant: not seventy-five years of prohibition, nor decades of reefer madness, nor forty years of war. Today, cannabis is legal as medicine in nearly half the country, legal for personal use in two states, but remains illegal under the federal umbrella. This dissonance between federal and state law has created uniquely murky legal territory whereby people who follow state law can still face federal prosecution and decades in prison. How did we get here, and how will cannabis prohibition continue to unravel?

1

A PLANT BY ANY OTHER NAME

Cultivation of cannabis is illegal in Mississippi. After a typical raid, officers weigh the plants, sometimes roots and all. That water- and dirt-soaked weight is used to decide charges, which are heavy themselves and can involve felony counts and tens of thousands of dollars in fines. But in Oxford, Mississippi, there's an exception to this rule.

Most students at the University of Mississippi probably don't realize that just past a road called Confederate Drive and the Ole Miss Softball Complex, cannabis is grown right under their noses. And that's the point. The Coy W. Waller Laboratory Complex is tucked away from student foot traffic. There, within concrete walls—and, some years, in a nearby field guarded by barbed-wire fences and a watchtower—grows the only federally legal cannabis in the United States as part of the federal government's cannabis research program.

Inside, on first glance, the complex fits in on a typical college campus. In one room of the low building, a black and white bong decorated with a dragon design graces a bookshelf. An issue of *High Times* rests on a table in another. In a room at the end of a hall, a researcher sits near a Volcano vaporizer, a grinder, a scale, and bags of cannabis, watching and mocking a YouTube video for a pocket vaporizer. Much in the facility would look familiar to a grower, too: a poster with the steps for making an extract; trash cans labeled "regular garbage only" and "marijuana trash only"; plants trimmed down to the buds under intense grow lights; some seedlings small enough for an herb garden and others the size of an office plant; a box of Miracle-Gro; watering cans.

Just about everything else here would bring a cannabis enthusiast to tears. Boxes upon boxes of DEA-confiscated cannabis, mementos of many growers' worst days, await the gas chromatography machine for a potency test. A cabinet museum displays hashish and cannabis seized as long ago as the 1970s, anywhere from Humboldt to Miami. Freezer vaults with steering wheel–sized handles house hundreds of seeds Americans will never plant and barrels of ground cannabis for joints they will never smoke—because, outside of this facility, none of this is federally legal. The differences between cannabis in this facility's grow rooms, a dispensary in California, or a basement in the Midwest start and end with its legality.

The genus *Cannabis* L. includes the species *Cannabis sativa* L. and the subspecies *sativa* and *indica*.[1] The strength of the stalk of a cannabis plant depends on the particular plant's size and need for support; some grow wide while others tower over the farmer. The leaves form different shapes, but they always bear some resemblance to an outstretched hand. On some plants the leaves are spindly, like thin Grinchy fingers; these are the *sativa* variety. Other plants have fatter leaves; generally, these are *indicas*. At the joint of these leaves is an inflorescence, commonly called a bud. These dense clusters may appear dusted in a white or amber confection—the sticky trichomes from which the plant's resins are released. (These trichomes contain the therapeutic components of the plant.)

Anyone who steps into a grow room and is overwhelmed by light, sugary, citrus scents or deep, spicy, earthy smells has encountered terpenes. "It's the same thing that's responsible for the smell of tomatoes and peppers and pine and roses and geranium and oregano," said Mahmoud ElSohly, director of the federal Marijuana Project in Mississippi, overseen by the National Institute on Drug Abuse (NIDA) since 1968. Due to this large group of essential oil components, dried buds can smell like fuel (the "diesels"), banana bread (in the case of banana kush), honey, tobacco, chocolate, bubble gum, black licorice, and so on. The terpene limonene, for example, generates the citrusy smell of some cannabis buds and is also present in lemon rinds; alpha-pinene (α-pinene) is found in both buds and pine trees.[2] While terpenes have nothing to do with potency, what one ultimately experiences is rooted in a complex blend of odors that the cannabis plant emits based on the terpenes within. Some find these aromas enjoyable; others think they stink.

For a century, this fragrant flowering shrub has lived at the center of passions and politics. One ongoing debate seeks to resolve whether cannabis is a medicine. Twenty states and Washington, D.C., nearly half the country, have passed laws that allow their residents to consume whole plant cannabis for approved medical conditions. The federal government disagrees, maintaining that cannabis is not a medicine and is illegal for that and all other purposes. The cannabis at the federal research farm is grown not as medicine, but for medicine—a nebulous but crucial distinction that defines the discord between the state and federal stances toward this plant.

The role of cannabis in medicine extends much further back in time than the half century the U.S. government has operated this farm. It's challenging to pin the exact origin of cannabis use, but archaeologists have traced it as far back as the Neolithic period (4000 B.C.) in China.[3] According to ancient records, cannabis was used as a therapy for various diseases in the Roman

Empire, as well as across Africa and the Middle East.[4] Modern exploration of medical cannabis picked up in the early nineteenth century, when doctors began to identify the plant's therapeutic potential. William O'Shaughnessy, an Irish physician whose name remains synonymous with the origins of Western medical cannabis, published his findings after years of practicing medicine and surveying cannabis use in India.

In his 1843 report in *Provincial Medical Journal and Retrospect of the Medical Sciences*, O'Shaughnessy observed that cannabis acted as an effective appetite stimulant when taken in small doses and as a sedative in larger doses.[5] In a test, O'Shaughnessy gave a cannabis solution ("one grain of the resin of hemp") to three patients with rheumatism. Two hours later, he noted the following effects:

> At four, P.M., it was reported that one was becoming very talkative, was singing songs, calling loudly for an extra supply of food, and declaring himself in perfect health. The other two patients remained unaffected.
>
> At six, P.M., I received a report to the same effect, but stating that the first patient was now falling asleep.
>
> At eight, P.M., I was alarmed by an emergent note from Nobinchunder Mitter, the clinical clerk on duty, desiring my immediate attendance at the hospital, as the patient's symptoms were very peculiar and formidable. I went to the hospital without delay, and found him lying on his cot quite insensible, but breathing with perfect regularity, his pulse and skin natural, and the pupils freely contractile on the approach of light.

This patient was in a cannabis coma, which is about as harmful as a food coma. While this is technically an overdose, cannabis has no toxicity so there's no risk of death. The patient's limbs were moved in every direction, but he remained unresponsive. His story has a happy ending: within an hour, he was more alert, and within two, he was "perfectly well and excessively hungry."

In each of O'Shaughnessy's patients, the cannabis somehow alleviated the pain associated with rheumatism. O'Shaughnessy concluded, "My object is to have it extensively and exactly tested without favor or prejudice, for the experience of four years has established the conviction in my mind, that we possess no remedy at all equal to this in anti-convulsive and anti-neuralgic power."

Due in part to O'Shaughnessy's work, cannabis extracts and tinctures became a new therapeutic medicine used throughout Europe and, eventually, the United States. One tiny bottle from the late 1800s read, "100 gelatine-coated pills: extract cannabis." Its contents were prepared by McKesson & Robbins, manufacturing chemists based in New York.

Medical cannabis went on to be listed in the U.S. Pharmacopeia for almost one hundred years before its removal, in 1941, due to rampant misconceptions about the plant's dangers.[6] Even after that point, however, the intrigue surrounding cannabis's medicinal properties didn't wane.

Cannabinoid science, the study of the active compounds in cannabis, was born in the late 1930s. The plant is thought to contain more than one hundred cannabinoids, but the exact number is unknown, as is the biological activity of each compound and which cannabinoids come from which strains. American scientist Roger Adams and British scientist Alex Todd in 1940 first isolated cannabidiol (CBD), one of the most common cannabinoids found in the plant. Cannabinoid science then accelerated when Raphael Mechoulam, now a professor of medicinal chemistry and natural products at the Hebrew University of Jerusalem, re-isolated CBD and elucidated its structure in 1963.[7] Tetrahydrocannabinol (THC), the foremost cannabinoid and the only one known today to be psychoactive, was isolated and synthesized by Mechoulam and Yechiel Gaoni in 1964, when the team also partially synthesized CBD.[8]

The isolated and examined compounds of cannabis were instrumental in advancing knowledge about the plant's therapeutic value. At the time, and until recently, researchers were most interested in THC, even though CBD also had promise, partly because of its abundance in the plant and effect on humans. Published articles in the 1970s reported that THC warded off nausea associated with cancer treatments.[9] In 1980, the Food and Drug Administration (FDA) approved the National Cancer Institute to give oral synthetic THC to cancer patients undergoing chemotherapy. The program's participants reported mixed results: most felt some anti-emetic relief, but some also said they experienced undesired side effects, like confusion or dizziness. In 1985, the FDA approved Unimed Pharmaceuticals's Marinol capsules (synthetic THC) for cancer patients to manage the nausea associated with chemotherapy; several years later it was approved to help AIDS patients gain weight. The modern pharmaceuticalization of cannabis was under way.

But Marinol was a forerunner medicine with an unsuitable delivery method that contained only the psychoactive cannabinoid THC, to the discomfort of some patients. Patients have stated a preference for inhaled whole plant cannabis, rather than swallowing a capsule and waiting thirty minutes or more for the anti-emetic to kick in. A patient on the verge of vomiting can typically take one or two puffs from a joint, pipe, or vaporizer and the feeling will wash away. Unlike Marinol, the cannabis plant also provides a complete cocktail of psychoactive and nonpsychoactive therapeutic cannabinoids that work in synergy. Perhaps the best measure of Marinol's efficacy has been the introduction of laws in twenty states and Washington, D.C., to legalize the whole plant as medicine.

While the effects and uses of THC were explored, why and how it and other cannabinoids worked remained unknown until Allyn Howlett, PhD, now a professor at Wake Forest School of Medicine, first discovered a cannabinoid receptor in the brain. In the early 1980s, Howlett came across a Pfizer report on cannabinoids and pain. When the company dropped the project, Howlett contacted Pfizer to ask if it would donate its compounds so she could pick up the research. (This was back before researchers and academic institutions were encouraged to patent their work and profit from it.) Pfizer agreed and provided Howlett with an array of about sixty different compounds to test. At the time, researchers using THC in animal and human studies tended to think of it like alcohol. THC is a lipid-soluble compound, so it was hypothesized that it would penetrate plasma membranes and act like an anesthetic or perturb different kinds of proteins, as alcohol would. In those cases, neurons just stop communicating with each other, and that is when sedation and pain alleviation kick in.

After testing how cells in tissue cultures responded to THC, however, Howlett sensed another possibility. She thought there might be a system of receptors in cell membranes within the human body that, like mailboxes, would be able to receive "messages" in the form of cannabinoids. When present, THC would be brought into the cell and cause a reaction. Howlett's research led her, in the late 1980s, to discover a receptor in the brain to which THC binds. "When we discovered there was a receptor, of course it was very exciting because I think that lent some legitimacy to these kinds of compounds as actual medicinal compounds. It means that the body has a system that works through these kinds of receptors," Howlett said. "A lot more researchers became interested. It could explain a lot of things that were going on in different areas of the brain."

Daniele Piomelli, professor of anatomy and neurobiology at the University of California–Irvine, described a desert surrounding cannabinoid-based research after Mechoulam's discovery of THC—and a subsequent "boom" after Howlett found the cannabinoid receptor. The reason? More was understood about the mysterious plant's behavior in the body. "People had the weirdest ideas as to how THC worked. They thought it was a kind of soap—like a detergent that interacted with membranes and caused membranes to change their property, and this somehow changed the activity of the neurons. But in reality, things don't happen like this in nature. They never do," Piomelli said of the years before Howlett's breakthrough.

The two primary receptors—CB1 and CB2, as they later became named—can be thought of as cannabinoid-binding targets found from head to toe in the immune, central, and peripheral nervous systems. Some cannabinoids, like THC, behave like Velcro on these sites; others, like CBD, don't adhere as well. CB1 exists in great abundance in brain and neural cells, while CB2 receptors are found in the immune system.[10] Researchers are also beginning to find both receptors in organs and tissues throughout the body, and they are trying to understand what those messages say in each cell type.

But what use is a mailbox without any mail? The discovery of receptors indicated the strong likelihood that an endogenous ligand, or naturally occurring binding molecule, must also exist to be sent to the receptors upon demand. William Devane, one of Howlett's students, went to Israel to work with Mechoulam. There, in late 1992, they discovered the human body's own production of a cannabinoid—an *endo*cannabinoid.[11] They called this endocannabinoid anandamide, a name derived from the Sanskrit word for bliss. This was fitting because anandamide works through the same pathways that offer feelings of security, comfort, or happiness that cause humans to seek social interaction, cozy homes, and sex. The purpose of those good feelings is to keep the species strong. A second endocannabinoid—with a less memorable name, 2-arachidonylglycerol (2-AG)—was also discovered. The network became known as the endocannabinoid system.

This system of receptors and endocannabinoids is present from before birth and acts as a motherboard to help the body control mood and appetite, for example. According to a 2010 report from the Center for Medicinal Cannabis Research at the University of California, San Diego, the endocannabinoid system is "implicated in nervous system excitability, movement, analgesia, neuroprotection, and feeding behaviors, including newborn suckling."[12] At any given time, the system is at work; receptors are activated by either the body's own production of endocannabinoids or by cannabinoids like THC or CBD.[13] Endocannabinoids are fascinating modulators that work like a dimmer switch for bioregulation. Anandamide and 2-AG operate "on demand": they are produced and released when the body needs them, perhaps during times of emotional stress.

In an article published in June 2000 in *Trends in Pharmacological Sciences*, a group of researchers, including Piomelli, noted, "It would be surprising if such a prominent signaling system, which gives every indication of serving key physiological functions in the CNS [central nervous system] and in peripheral tissues, will fail to prompt the development of new medicines in the not too distant future."[14] The study of the endocannabinoid system continues to be a pioneering field. And without the cannabis plant as a guide, it is likely that researchers still would not know about this vital human system.

For those wondering, there's no comparable high in the natural endocannabinoid process. We get high when cannabinoids within cannabis, primarily THC, interact with the human body's endocannabinoid system. Essentially, plant cannabinoids send unsolicited messages to receptors that cannot tell the difference from a bona fide message (an endocannabinoid, like anandamide). While endocannabinoids keep humans stable, plant cannabinoids make them feel more than satisfied, or high. Most people don't think about their endocannabinoid system when they inhale—or that cannabis, which is often called a simple weed, seems made to interact with it.

The common way to consume cannabis is to smoke the dried bud from a pipe or bong or rolled in a joint. Some people, especially those with lung problems or compromised immune systems, prefer to use vaporizers, which heat cannabis (or prepared cannabis oil) to a temperature that forces trichomes, the sticky white or amber flecks on cannabis buds that are filled with cannabinoids, away from the plant and into the vapors. These vapors are clean and smooth, and devoid of the hot, scratchy smoke one can inhale through a joint or pipe.

As soon as cannabis is inhaled, a chain reaction commences. The cannabinoids move quickly from mouth to lungs and through the alveoli into the bloodstream, which then carries them to organs throughout the body. There, the cannabinoids bind to receptors in various cells, influencing the activity of those cells. This all happens very quickly: cannabinoids are so rapidly absorbed that one can take a small puff and feel a lightness seconds later.

What does it feel like to be high? The experience often depends on the person. Some people who consume too much become marooned on their couches, starfishing the evening away. Someone with severe anxiety who consumes the right strain of cannabis may find that his self-critical executive function shuts off; suddenly, he is more outgoing and personable. Just as there are happy, sad, angry, tired, and energetic drunks, the spectrum of cannabis users is wide. Additionally, different subspecies—and strains within those subspecies—of cannabis have unique effects. *Sativas* are often described as energizing, bright, and mentally stimulating, while *indicas* are mellow and sometimes heavy. Most cannabis consumed is a hybrid.

Cannabis's effects are also dependent on dose. In the same way that there's a difference between a glass of wine and ten shots of whiskey, there's a big difference between a puff from a pipe and a hit from a six-foot bong. If too much cannabis is consumed, one may experience unpleasant effects; agitation and anxiety are common, especially for those predisposed to such feelings. Deliberate adjustment of dosage, or titration, is key and the couch-lock is not inevitable. Though some may have a negative experience, no one will die from a cannabis overdose. No one ever has. In fact, an overdose looks quite like a nap, and there's also no hangover period.

Because cannabis is fat- and alcohol- (but not water-) soluble, food makes an able vehicle for consumption. When consumed with food, cannabis's effects are longer-lasting, sometimes more intense, and can take an hour, more or less depending on each person, to kick in. Ingested cannabinoids travel through the digestive system. Instead of taking the typical route of, say, a burrito, the cannabinoids leave the stomach to be metabolized in the liver in what is referred to as first pass hepatic absorption.[15] The euphoric feeling is often transferred more to the body than the head, and it usually lasts longer than when cannabinoids reach the bloodstream through the lungs. While inhaled cannabis is felt immediately and the effects fade within an hour or so, the effects of ingested cannabis can last an afternoon.

Cannabinoids translate differently in the human body when cannabis is used as a medicine. The same cannabinoids that might cause a healthy person to have the munchies encourage someone with AIDS to eat. Someone who smokes for pleasure probably wouldn't notice the same nausea relief as a patient undergoing chemotherapy. "It would be useful to provide a drug like cannabis in an event where you want some of those effects to take place," Howlett said, in reference to the pain relief and sedation for those who need it. "That would probably be an excellent drug to use in a hospice setting."

Patients often say that cannabis mostly disassociates them from the pain, which is placed in another room instead of eliminated. Diane Riportella, who died on August 31, 2012, was a former marathon runner in the late stages of amyotrophic lateral sclerosis (ALS), often called Lou Gehrig's disease. Her once strong legs stopped working as the disease made its way up her body; her gastrocnemius muscles and hamstrings shrank away from their bones. "I have a medicine cabinet that would be a junkie's dream. I'm on morphine. I'm on lorazepam, sleeping pills. I'm on everything. But my best time when I'm real [anxious]— and I have a lot of anxiety—I just smoke. It just makes me calm. And when I have a partner, she makes me laugh," Riportella said in her bed, as she and her aide laughed.

Riportella struggled with ALS since her diagnosis in 2007, and she didn't understand why her life had taken such an unexpected and difficult turn. "I ask why sometimes," she said, beginning to cry. "I feel like I'm getting punished, but I know I'm not. I don't know why me. And the only answer everybody can say: that it's bigger than me." Riportella's aide had recently moved in with Riportella and her husband to help with the advancing illness. The aide lit and held a pipe filled with cannabis. Riportella inhaled, leaned back, exhaled, and smiled about ten seconds later. "I don't know," Riportella said in a thick, comic accent, smirking. She was louder than before and seemed to find strength from the puff. "If you hear me say, 'I don't know,' that's the guy from My Big Fat Greek Wedding." Her aide laughed and said, "She's trying to make it seem like I'm the only person who's funny when I'm high. She's funny when she's high, too. She's even funnier."

An Oxford University study released in December 2012 confirmed Riportella's and other patients' experiences.[16] For the

Diane Riportella, a New Jersey resident with late-stage amyotrophic lateral sclerosis, is shown moments after she smoked medical cannabis. ALYSON MARTIN

study, subjects were given THC pills. Then they rubbed one of two creams on their legs, either a placebo or a cream that contained 1 percent capsaicin, the ingredient in chili peppers that makes them burn. The subjects reported that the pain didn't necessarily go away after consuming a THC pill—it just didn't bother them as much. MRI imaging of the subjects' brains supported their reports. There was less activity shown in the amygdala and the anterior midcingulate cortex areas of the brain, which are associated with the emotional side of pain. The study showed that there's more to pain management than physical pain relief. Pain distraction can be just as essential.

While THC took center stage for many decades, there has been a resurgence of interest in the first discovered cannabinoid, cannabidiol (CBD). Its therapeutic properties range from anti-inflammatory to analgesic to anti-spasm, but unlike THC it is precisely high-less.[17] Some who use cannabis for medicinal relief do not necessarily want the mental effects along with the physical, and CBD can promise that. Patients in states with medical cannabis laws have recently taken a deeper interest in CBD, but that was not always the case. The majority of cannabis use over the last half century has been recreational, and because those users demanded plants abundant in THC, the underground market created cannabis-to-get-you-high. Growers bred high-THC plants with such gusto that they nearly choked out CBD. Now, a firm in Israel, where medical cannabis is legal, has produced a strain of cannabis with trace amounts of THC and plenty of CBD.[18] Researchers are increasingly focused on CBD as they understand more about its potential.

The UK-based GW Pharmaceuticals changed the conventional pharmaceutical formula with an increased role for CBD.[19] Previously, cannabinoid-based medicine was synthetic or included only THC. The GW product Sativex is the first cannabinoid-based medicine that is created directly from cannabis plants (grown by GW in secret greenhouse locations in England) and uses equal parts THC and CBD. Sativex is taken through an oral spray and absorbed into the bloodstream through the soft tissue in the mouth. Sativex is currently available in eight countries for spasticity associated with multiple sclerosis and is in clinical trials for neuropathic pain and cancer pain.

"When we started out, we thought that really, the only role for CBD was to modify the effects of THC," said Mark Rogerson, a GW spokesperson. "We now know that CBD may well have therapeutic applications in its own right. And the significant number of other cannabinoids, which only appear in tiny quantities typically in the plants, may have very interesting roles to play, as well. So I think it's that breadth of what one plant has to offer that's the real surprise." This uncharted territory has scientists at GW excited. Of the more than one hundred or so cannabinoids within the cannabis plant, GW has studied about twenty of them in some detail. To study specific cannabinoids, GW has modified the plant over successive generations to amplify certain scarce cannabinoids. "It's what gardeners do to get the perfect rose. It's the same basic principle. We're not creating new plants so much as drawing out one particular aspect of an existing plant," Rogerson said. In fact, the specific nature of Sativex is its strongest point. For patients who aren't comfortable with homegrown medicine, the benefit of Sativex is that they can know, exactly, what they've consumed.

Predictably, the more scientists learn about cannabinoids and cannabinoid receptors, the more pharmaceutical companies are inspired to explore them. Over decades of research, several methods have emerged. One is the use of agonists, compounds that bind to receptors. Examples of agonists are a single synthetic cannabinoid like Marinol or a cannabis-based extraction like Sativex.[20]

Yet another means is the manipulation of the endocannabinoid system with compounds, called antagonists, that block or shield the receptors. As the workings of the endocannabinoid system were revealed, pharmaceutical companies Sanofi and Merck began to focus on the development of antagonists with the hope of finding a treatment for obesity.[21] While Rimonabant, developed by Sanofi to suppress appetite, did just that, it brought a host of side effects, including depression, anxiety, and irritability. "All cannabinoid antagonists that enter the central nervous system to access the brain have a very significant problem," Piomelli said. "They block the endocannabinoid system in the brain; of course, that's what they are meant to do. And the endocannabinoid system in the brain is very important for keeping us happy, for keeping us in a good mood. When you block it, you have a plethora of effects which are not good for people." Rimonabant was eventually deemed a failure.

A newer approach to cannabinoid-based medicine is focused on the inhibition of anandamide degradation. Degradation prevention leads to a buildup of endocannabinoids within the body, which creates a similar effect as the consumption of cannabinoids, but without having to consume them and without the high. Piomelli has focused his research on the potential of these inhibitors to increase anandamide's analgesic, anti-anxiety, and antidepressant effects. He also hopes to find that enhancing anandamide's effects will block cravings for certain drugs, like nicotine.

The federal government has never approved a plant in its entirety as medicine, and it's unlikely it is going to begin with the controversial cannabis plant. "For cannabis as a plant, I don't think there is a future. Honestly," said Mahmoud ElSohly, director of the University of Mississippi cannabis farm. "But cannabis as a source of pharmaceuticals? There is a very bright future for the plant."

ElSohly, who worked on a cannabinoid-based suppository that never took off, has partnered since 2003 with Dr. Michael Repka, chair of the department of pharmaceutics at the school of pharmacy at the University of Mississippi, to create a fast vehicle for THC. The pearl-sized patch would allow pure THC—not synthetic—to be absorbed through the mucosal tissue in the mouth. Unlike Marinol, which must travel through the stomach, the effects of this patch will be felt, Repka hopes, as quickly as inhaled cannabis. Human clinical trials for this product have not yet begun, and THC in pill form remains the only pharmaceutical option in the United States.

While there are many ongoing studies on cannabinoids, fewer have been approved for cannabis itself. In addition to the federal stance, pharmaceutical companies are unlikely to bother with efforts to bring a whole plant product to the market; they deal with components. That leaves the analysis of whole, raw cannabis in the United States—and related time-consuming, bureaucratic latticework—to independent and academic researchers.

Cannabis is grown and labeled under federal contract at the University of Mississippi. ALYSON MARTIN

Cannabis is federally classified as a Schedule I drug, a categorization reserved for substances with zero medical value and "high potential for abuse," including heroin.[22] Opium, which is used to make morphine and heroin, is listed as a Schedule II substance. Opioid pain relievers were responsible for nearly 74 percent of the 20,000 prescription drug–related deaths in the United States in 2008.[23] Even methamphetamine is Schedule II, and few would argue that meth is safer or less addictive than cannabis. Schedule III substances, like Vicodin, have less potential for abuse than Schedule I and II, but still may have a "moderate or low physical dependence or high psychological dependence," according to the Drug Enforcement Administration (DEA). Even that scheduling seems unreasonable for cannabis.

The placement of cannabis in Schedule I creates significant barriers to research because studies on substances with this categorization involve the most tedious restrictions; as the class becomes stricter, access to the substance involves more hoops.

But the federal government has imposed additional and unique restrictions on cannabis research, with little rationale—beyond politics. The federal government has enabled only one institution, the University of Mississippi, to legally grow cannabis for research on its behalf, although it is free to award additional and alternative contracts. And cannabis is the only research substance for which the government is the sole supplier.[24] For a scientist to receive cannabis from the federal farm at the University of Mississippi, a trifecta of approvals—not required of any other drug—must be obtained from the FDA, DEA, and a Public Health Service panel (and NIDA must approve the requested supply). Two of these four agencies exist, in part, to squash cannabis. The DEA aims to eradicate cannabis and arrest growers and traffickers, and NIDA actively works to educate people about the perils of cannabis consumption. ("As the National Institute on Drug Abuse, NIDA's focus is primarily on the negative consequences of marijuana use. We generally do not fund research focused on the potential beneficial medical effects of marijuana," Shirley Simson, a spokesperson, wrote in an e-mail.) These are odd umbrellas under which to place cannabis research, which should perhaps be overseen by a more objective body.

The American College of Physicians wrote in a 2008 paper that, "Unfortunately, research expansion has been hindered by a complicated federal approval process, limited availability of research-grade marijuana, and the debate over legalization."[25] The paper continued, "Marijuana's categorization as a Schedule I controlled substance raises significant concerns for researchers, physicians, and patients."

Cannabis is Schedule I because there is not enough federally approved research, but there is not enough federally approved research because cannabis is Schedule I. In response to NIDA's refusal to supply cannabis for a clinical trial proposal approved by the FDA in 2011 to study how cannabis could help post-traumatic stress disorder (PTSD), John H. Schwarz, former MacArthur fellow and California Institute of Technology physicist, said, "Consider what American science might look like if all research were run like marijuana research is being run now. Suppose the Institute for Creation Science were put in charge of approving paleontology digs and the science of human evolution. Imagine what would happen to the environment if we gave coal and oil companies the power to block any climate research they didn't like."[26]

One state has managed to forge ahead. In 1999, California passed legislation to funnel millions ($8.7 million by 2012) to create and sustain the Center for Medicinal Cannabis Research (CMCR) at the University of California–San Diego, the longest and most well-funded program to date.[27] Before these studies were completed in 2012, scientists at CMCR used cannabis from the University of Mississippi farm for consistency in both supply and potency. The goal, set by the California legislature, was to assess the safety and efficacy of cannabis in treating various medical conditions. Its findings showed that whole inhaled cannabis had an analgesic effect. The noted undesired effects were dose-related and faded once the subjects ceased smoking.[28]

Igor Grant, the director of CMCR, was one of the authors of a 2012 article published in the *Open Neurology Journal*, which stated,

> The classification of marijuana as a Schedule I drug as well as the continuing controversy as to whether or not cannabis is of medical value are obstacles to medical progress in this area. Based on evidence currently available the Schedule I classification is not tenable; it is not accurate that cannabis has no medical value, or that information on safety is lacking. It is true cannabis has some abuse potential, but its profile more closely resembles drugs in Schedule III (where codeine and dronabinol are listed).[29]

The cannabis plant plays a role in three very different spheres: cannabinoid and endocannabinoid system research, whole plant research, and state medical cannabis programs. Dr. Repka at UMiss believes the medical cannabis movement has actually helped those seeking to develop cannabinoid-based pharmaceuticals and says that interest has increased tenfold since around 2008. "There are a lot of people in the medical sense, the strict medical sense, that are still totally against legalizing marijuana for whatever reason," he said from his office in Oxford. "But, really, what's happened is it's brought so much exposure that that interplay has benefited the medical push."

But these same divergent roles for the plant are at the core of the confusion about the future of medical cannabis. Often, research conducted on the endocannabinoid system is mistaken as research conducted on the whole plant, which is understandable. As scientists research cannabinoids and the endocannabinoid system to uncover potential future pharmaceutical products, voters in nearly half of the country have passed laws that validate whole plant cannabis as medicine.

The overarching federal stance further blurs lines. When the federal government reiterates that cannabis is not a medicine, it means that inhaled or consumed whole plant cannabis is not an acceptable form of medicine—that there ought to be a great divide between the plant and the compounds within. In fact, NIDA, which oversees the federal cannabis farm and discourages whole plant cannabis for any use, is a regular sponsor at the annual symposiums of the International Cannabinoid Research Society.[30] Other sponsors have included GW Pharmaceuticals, AstraZeneca, Cayman Chemical, and ElSohly's very own ElSohly Laboratories, Inc., to name a few.

At a hearing on April 1, 2004, on state medical cannabis laws, Dr. Nora Volkow, the director of NIDA, attempted to clarify the difference between cannabis and cannabinoids, as far as the federal government is concerned.[31] "The scientific evidence is clear, marijuana is an addictive substance that has adverse health and behavioral consequences," she said. "It is also true that the cannabinoid system through which marijuana asserts its effects offers a wide range of potential therapeutic applications." In a 1999 Institute of Medicine report, *Marijuana and Medicine: Assessing the Science Base*, commissioned by the White House Office of National Drug Control Policy (ONDCP), the authors came to a similar conclusion.[32] The report, one of the most comprehensive to date, noted, "If there is any future for marijuana as a medicine, it lies in its isolated components, the cannabinoids and their synthetic derivatives." But this report included a crucial caveat: "However, it will likely be many years before a safe and effective cannabinoid delivery system, such as an inhaler, is available for patients. In the meantime there are patients with debilitating symptoms for whom smoked marijuana might provide relief."[33] Former U.S. surgeon general Joycelyn Elders added to this important point about the role of whole plant cannabis, particularly in the absence of a comparable pharmaceutical product, saying, "For many who need only a small amount—like cancer patients simply trying to get through a few months of chemotherapy—the risks of smoking [marijuana] are minor."[34]

Most Americans don't buy the notion that raw cannabis is bad, but the stuff inside might be good. Increasingly, patients are choosing whole plant cannabis for a number of reasons: they can't find equal pain relief elsewhere, they're frustrated with pharmaceutical side effects, or they prefer plant-based medicines and holistic health care. Common side effects for anti-nausea drugs are muscle spasms, uneven heart rate, painful urination, shortness of breath, fever, blistering or skin rash, chest pain, unusual bleeding, fainting, and, though they are meant to curb these very things, increased nausea or vomiting.[35] Compared to all that, the expected side effects of a joint—increased appetite, euphoria, and nausea relief—sound more appealing.

A slice of history shows that the federal government was once, perhaps, more open-minded. In the late 1970s, Robert Randall, a glaucoma patient, took the federal government to court for access to whole cannabis and won. He became the first federal medical cannabis patient and, with several other patients over the course of a decade or so, was entered into an FDA Compassionate Investigational New Drug program. Today, four of the living patients who were grandfathered into the now-defunct program still receive tins of cannabis cigarettes from the cannabis farm in Mississippi, care of the federal government. If the government truly does believe that whole cannabis is detrimental to health, why continue to allow these men and women to receive tin after hazardous tin of cannabis for decades? Conversely, if the tins

An employee at the University of Mississippi, where cannabis is grown under federal contract, pulls joints from a tin. The four remaining patients grandfathered into the IND program receive their supply in these tins.
ALYSON MARTIN

of cannabis are safe for *them*, shouldn't they be safe for *everyone?* While these four patients are not a large enough sample for comprehensive clinical trials, there has been no federal effort to study the effects of decades of whole plant cannabis use on them, even as a starting point.

In a letter to a longtime friend and cannabis activist, Roger Winthrop, in 1981, a frustrated Randall wrote:

> Unfortunately, the desire to tinker with synthetics always gets the best of them—if not d-9 then maybe d-8 or XXX or YYY or anything but cannabis. I unkindly translate this to "Let 'm go blind, there's a grant here somewhere." Alas. . . . Marijuana, with its "ghastly" array of 400 or more all-natural chemical compounds is a sheer pharmacologic terror. Never mind that Mother's milk contains 400 chemicals—and more since toxins abound—or the simple potato is a hazard of lurking possibilities. The idea "what works works" is alien. The question is not "Does THC really help?" The thought, "What's best?" is not avoided—it never occurs. THC is automatically, quite "naturally" and absolutely "better" because it is pure and "refined" and whatever other technocratic, collegese numbness you [want] to call it.

Lester Grinspoon, associate professor emeritus of psychiatry at Harvard Medical School and author of two books on cannabis (the first, *Marihuana Reconsidered*, published in 1971), wonders if raw cannabis really needs to be tested with the same rigor as any other new medicine or to navigate the regulatory channels of the FDA. "There's no point in going back and doing double-blind studies to replicate results that we already know," Grinspoon said of cannabis, noting that aspirin has been used since long before the days of double blind.

There may come a day when patients have the option between whole plant medical cannabis and effective cannabinoid-based medicines that contain selected cannabinoid combinations tailored to specific illnesses. Until then, in the absence of such medicines, twenty states and Washington, D.C., have decided to allow whole plant medical cannabis as an option—and they are not alone. More than three-quarters of Americans believe that cannabis has therapeutic value. A 2013 article in the *New England Journal of Medicine* revealed that 76 percent of readers polled in seventy-two countries support medical cannabis. Further, Israel, Canada, the Netherlands, and the Czech Republic have national systems for the distribution of whole plant medical cannabis.

No matter the outcome, the scientific role of cannabis remains significant: the plant has led researchers toward discoveries essential to the field of medicine.

Raphael Mechoulam, the researcher who has spent four decades studying cannabis and who discovered THC, closed an editorial titled "Cannabis—A Valuable Drug That Deserves Better Treatment" for *Mayo Clinic Proceedings* in February 2012 with, "I believe that medical marijuana as a therapeutic entity is here to stay. It is being used in numerous medical conditions, at times with considerable success. Are we entitled to neglect a valuable drug?"[36]

2

HISTORY REPEATING

There was a time when cannabis grew freely in America. Green leaves blanketed fields where farmers now sow golden rows of wheat and corn. The cannabis plant likely originated in Asia and traveled westward with British colonial expansion until it arrived in the 1600s in what would become the United States.[1] Hemp from cannabis made the ropes and sails of ships that brought settlers to places unknown, the tents these men and women slept in, the fabric that kept them warm, and, perhaps, the oil that lit their lamps.[2]

For many years, cannabis was called the hemp plant because that was its primary utility. While hemp is of the genus *Cannabis*, which also includes plants abundant in THC and other cannabinoids, plants grown for hemp are distinct because they have negligible traces of THC and are valued for their seeds and meaty and fibrous stalks.[3] Therefore, it is accurate to call both industrial hemp and marijuana "cannabis," but each has been given distinguishing nomenclature.

In 1854, Englishman Edmund Saul Dixon described hemp as a "crop of lances."[4] This stiff, upright plant, he wrote, was "destined for robust purposes, becoming almost a weapon in the hands of man." But his admiration was directed only at the plant's stalk, which contains the useful fibers. Of the flowers and leaves, he wrote: "it furnishes, in the shape of 'bang,' a poisonous as well as an intoxicating agent." Hemp is not intoxicating, so it seems that the precise differences between varieties of cannabis were unclear at the time. In an 1801 essay, Dr. William Roxburgh, who oversaw the cultivation of hemp for the East India Company in Calcutta, compared hemp plants grown using European seeds with hemp plants found in India; he wrote that he "can discover no difference whatever, not even to found a variety on."[5] He added, "Yet, I cannot discover, that the fibres of the bark have ever been employed by them for any purpose. It is cultivated in small quantities every where (in India) on account of its narcotic qualities." The *Encyclopaedia Britannica* of 1856 inaccurately suggested in the entry for hemp that the "intoxicating properties of hemp" (likely the cannabis Americans know today) resulted solely from the climate in which it was grown.[6] Then the text reiterated, "But it is not as a narcotic and excitant that the hemp plant is most useful to mankind; it is as an advancer rather than a retarder of civilization, that its utility is made most manifest."

England relied on colonies to produce an abundance of hemp and began to lose access to hemp grown in the soon-to-be United States as tensions rose in the mid-1700s.[7] Founding Father Benjamin Franklin backed the colonists' refusal to send hemp to London, saying, "We have not yet enough for our own consumption." In some regions, individuals could be penalized for not producing hemp during those crucial years.

Thomas Jefferson grew hemp, which he said was "abundantly productive, and will grow forever on the same spot."[8] Jefferson's letters from 1815 reveal that he dithered between hemp and cotton, which would later come to replace hemp. "But the breaking and beating it," Jefferson wrote of hemp, "which has been always done by hand, is so slow, so laborious, and so much complained of by our laborers, that I had given it up and purchased and manufactured cotton for their shirting." Over time, as cotton was increasingly used for such essentials as clothing and rope, the nation curtailed its dependence on the hemp crop.

After the cultivation of cannabis for hemp products declined, its cultivation for consumption steadily increased. Recreational cannabis smoking in the United States is often traced back to Mexican immigrants in the early twentieth century.[9] It is possible, however, that some Americans partook of the "intoxicating properties of hemp" long before.

Prohibitionist ideology also overtook the country at the turn of the twentieth century, with some of the first legislative efforts to ban or regulate alcohol and drugs. Efforts to specifically curb recreational cannabis use began state by state.[10] Between 1911 and 1933, thirty-four states changed their laws so that the plant could be manufactured only for medicine and industrial use.[11] Cannabis was almost included in the 1914 Harrison Narcotics Tax Act, a federal law requiring those who manufactured or dealt opium, coca, and their derivatives outside of a medical practice to register and pay an annual tax.[12] The act represented the first time the federal government enforced substance regulation.[13] Indirect control through taxation also allowed the federal government to engage the criminal justice system in drug control but avoid full-on prohibition. Those who sold or possessed but did not register or pay taxes—which dealers and addicts were unlikely to do—faced arrest. Individuals who abused these substances were not given treatment, but time behind bars (fifteen years would pass before mention, in 1929, of opening the first federal drug rehabilitation centers).[14] The seed for the war on drugs mentality was planted.

The Harrison Narcotics Tax Act was inspired by the 1912 International Opium Convention at The Hague, one of the first international drug control efforts, which was led by the United States and aimed to unify countries in restricting opium and coca leaves and their derivatives.[15] While cannabis was not included in this treaty, it was in subsequent international drug control efforts beginning in 1925. A cannabis law for the United States would soon follow.

Many factors led to America's newly hostile attitude toward cannabis. The popularity of temperance—a movement that targeted alcohol as the root of excess and ruin, placing abstinence at the heart of a fulfilling life—likely contributed to states' willingness to outlaw the plant. Although the aim of the movement was alcohol prohibition, there was no such thing as a good intoxicant. And with the tracks already built, it was easy to add another boxcar. But as alcohol prohibition came and went between 1920 and 1933, states continued to pass anti-cannabis laws.

What is unclear is why the United States would declare one prohibition a failure and then choose to embark on another. Perhaps drug prohibition was considered dissimilar because it dealt with unfamiliar substances and, in minorities, unfamiliar targets. Temperance, while it had some racist roots (it was argued that alcohol turned a black man into a "beast" or a violent rapist), was primarily built on religious rhetoric meant to save whites from themselves.[16] The new state and national drug laws, on the other hand, were framed as saving whites from minorities and righteously saving minorities from their own supposed lack of self-control. The narrative behind these early laws was that blacks, Mexicans, and Chinese were going mad, turning murderous, and luring whites with cocaine, "marihuana,"* and opiates.[17]

In addition to race, panic played into the misunderstanding around certain drugs. It's now known, for example, that cannabis doesn't turn people into murderous lunatics. Did people truly

---

* From around the time of the Marihuana Tax Act and for the next several decades, the plant was referred to as "marihuana," then later also "marijuana." Only recently has language begun to change in the U.S. to reflect the plant's scientific and most accurate name, "cannabis." We have chosen to refer to the plant as cannabis throughout this book, except where necessary to indicate historic nomenclature or within a quote.

believe that then and, if so, why? Was it racism gone rampant, an irrational hysteria among the misinformed? Evidence suggests it was both.

Certainly, at the sensationalist height of yellow journalism, horror stories about "loco weed" proliferated. As early as 1901 the *New York Times* wrote that cannabis "sends its victims running amuck."[18] In 1905, the *Los Angeles Times* reprinted an article that claimed cannabis made smokers' "brains dry up and they die, most of the time suddenly." A cannabis user in El Paso, Texas, killed a policeman.[19] A California man decapitated his friend in a cannabis-induced craze. A young boy in Florida axed his parents and three siblings to death. On the streets of New Orleans, a man killed his wife while under the influence. Word from Colorado was that "Mexicans" were cultivating and selling "the weed" to "white school students." Floyd K. Baskette, city editor of the *Alamosa Daily Courier* in Colorado, wrote to the Federal Bureau of Narcotics about hundreds of "murders, rapes, petty crimes, insanity" that he linked to cannabis. "I wish I could show you what a small marihuana cigarete [*sic*] can do to one of our degenerate Spanish-speaking residents," Baskette wrote. "That's why our problem is so great; the greatest percentage of our population is composed of Spanish-speaking persons, most of whom are low mentally, because of social and racial conditions."

Most of these tales about cannabis were brought to national attention by Harry J. Anslinger, who in 1930 became the first commissioner of the U.S. Treasury Department's Federal Bureau of Narcotics.[20] If the story of cannabis prohibition were told in a comic book, Anslinger would be a formidable villain. Anslinger didn't investigate the panicked rumors. Instead, he became a federal megaphone for these accounts during his exaggerated and impassioned testimonies against the "killer weed." Already tasked with enforcing the Harrison Act, Anslinger pushed for similar legislation for cannabis.

The proposed law was closely modeled after the Harrison Act. Instead of prohibiting cannabis outright, HR 6385, better known as the Marihuana Tax Act of 1937, aimed to tax the plant out of existence.[21] An annual tax of $50 was imposed on manufacturers, compounders, and importers; $15 for dealers; $25 for producers (growers); and $1 for researchers and medical professionals who sought to prescribe it. All of the above were required to register and file returns to "the collector of internal revenue." Additionally, the transfer of cannabis to a registered user required an additional $1 tax per ounce and transfer to a nonregistered user $100 per ounce. For perspective, fair market value of one ounce of cannabis was $1. Dealers had to self-incriminate and pay the taxman out of pocket to sell cannabis at a loss.

The Marihuana Tax Act passed within a year of the release of the propaganda film *Reefer Madness*. The rationale behind the act as well as the mind-set of the time can be summed up by a statement Anslinger gave during hearings for the act: "The deleterious, even vicious, qualities of the drug render it highly dangerous to the mind and body upon which it operates to destroy the will, cause one to lose the power of connected thought, producing imaginary delectable situations and gradually weakening the physical powers. Its use frequently leads to insanity."

So began the wrongful banishment of cannabis. It may be tempting to excuse the missteps of the time with the reasoning that no one knew better. But Anslinger was presented with alternative views; he chose to ignore them. The American Medical Association's legislative counsel, Dr. William C. Woodward, expressed particularly vocal opposition during hearings for the act. Importantly, he noted that using the term "marihuana" in the name of the act, instead of the scientifically correct "cannabis," led to misconceptions. In his words, "It was the use of the term 'marihuana' rather than the use of the term 'Cannabis' or the use of the term 'Indian hemp' that was responsible . . . for the failure of the dealers in Indian hempseed to connect up this bill with their business until rather late in the day. So, if you will permit me, I shall use the word 'Cannabis,' and I should certainly suggest that if any legislation is enacted, the term used be 'Cannabis' and not the mongrel word 'marihuana.'" The word "marihuana" remained in the act—and therefore in American vernacular for decades to come, maintaining a stigma that "cannabis" did not carry.

Anslinger's deceptive efforts didn't end there, and Dr. Woodward expressed even deeper concerns about the haste and hysteria surrounding the act. "It has surprised me, however, that the facts on which these statements have been based have not been brought before this committee by competent primary evidence," he said. "We are referred to newspaper publications concerning the prevalence of marihuana addiction. We are told that the use of marihuana causes crime. But yet no one has been produced from the Bureau of Prisons to show the number of prisoners who have been found addicted to the marihuana habit. An informal inquiry shows that the Bureau of Prisons has no evidence on that point." Dr. Woodward proceeded to note that not only was the Children's Bureau not present to testify in response to Anslinger's tales of schoolchildren on "marihuana," but that they and the Office of Education had heard no such complaints. He added, "The Bureau of the Public Health Service has also a division of pharmacology. If you desire evidence as to the pharmacology of Cannabis, that obviously is the place where you can get direct and primary evidence, rather than the indirect hearsay evidence."

Dr. Woodward's statements were not taken into consideration, and the act was passed in 1937. By 1942, cannabis was removed from the U.S. Pharmacopeia. Anslinger was not satisfied. He pushed for the Boggs Act of 1951, which lumped cannabis with narcotics (the drugs included in the Harrison Act), and subsequently the Narcotics Control Act of 1956.[22] Both acts increased penalties and marked the first efforts to determine mandatory minimum federal criminal sentences for those who possessed or distributed narcotics. By 1956, conviction for first-time possession of cannabis led to a two-year mandatory sentence; second-offense possession or first-time sale resulted in five years with no option for parole or probation; and a third-time possession or second-offense sale resulted in ten to forty years with no option for parole or probation. An infrequent user caught in possession of just enough cannabis for personal use on three occasions was required to spend a minimum of ten years in prison. Convinced that the increased threat of incarceration would work as a deterrent, Anslinger insisted that these penalties would reduce drug abuse in America by 60 percent.[23]

Of course, these laws didn't stop the increasing use of cannabis—they just put more people behind bars. In 1958, just after these laws were passed, there were 3,287 reported state and local "marihuana arrests."[24] In 1967, there were 54,468, a third of whom were offenders under twenty-one years old. If cannabis was as lethal as Anslinger claimed, that alone would have been more effective at curbing use than his laws. Most people, though, understand the difference between self-destruction and self-indulgence; a 2011 survey showed that roughly 300,000 people used heroin in the previous month while more than 18 million used cannabis.[25]

Cannabis use continued to climb not because the plant is so overpoweringly addictive, but because people began to realize that the weed wasn't so loco after all. By the 1960s, cannabis had become an integral part of counterculture. Hundreds of thousands of people (many of them white, middle-class, and college-aged) reclaimed the plant as a political symbol of peace, love, and protest during a time of turmoil and progressive change. A writer described the use of cannabis during these years in a 1967 issue of *Life* magazine as "the greatest mass flouting of the law since prohibition."[26]

By the late 1960s, with early breakthroughs in cannabinoid research under way, many more doctors and officials spoke out against the reefer madness narrative. But those who advocated for cannabis law reform during legislative hearings throughout the 1960s and 1970s, prompted by the rise in Americans' consumption, were mostly shamed and ignored by the (shrinking) majority. One progressive doctor summed up this hostility when he said, "I have come under a lot of attack simply because I am saying the Emperor has no clothes on."[27]

In 1967, Dr. James L. Goddard, the U.S. commissioner of Food and Drugs (head of the Food and Drug Administration), stated that he was unsure if cannabis was more dangerous than alcohol. This sentiment, bold for its time, shocked members of the House of Representatives who called him unfit for office. His underlings at the FDA even penned a limerick:

> A well-known physician named Jim,
> Has really gone out on a limb.
> Believe it or not
> He's decided that pot
> Is better than drinking straight gin.[28]

When confronted about his views during a hearing, an exasperated Dr. Goddard made a point that still resonates decades later, as hundreds of thousands of nonviolent drug offenders sit behind bars and millions are haunted by a possession arrest record: "All I have to ask is what price are we attaching to this as far as the future cost to society by making felons of these people, by arresting juveniles, whether they actually technically become felons or not? Do we not tend to cast them in the role of involvement with drugs for the rest of their lives, involvement with criminals? Now, are there not better ways of getting at this particular problem?"

Year after year, these rather theatrical hearings played out more like interrogations of government officials who spoke out against common prohibitionist views surrounding cannabis than balanced discussions about a national issue. Attempts at rational and factual conversation often regressed into bickering. When one doctor said cannabis was technically not a narcotic, as it was often called, a committee member suggested changing the definition of narcotic so it would fit; when another doctor clarified that cannabis does not cause physical addiction, a committee member launched into a conversation about how psychological dependence was worse.[29] If, like Dr. Goddard, someone was less than disparaging about cannabis, they were told that they were responsible for encouraging youth experimentation with drugs.[30]

The following exchange between Dr. Stanley Yolles, the director of the National Institute of Mental Health, and South Carolina representative Albert W. Watson, from a 1969 hearing, illustrates what often resulted from these tiresome battles of opinions, in this case about the gateway drug theory:

> Mr. Watson: The fact that 80 to 95 percent of present hard narcotic and heroin users started with marihuana, that is a specious argument or relationship?

> Dr. Yolles: Some of them had mothers' milk, some of them have used alcohol.

> Mr. Watson: Doctor, that is the most absurd thing. Are you now intimating that we are comparing the use of marihuana with mothers' milk? Now, let's don't get ridiculous on this.

> Dr. Yolles: Mr. Chairman, the World Health Organization itself has stated there is no relationship between the use of marihuana and a progression to heroin.[31]

During that hearing, Dr. Yolles reiterated what Dr. Goddard had said two years prior, which bears repeating. "The major point I wish to make," he said, "is that in the case of marihuana, legal penalties were assigned to its use that are strict enough to ruin the life of a first-time offender, with total disregard for medical and scientific evidence of the properties of the drug or its effects. I know of no clearer instance in which the punishment for an infraction of the law is more harmful than the crime."

Up until this point, no president had led a major national rewrite of drug policy. But in 1969, Richard Nixon's first year in office, he detailed his plans for what one newspaper referred to as a "war on drug abuse," which would include the passage of a new federal drug control act and an increased budget for enforcement.[32] Nixon's actions were mixed: he amended harsh past policies and then created some harsher new ones. For example, despite the conversations during the cannabis hearings that attempted to link the plant to alcohol and distance it from narcotics, Congress, with Nixon's support, passed the Comprehensive Drug Abuse Prevention and Control Act of 1970 that officially placed cannabis in Schedule I with heroin, where it remains to this day. (It is worth noting that at the time this legislation was passed, the cannabis plant was so misunderstood that a report misstated that cannabis resin could be injected, like heroin, into a person's arm.)[33] Substances were listed in one of five schedules—one being the most restrictive and five being the least—based on harm and medical potential. Schedule I, the most tightly regulated and home to cannabis, was reserved for substances with no medical utility and high abuse potential. This act, most often referred to as the Controlled Substances Act (CSA), still dominates the federal approach to drugs.

Conversely, the CSA reduced mandatory minimum drug sentences.[34] First-offense simple cannabis possession, for example, fell from a minimum of two but up to ten years behind bars to up to one year. This was an improvement, though by no means the total decriminalization recommended in 1972 by the National Commission on Marihuana and Drug Abuse, created by Nixon to research cannabis and suggest sound policies. The commission wrote in its report, "Unless present policy is redirected, we will perpetuate the same problems, tolerate the same social costs, and find ourselves as we do now, no further along the road to a more rational legal and social approach than we were in 1914."[35] Nixon ignored the very advice he sought.

Nixon's budget to fight what was in 1971 first referred to as the "war on drugs" increased from $81 million at the start of his presidency to nearly $800 million by the time he left office.[36] (The budget has continued to increase, reaching $25.4 billion for 2014.) In a departure from prior (and subsequent) federal drug control efforts, though, Nixon made treatment a financial priority. As he said to Congress in 1969, "It has been a common oversimplification to consider narcotics addiction or drug abuse to be a law enforcement problem alone."[37] While many presidents have since repeated versions of this sentiment, Nixon was the only president to spend more money on drug treatment and prevention than on enforcement. But what eventually survived of Nixon's approach, and what required the bulk of his budget by the time he left office, was an extension of the Anslinger method of federal drug control: the use of law enforcement (Nixon created the DEA in 1973) to "tighten the noose around the necks of drug peddlers, and thereby loosen the noose around the necks of drug users."[38]

Gerald Ford took office post-Watergate in 1974, and he received a white paper in late 1975 stating that the war on drugs could not be won and that any progress made between 1972 and 1974 had reversed.[39] The paper acknowledged the need for a new direction because drug supply and use could not be eliminated and the aim of the government should be to contain it. "Quality arrests" should come before the number of arrests. While this war would mellow for a decade or so, Ronald Reagan would later reignite it with calls for "a drug-free America by 1995."[40]

Despite Nixon's launch of the war on drugs, one man's misfortune sparked the movement that has now breached the castle walls of cannabis prohibition. In 1972, Robert Randall, an energetic twenty-four-year-old, had just moved to Washington, D.C., to be a speechwriter when he was devastated by a glaucoma diagnosis and informed that he would likely be blind by thirty. One evening a year later, after smoking a joint obtained from a friend, he noticed the blurry halos around the streetlights were gone. After a string of similar experiences, Randall concluded, though it was difficult for him to believe, that cannabis reduced the pressure in his eyes that caused the halos and would hasten his blindness. No medicine alone had had the same effects.

Randall continued to self-medicate with cannabis until he was found with plants and arrested in 1975. As Randall explained to his lawyer that he used cannabis for medicine, his lawyer challenged him to prove it. With the help of the National Organization for the Reform of Marijuana Laws (NORML), then a five-year-old cannabis lobby and now the oldest in the country, Randall set out to do just that. (Other groups had formed prior to NORML, and a notable one was the short-lived Legalize Marijuana, or LeMar. Beat poet Allen Ginsberg and several of his friends started the New York City chapter in the mid-1960s.)[41] It just so happened that the same year Randall was diagnosed with glaucoma, NORML filed a petition to move cannabis out of Schedule I and into Schedule II so it could be considered a medicine, as it had been until thirty years earlier, when it was removed from the U.S. Pharmacopeia.

Randall visited Keith Stroup, the young lawyer who founded NORML with funding from the Playboy Foundation, for any information that would help his case. Stroup handed him a folder that contained documents about the potential therapeutic uses of cannabis. Randall had never heard of cannabis in a medical context before. With this as a starting point, Randall found information from NIDA about a study conducted at the University of California–Los Angeles on cannabis and glaucoma. The researcher, Dr. Robert Hepler, had obtained his cannabis from the federal research farm at the University of Mississippi. By the end of 1975, four months after his arrest, Randall became the subject of one of Dr. Hepler's glaucoma studies as a part of the Marijuana Research Project at UCLA. The results revealed that, indeed, smoking cannabis reduced the pressure in Randall's eyes that would have accelerated his blindness. In the absence of another therapy that offered the same results, Randall decided that he would challenge his arrest by arguing that his use of cannabis was a medical necessity. In a separate and pioneering move, he would petition for a supply of cannabis as medicine from the federal farm.

A continued "mass flouting" of drug laws in the 1970s would eventually come to aid Randall's case. Americans felt more lenient toward cannabis than ever before and between 1968 and 1970, laws in thirty-three states were amended to make cannabis possession a misdemeanor instead of a felony.[42] By 1975, the penalty for possession of under an ounce in California and Oregon had been reduced to a violation—a slap on the wrist—with a fine of up to $100. Jimmy Carter, elected in 1976, was the first (and only) president to seriously consider the decriminalization of cannabis possession. Within months of when Carter took office, congressional hearings were held to discuss the possibilities. Peter Bourne, director of the Office of Drug Abuse Policy (the equivalent of today's drug czar), said at one of these hearings, "We believe that the mechanism for discouragement should not be more damaging to the individual than the drugs themselves. We will continue to discourage marihuana use, but we feel criminal penalties that brand otherwise law-abiding people for life are neither

an effective nor an appropriate deterrent." Representatives from
the Department of Justice and the DEA said that such a move
would not negatively impact their organizations' efforts.[43]

The novelty of a president advocating for the decriminalization
of cannabis was amplified by an unprecedented bond between
cannabis activists and the White House. NORML's Stroup was
friends with Carter's son, Chip, with whom he says he smoked
cannabis. Just as Randall felt like he could go directly to the federal government for medical cannabis, Stroup went directly to the
White House when he sought change. (Today, cannabis advocates
circumvent the federal government to seek change at the state
level.) While NORML's cannabis rescheduling petition remained
unattended to, another issue distressed Stroup at the time: the
U.S. government encouraged and funded the spraying of paraquat, a toxic herbicide, to destroy cannabis crops in Mexico. This
wasn't the first time the U.S. government turned a forbidden substance poisonous in an attempt to destroy the supply and discourage use. During alcohol prohibition, an estimated ten thousand
people died as a result of alcohol adulterated by the government
with such substances as methyl alcohol.[44] Stroup was concerned
that the contaminated cannabis was not being discarded by growers, but instead sold in the States. The fear of unintentionally in-
gesting sprayed cannabis was widespread. One poster promoting
a *Village Voice* cover story written by Fred Gardner about Bourne
and paraquat cautioned, "Poison Pot: Even Your Dealer Doesn't
Know for Sure." Stroup said he met with Bourne to discuss what
he considered a major potential health hazard. But as the spraying continued, Stroup felt that Bourne wasn't taking his concerns
seriously enough. Their relationship became strained.

In December 1977, NORML held a swank holiday party for hundreds of influential people in a D.C. town house. The celebration
encapsulated the soul of the decade—but that decade was coming
to an end. There are many versions of how events unfolded that

night. This is what Stroup remembers: As a band played, Stroup and a female friend were talking when Bourne showed up and began to flirt with her. Stroup walked away to entertain other guests when the woman came to him and said that Bourne wouldn't mind getting high. "What do you mean?" Stroup remembers asking. "I think he might like to snort some cocaine," she replied. Stroup, Bourne, Hunter S. Thompson (on the NORML advisory board), and a couple of journalists from *High Times* (one of the first go-to publications for cannabis enthusiasts) went to the top floor of the town house together. "So we went up and did what people did in those years. We sat around and chatted and passed a joint around and somebody laid out a couple of lines of cocaine," Stroup said as he described this very extraordinary example of what was at the time a rather ordinary activity. Yes, Stroup said America's drug czar got high with the head of the nation's largest pro-cannabis group—and they would both come to regret that decision.

Months passed with no public mention of what happened at the NORML party. One Wednesday the following summer, newspapers reported that Bourne illegally wrote a Quaalude prescription for an aide.[45] The next day, the secret kept for months by the journalists who had been there came out, and the cocaine story broke on *Good Morning America*. The *Washington Post* also covered the cocaine story.[46] Journalists from both had been at the party, and at least one from the *Post* was in the room when the snorting occurred. It is unclear why the journalists withheld this story for so long. Maybe they were uncertain of what they heard or saw. But once the Quaalude story broke, perhaps they piled on. Friday newspapers reported that Stroup wouldn't deny the cocaine allegations. Bourne had taken a leave of absence in the wake of the prescription incident, but resigned once the cocaine story was out, though he never admitted to the events. At the time, Stroup felt no remorse about the resignation and said to reporters, "I do not see it with any great sadness."[47] Stroup believed he owed no loyalty to Bourne, who still wasn't paying much attention to the paraquat issue.

Today, Stroup recalls the incident with apparent sorrow. He said that allowing his anger to override his better judgment to deny Bourne's cocaine use remains the greatest embarrassment of his career and that he didn't foresee the consequences for NORML. As a result of this betrayal and Bourne's resignation, a much less cannabis-sympathetic drug czar took Bourne's place. The White House no longer wanted anything to do with NORML, which, as Stroup remembers, became "persona non grata." Stroup had no choice but to step down as executive director of NORML.

The Bourne-Stroup scandal—and Stroup's response— potentially altered the course of an entire movement. Any progress that could have been made at the federal level during Carter's term vanished, and decriminalization never came to pass. In hindsight, it is hard to pin too much blame on Stroup. Bourne's prescription incident could have eventually forced his resignation, or at least lessened his credibility as an advocate for decriminalization. Even if Stroup's revelation hadn't turned the tide against NORML then, the link between the cannabis lobby and the White House would have been severed with Carter's departure. And with Reagan's election, the Dark Ages, as cannabis activists have retrospectively named the decade to come, was inevitable.

In 1982, Ronald Reagan declared a new war on drugs, nullifying much of the progress that had been made during Carter's term. "The mood towards drugs is changing in this country and the momentum is with us," he said. "We're making no excuses for drugs, hard, soft, or otherwise. Drugs are bad and we're going after them."[48] In just a few years, discussions about cannabis decriminalization gave way to efforts to eradicate cannabis at any cost.

While the White House post-Nixon had conceded that containment was a smarter approach to drugs and drug use, Reagan believed he could wipe this cockroach of a plant off the map if he just tried hard enough. In 1981, the DEA was involved in six states' aggressive "cooperative eradication programs" for cannabis; by 1983, the DEA expanded the programs to forty states. That year, the number of "DEA-sponsored training schools," which taught local law enforcement about "aerial observation techniques, the legal requirements to obtain search warrants in their state, methods to conduct raids to destroy the cannabis crop, and procedures to arrest and prosecute those individuals identified with the cultivation," expanded from four to seventeen. By 1983, ten states had signed memorandums of understanding and received support from their local National Guard units to go after domestic cannabis growers. Thomas G. Byrne, chief of the Cannabis Investigations Section of the DEA, insisted that "the military should be encouraged to incorporate marijuana production detection as a regular part of their ongoing air training activities." When Reagan declared war, he meant it.

Although the Posse Comitatus Act of 1878 had been written explicitly to limit U.S. military interference in local law enforcement, in December 1981 Reagan amended it to allow for unprecedented military involvement in "civilian" (federal, state, and local) law enforcement efforts.[49] According to a 1983 hearing, "Underlying the action of the Congress was the notion that even though the times called for fiscal restraint, all possible resources should be utilized to combat narcotics trafficking; all involved agencies should cooperate, and perhaps the greatest untapped resource was the Department of Defense." There was some concern that shifting the military's attention to the drug war had the potential to interfere with their preparedness. But with Reagan's amendment to the act, the U.S. Army, Navy, and Air Force increasingly lent troops, facilities, and aircrafts previously marked for international defense to domestic drug law enforcement.

Reagan's war made Nixon's look like a play fight. He pushed for laws allowing seized assets involved in illegal drug operations to be reinvested into the drug war.[50] From the mid-1980s to the mid-1990s, over $3 billion worth of stuff was seized by the Justice Department, a dramatic increase compared to the years before the new law.[51] One stated objective was to let the drug war help pay for itself. But when Americans guilty of nothing lost anything from tens of thousands of dollars to their homes and their supposedly suspicious possessions were not returned, some experts suggested that the rewards gained from such seizures had become a corrupting incentive. A bust, warranted or not, was a guaranteed windfall.

Reagan also reintroduced and increased the mandatory minimums that had all but disappeared under the original CSA, including mandatory life imprisonment.[52] In a move that seemed to target minority communities, five grams of crack cocaine led to a minimum of five years in prison, while it would take five hundred grams of powder cocaine to warrant the same sentence.[53] The core difference between the two substances was their markets; one was popular on Wall Street and the other on backstreets. As a result of penalties introduced during Reagan's administration, anyone convicted of a drug offense, even simple possession, could be denied federal benefits—including student loan aid, subsidized housing, and access to welfare—over their lifetime.[54] In many cases, drug charges can also revoke one's right to vote. According to Michelle Alexander in The New Jim Crow, these new drug policies served as a way to foment race-based fear and build a solid, white working-class voting bloc, as well as a backdoor way to disadvantage and disenfranchise minority populations over the long term.[55] To this day, one bad choice could mean a lifelong burden; it's the conviction that keeps convicting.

While Reagan pushed law enforcement and legislation, his wife Nancy went mainstream with her First Lady cause: Just Say No. This phrase, still chanted in grade schools today, came to represent a symbiotic relationship between the First Lady and a parent-driven anti-drug movement, notably less present in earlier decades. As Carla Lowe, vice president of the National Federation of Parents for Drug Free Youth, said in a 1983 hearing about cannabis eradication, "Marihuana has been the impetus for the parent movement."[56] From the late 1970s to the early 1980s, a handful of parents' groups grew to a few thousand. Their battle cries of "D.A.R.E." and "Drug-Free" and "Just Say No" were loud and influential as their mission spread from the White House to popular culture. These groups pushed legislation that criminalized drug paraphernalia. *The New Teen Titans* comic book's anti-drug series ("in cooperation with the president's drug awareness campaign") included a letter from Nancy Reagan herself that told kids they were in combat.[57] "The battle is against drug abuse," she wrote. "Declare that you will stay drug-free. At any cost. You're guaranteed to win. And you'll be a hero to your mother and father, family and friends, but most of all, to yourself." By the 1990s, after Reagan left office, drug-related Public Service Announcements were added to the end of popular television shows; one *Saved by the Bell* episode about cannabis use was called "No Hope with Dope."[58]

The Reagans' manifold approach might have halted cannabis reform for decades if not for Robert Randall's ambitious pursuit of federal medical cannabis, which was well under way before Reagan took office. Randall's expectations must have sounded delusional: he wanted a medical exception to cannabis laws *and* for the federal government to bestow upon him an abundant and consistent supply of joints. But he was armed to make those demands with proof in hand that cannabis helped reduce the pressure in his eyes and with testimony from a doctor who was supplied with federal cannabis to conduct such research. Certainly, neither Randall nor the federal government knew just how much water was building behind the dam when Randall's crusade began in the 1970s, or else this crack in the drug war would have been promptly sealed.

The course for cannabis in America had been irreversibly altered in November 1976. That month, Randall's arrest case was
dismissed due to medical necessity and he soon became the first
person with access to a federal supply of cannabis for medical
use. The original process through which Randall obtained federal cannabis was makeshift because no program yet existed.
Cannabis joints were shipped each month from the federal farm
to the physician who applied on Randall's behalf and who gave
them to him as medicine. Randall was urged to keep quiet about
his new privilege and was even briefly cut off from his cannabis
supply after appearing on national television to smoke his medical
joints. The media couldn't get enough of Randall, and they could
hardly be blamed—the idea of federal medical cannabis is still
somewhat unfathomable decades later. In 1978 Randall fought
back and was officially entered into an FDA Investigational New
Drug (IND) program that allowed him to go to pharmacies in
Washington, D.C., to pick up his cannabis.

The push to silence Randall only intensified his desire to extend medical cannabis access to other patients. While speaking
about medical cannabis in New Mexico, Randall met a termi-
nally ill twenty-five-year-old, Lynn Pierson, who wanted cannabis to relieve nausea from chemotherapy. After thinking through
many possibilities together, Randall suggested that Pierson and
his supporters in the New Mexico legislature pass a state medical cannabis research law. Federal cannabis could be obtained
for research purposes only, so the state had to pass a law that
indicated its intent to collect data and learn from the patients'
use while supplying the patients with federal cannabis. Randall
believed that the resulting research would once and for all prove
cannabis's medical value. This strategy was used to pass the first
state medical cannabis research law, the New Mexico Controlled
Substances Therapeutic Research Act, in early 1978. Pierson
died before his cannabis supply arrived the following year.

The dam had burst: the first wave of medical cannabis was underway in America. Access to federal cannabis was now available to individuals either through the federal IND program or through New Mexico's research program. Over the next decade or so, thirty-three additional states passed similar research laws, and a total of six managed to actually procure federal cannabis for hundreds of patients: New Mexico, Tennessee, New York, Michigan, Georgia, and California. Fifteen patients (of the dozens approved) received cannabis through the federal IND program.

This turned out to be too much, too soon. With increasing demand in the 1980s, NIDA faced a supply problem and stalled. To grow more plants in response to increasing IND applications and state medical cannabis research laws would have threatened to contradict Reagan's (and then George H.W. Bush's) national push to eradicate cannabis. The implications of Reagan's presidency were not lost on Randall, who had written in 1982 to his friend Roger Winthrop, coordinator for NORML in Michigan, "The news is not good . . . The White House is bonzo over pot." Two years prior, in 1980, the National Cancer Institute got approval to do its own version of the IND, with plans to distribute capsules of synthetic THC to cancer patients. Randall also saw this as an ominous sign. THC hadn't worked for him in studies, and he didn't want a pharmaceutical product in development to replace his or anyone else's plant-based medicine.

Activists were hopeful, though, when the languishing petition NORML had proposed in 1972, to move cannabis from Schedule I, was finally heard in 1986. After two years of hearings, DEA chief administrative law judge Francis L. Young agreed that cannabis should be rescheduled and wrote in his recommendation that "marijuana, in its natural form, is one of the safest therapeutically active substances known to man."[59] In what was likely a top-down directive, a higher-up DEA judge rejected that ruling within a year.

While support for state medical cannabis research laws and individual INDs was at its peak, Randall thought he could encourage NIDA to increase the federal supply of cannabis if he could quickly demonstrate need—and there was unprecedented need due to the emerging AIDS crisis. Cannabis's anti-nausea and appetite-inducing properties were well suited for this population. In 1991, Randall bundled hundreds of individual IND applications from AIDS patients and sent them to the FDA. The response was not what he'd expected: denial, because the federal supply program would soon shut down. States were cut off and their medical cannabis research laws essentially voided. The individuals in the IND program already receiving cannabis from the federal farm would be grandfathered in; everyone else could pursue the THC capsules.

Yet a resilient medical cannabis movement was budding. As the federal government withdrew, the majority of Americans sided with medical cannabis because the concept had grown increasingly familiar and acceptable over years of exposure. Patients remained dissatisfied with synthetic THC. If the federal government wouldn't supply patients' cannabis, they would just grow it themselves. Just as the states were first to outlaw cannabis in the early 1900s, progress would henceforth be initiated from within the states.

At least, this was the bold logic of Dennis Peron, well known in the Castro area of San Francisco for selling cannabis and for his gay rights advocacy (he had been a friend of the late Harvey Milk). In 1991, San Francisco, which had been particularly devastated by the AIDS epidemic, passed Peron's citywide Proposition P with 80 percent of the vote. This law was mostly symbolic. It did not actually legalize the use of medical cannabis, but it suggested that patients who cultivated or used it with a physician's recommendation be the "lowest priority" for law enforcement. The San Francisco Board of Supervisors wrote a resolution in response to Prop P: "Federal agencies have refused to recognize marijuana's important role in medical therapy, continue to maintain legal prohibitions against marijuana's prescriptive medical use, and recently cancelled the nation's federal marijuana-as-medicine program."[60] Prop P was the unprecedented solution to this clearly stated dilemma. One year later, Santa Cruz County passed a similar measure.

The fuel behind these propositions came from the AIDS community, which had essentially created alternative treatment plans when the medical field could not catch up quickly enough.[61] Groups like ACT-UP (the AIDS Coalition to Unleash Power) had started "buyer's clubs," which were illegal but tolerated, so patients could access experimental drugs not yet available in the United States. Soon enough, cannabis was on the menu. Then cannabis-only buyer's clubs—essentially the country's first dispensaries—began to emerge.[62]

After the IND program phased out and Californians prepared for a statewide vote on medical cannabis, Randall neared his fiftieth birthday and was exhausted by the years-long fight for cannabis. The state law strategy was, in his opinion, piecemeal and unsustainable. He'd worked hard for the federal medical cannabis model, but it had slipped away. By the time Randall died from AIDS in 2001, however, the movement he helped create had garnered unstoppable support and strength as it spread from coast to coast.

This state-by-state approach led by Californians was, and continues to be, the only way for new patients to legally obtain medical cannabis. In 1996, almost twenty years after Randall first accessed federal cannabis, Californians passed the statewide Proposition 215, also known as the Compassionate Use Act. The one-page proposition was simple and straightforward: with a doctor's recommendation, patients could legally cultivate, or have a caregiver cultivate on their behalf, cannabis for medical use. This is the version of medical cannabis most Americans know today.

3

HALF-BAKED LAWS

Following California's lead, medical cannabis laws passed in nearly one half of the United States from 1996 to the present. By no means was the road easy: the passage of just one law could take a decade of strategy, patience, and endurance. In addition to the gale of federal opposition every step of the way, many complications came from within each state. The medical cannabis movement tried to reconcile the conflicting desires of the sick, the fake-sick, covetous entrepreneurs, obstinate law enforcement, hesitant regulators, agenda-pushing activists, NIMBY citizens, open-minded physicians, and, of course, billionaires. In this ambitious endeavor, the path was often precarious—and the resulting laws sometimes far from perfect.

Money can't buy love, but it can buy a law. While passionate grassroots activism has long been the heart of the medical cannabis movement, its successes are owed in part to a key catalyst: big money. This has held true since nearly $2 million helped push through California's Proposition 215, the country's first state medical cannabis law, in 1996. Dennis Peron and some others behind Prop 215 initially declined outside help, determined to rely solely on their community and volunteers to get the initiative on the state ballot. The first offer came in late 1995 from Ethan Nadelmann, a Princeton professor turned founder of the drug policy reform–focused Lindesmith Center. (In 2000, the Lindesmith Center merged with the Drug Policy Foundation to create the Drug Policy Alliance, and Nadelmann remains at the helm.) By early 1996 Nadelmann had offered again and says that Peron reluctantly accepted; money would bring in experts to lead a professional—and successful—campaign. Nadelmann was in an opportune position to help with Prop 215. His skills as a closer complemented his ability to connect very different and very influential individuals who cared about drug policy, in this case: Bill Zimmerman, a political consultant with experience running ballot initiatives; George Soros, a billionaire investor and philanthropist who funded the Lindesmith Center; Peter Lewis, chairman of Progressive Insurance; George Zimmer, founder of Men's Wearhouse; and, later, John Sperling, founder of the University of Phoenix.

California's size and diversity make it one of the more difficult states in which to run a ballot initiative. The cost to gather signatures to place Prop 215 on the ballot and run an effective campaign amounted to just under $2 million, which came mostly from the wealthy donors (excluding Zimmerman) and the Life AIDS Lobby, one of the first groups to represent the AIDS community in California.[1] Nadelmann hired Bill Zimmerman to oversee Prop 215. The professionalization of the campaign under Zimmerman was not an entirely smooth transition. Some activists were "troopers," Nadelmann recalled, while others wound up in the way. Cannabis reform had been largely bottom-up and on the fringes, so once money and Zimmerman came in, "it was like, all of a sudden, they had this 800-pound gorilla, at least it felt that way to them, in bed with them." Nadelmann continued, "Here was the first time we actually had a chance to win . . . [but] the challenge was making sure to maintain good relations and keep a lot of the longtime activists involved."

Only with this budget and degree of collaboration did the pipe dream of legal, homegrown medical cannabis become a possibility that election year. Proposition 215 passed with 56 percent of the vote. As a result of California's landmark initiative (and others on the way), the federal government lost a good deal of authority because it could no longer rely on local law enforcement to impose federal cannabis laws (though some still continued to do so).[2] And, unlike the federal cannabis program that was abruptly discontinued after fifteen years, this state-by-state access to medical cannabis could not easily be reversed.

Nadelmann wanted to replicate this success while the majority of Americans supported medical cannabis (though he didn't have to worry, as the issue has retained majority national support since). In the summer of 1997, Nadelmann convinced Soros, Lewis, and Sperling to agree to an $8 million partnership that would allow Zimmerman to pursue ballot initiatives—since voters were polling more supportive than legislators—in an additional six states. The team selected states that were not too big or expensive for a campaign, with 60 percent or higher support for medical cannabis and a motivated group of activists: Alaska, Oregon, Washington, Colorado, Nevada, and Maine.

State by state, the initiative drafting process required a balance between the restrictive but passable initiatives preferred by Zimmerman and the laissez-faire but potentially objectionable initiatives desired by many activists. It was at least clear that the language for these initiatives had to be more specific than the open-ended Proposition 215, a surprise victory that would have likely been emphatically rejected elsewhere (more on this later). This process, Nadelmann said, was easier in states with fewer opinionated activists, like Nevada, because "more players at the table" meant more positions to take into account.

These early states confronted a long and uncertain road as they followed California in opposition of federal law. Alaska,

Oregon, and Washington passed medical cannabis initiatives in 1998, Maine in 1999, and Nevada (whose initiative was originally approved by voters in 1999 but needed to get majority support in two elections to become law) and Colorado in 2000.[3]

All but a couple of the country's medical cannabis laws can be traced to either Marijuana Policy Project (MPP), started in 1995 by former NORML employees, or Drug Policy Alliance (DPA). While MPP focuses solely on cannabis, DPA seeks to end the broader drug war in favor of more rational, health-focused drug policies. The groups work parallel to each other on cannabis laws to deploy their limited resources in a strategic way. One legislative analyst for MPP joked that they don't just sit around and throw darts at a map when selecting states for medical cannabis laws: either legislators or public officials must indicate support or there must be a local culture of acceptance. For instance, the Freedom Rally, an annual gathering of thousands of cannabis enthusiasts on the Boston Common, indicated that Massachusetts would be a better target than, say, Nebraska. A poll showing greater than 55 percent support is considered the ultimate green light. On the other hand, a qualified and influential sponsor must be willing to champion a bill in order for MPP or DPA to pursue the legislative route. One good example is the late Representative Thomas Slater, who pushed a bill through to allow medical cannabis in Rhode Island as he battled cancer and, the year he died, a bill to allow dispensaries.[4]

The initiative and legislative processes each have their benefits and drawbacks. The legislative process is lengthier and requires many compromises on the language of a bill, but it is often seen as more legitimate as a result of that process. Initiatives are usually quicker and allow for more control—but it costs money to influence minds, and it's far cheaper to speak to a few politicians than it is to inspire the masses through pricey campaigns. To secure continuing political support for a cannabis law once it has passed, DPA and MPP also contribute to the campaigns of candidates who have open minds about cannabis. MPP gave $14,000 toward Vermont governor Peter Shumlin's 2010 campaign because he said he supported decriminalization; in 2012, Drug Policy Action, DPA's political arm, gave $80,000 to Ellen Rosenblum's successful campaign for Oregon attorney general (and facilitated an additional $70,000 from Sperling) because she said on her campaign website that she would "protect the rights of medical marijuana patients."[5]

While the first seven medical cannabis laws were passed through the voter initiative process, Hawaii's, a local effort in 2000 with some input from MPP, was the first to pass through the legislature.[6] From there laws passed in: Montana (2004, MPP, initiative); Vermont (2004, MPP, legislature); Rhode Island (2006, MPP, legislature); New Mexico (2007, DPA, legislature); Michigan (2008, MPP, initiative); New Jersey (2010, DPA, legislature); Arizona (2010, MPP, initiative); Delaware (2011, MPP, legislature); Connecticut (2012, local and DPA, legislature); Massachusetts (2012, MPP groundwork, initiative funded directly by Peter Lewis); New Hampshire (2013, MPP, legislature); and Illinois (2013, MPP, legislature). Ten of these states allowed dispensaries by 2012, but they cropped up in six others. Though dispensaries first appeared in California, they are not explicitly allowed. New Mexico's law was the first to allow for state-licensed cultivators and dispensaries. The law was named after Lynn Pierson, Robert Randall's friend who died of cancer during their early medical cannabis research efforts in the state. In non-dispensary states, patients must grow their own cannabis or designate a caregiver to do so for them.

One additional medical cannabis law took a peculiar course. In 1998, ACT-UP, the AIDS organization that pushed for medical cannabis in California after the federal program was shut down, placed a medical cannabis initiative on the Washington,

D.C., ballot on a shoestring budget. In response, then Georgia representative Robert Barr added an amendment to a 1999 D.C. appropriations bill that barred (pun intended) Congress from using any money to count the votes.[7] Barney Frank, then a Massachusetts representative, referred to this unwarranted disruption of democracy as "the least intellectually valid enactment of the United States Congress in its history."[8] A U.S. district judge challenged Barr's amendment in 1999, and counted votes revealed that ACT-UP's initiative had received 69 percent support. Then, in 2000, Representative Barr and others added an amendment to the D.C. budget stating that the initiative "shall not take effect." That language was attached to D.C. appropriations bills every year until 2009; the initiative finally became law in 2010. (Arguing for states' rights, Barr switched his position by 2007 and supported MPP.)[9]

The stark discrepancy between public support for medical cannabis and the number of vocal advocates in Congress has been evident since the passage of the first law. Today, while nearly three-fourths of the country is pro medical cannabis, congressional support remains in the minority. The Barr Amendment, as it came to be known, was only one example of early congressional pushback. In another show of resistance, in 1998 Congress reiterated its support for the FDA drug approval process, speaking out against medicine by ballot box. Perhaps legislators' time would have been better spent asking themselves then—and today—why voters would feel the need to bypass the federal drug approval process in the first place. Are voters breaking the system or is the system broken?

The federal resistance continued when Bill "I didn't inhale" Clinton's administration warned that it would withdraw doctors' licenses to prescribe medication if they suggested their patients participate in a medical cannabis program.[10] The issue remained in the courts until 2002, when federal judges ruled that a doctor who *recommends* that her patient try medical cannabis is protected by First Amendment freedom of speech.[11] It is incorrect to say that someone has been "prescribed" medical cannabis; due to its placement in Schedule I, this would violate federal law. A "recommendation" protects the doctor and allows the patient to obtain cannabis (homegrown or dispensed) by legal means in his state of residence. (Arizona residents passed a law allowing medical cannabis alongside California in 1996—by an even wider margin—but it was void because the initiative included the word "prescribe" instead of "recommend."[12])

The crucial and fundamental distinction between "prescription" and "recommendation" for medical cannabis is often lost, even in states where laws have most recently passed. The Connecticut Pharmacists Association asked that the state "track *prescribers*, patients and dispensaries through the *Prescription* Monitoring Program" (emphasis added).[13] An editorial in the *Gloucester Daily Times* suggested Massachusetts pharmacies serve as dispensaries and wrote that cannabis "will have to be signed off upon by a physician through a patient *prescription*" (emphasis added).[14] These aren't bad ideas—subjecting cannabis to certain pharmaceutical protocols would help legitimize it—but they involve privileges bestowed only by the FDA, and the federal government opposes medical cannabis. Original nomenclature and unique legislative processes are repeatedly called for because the medical infrastructure set by the federal government is not yet built to accept cannabis. This resistance has made the process of legalizing cannabis as a medicine more complicated from day one.

While California stood at the vanguard of the medical cannabis movement, the state also served as a warning for trailing states. Proposition 215, as written and passed, was exceedingly vague.[15] The law allowed unlimited medical cannabis for any condition.

Odorous flatulence? A viable excuse. Chronic hangnails? You bet. Only a doctor's note stood between Californians and legal cannabis; for the first time, they were able to possess, grow, or consume as much as they wanted. No department was selected to oversee implementation of the law. There was nothing to guide law enforcement, no quality controls on the product, and the proliferation, which extended beyond medical use, made the medical cannabis movement look like an uncontrollable farce.

In the courts, too, the law was as open to interpretation as modern performance art. Dennis Peron's five-story San Francisco Cannabis Buyers' Club, also known as the Cannabis Cultivators Club, was raided and shut down in 1996.[16] He reopened the club (a dispensary) and returned volley in what became a prolonged judicial Ping-Pong match.[17] First, a state judge ruled that the club fit under the term "primary caregiver" (previously understood to be an individual) in the law and could remain open. Then, another court countered that the club was not a caregiver and needed to shut down. Yet another judge said the club could temporarily stay open, then that it needed to shut down, then that it could stay open while a jury debated if it was truly a caregiver—and finally, two weeks later, that the club needed to promptly close. Peron then renamed his club the Cannabis Healing Center and put an elderly cannabis patient in charge. In the end, the club was shut down anyway.

In the two years after Prop 215, a couple of dozen cannabis buyer's clubs (CBCs) appeared across California.[18] Unsurprisingly, the federal government intervened in 1998, to the relief of some cities and dismay of others. In places like Berkeley and Marin County, local governments had set guidelines for CBCs, which weren't explicitly permitted to exist, and built the groundwork for a local culture of tolerance. Places like Sacramento and Ventura County, on the other hand, promptly moved to shut CBCs down. A 1998 federal lawsuit against six CBCs (*United*

States v. Cannabis Cultivators Club et al.) argued that the clubs
violated federal law (the CSA) and were therefore open to federal prosecution despite state law. The mayors of San Francisco,
Oakland, West Hollywood, and Santa Cruz, as well as officials
in Mendocino County, said they opposed the intrusion.[19] One of
the CBCs, the Oakland Cannabis Buyers' Club, fought through
appeals for three more years and argued medical necessity, with
the city of Oakland at the side of owner Jeffrey Jones, but was
forced to close for good in 2001.[20] Ten years after the law was
passed and hundreds of dispensaries dotted the state, the turmoil continued: in late 2005, San Francisco created a citywide
system for permitting dispensaries while in early 2006 San Diego
sued the state to overturn the law because it conflicted with federal law.[21]

Passive state legislators worsened the consequences of the half-
baked law. No effort to enact comprehensive regulations or to
elaborate on the law succeeded until 2003—in other words, until
it was too late to rein in the dispensaries. By that point, the law
had become a sort of legal Rorschach test, so ill-defined that anyone opposed to certain changes could argue that the attempts to
clarify pushed against the voters' original intent. The initiative,
which from the beginning was neither comprehensive nor clear,
could not offer guidance on voters' specific desires or legal rights.
California Senate Bill 420, meant to clarify issues from Prop 215,
signed in late 2003, was overdue but still lacking.[22] The bill asked
that each county distribute patient and caregiver ID cards for arrest protection, and set a limit on how much cannabis a patient
or caregiver could grow or possess. In true California form, the
bill all but negated itself when it made the ID cards optional, provided that individual counties and cities could create their own
cannabis possession limits, and also permitted doctors the option
to override those possession limits with their recommendations.
The bill failed to address the CBCs and other storefronts that

had appeared throughout the state but allowed patients to create cooperatives or collectives where cannabis could be grown and distributed among members.[23]

Nearly two decades after California legalized medical cannabis, there is still little statewide standard. There could be hundreds of these dispensaries or there could be thousands; there could be tens of thousands of patients or there could be hundreds of thousands; a patient's cannabis could be moldy from a closet in Los Angeles or pesticide-free from a farm in Humboldt County; one patient could be on hospice care and another a high schooler with headaches. As for the legality of dispensaries, the state's medical cannabis industry currently operates under additional guidelines issued by Jerry Brown in 2008 when he was attorney general—but they are still only guidelines, and Brown's language is still ambiguous.

> It is the opinion of this Office that a properly organized and operated collective or cooperative that dispenses medical marijuana through a storefront may be lawful under California law, but that dispensaries that do not substantially comply with the guidelines set forth in sections IV (A) and (B), above, are likely operating outside the protections of Proposition 215 and the MMP [Medical Marijuana Program Act], and that the individuals operating such entities may be subject to arrest and criminal prosecution under California law.[24] [Emphasis added.]

As a result, the answer to the question of whether dispensaries, in their now semi-tolerated form, can be considered nonprofit cooperatives or collectives changes from one municipality to another. These were intended to be intimate, compassionate arrangements in which people were reimbursed for their efforts

but never made a profit. But many of the intended cooperatives and collectives resemble retail outlets operated by any Joe
or Jane Schmo who sells cannabis from any number of gardens.
A patient walks in with a recommendation, becomes a member, purchases cannabis, and leaves. This patient could do the
same routine all over Los Angeles dozens of times in one day. So
what degree of participation is required of a true "member"? To
how many of these storefronts can a patient legitimately possess
"membership"?

Tales of the legal chaos in California traveled east and led
to more restrictive medical cannabis laws with every passing
year. With no medical cannabis blueprint, at least one state was
bound to go astray and provide the cautionary example before
other states could slowly get it right. But DPA and MPP knew
that problematic precedents would make it more difficult to convince new states to consider medical cannabis, which is why
Nadelmann immediately insisted that subsequent draft initiatives be more detailed than Proposition 215. While Proposition
215 went into effect as a single page of untouched text, newer
laws like New Jersey's were not implemented until more than one
hundred pages of rules were added.

MPP uses a model bill for its efforts that evolves as states' experiences provide lessons.[25] The text defines terms like "bona fide
practitioner-patient relationship" and provides several examples
of illnesses that can be considered a "debilitating medical condition" and qualify for medical cannabis. It addresses who can
be a caregiver, where and how much cannabis can be grown,
where cannabis can be consumed, and patient registries and protections. Still, everyday nouns like "plant" or "enclosed, locked
facility" are not indisputable, said Dan Riffle, previously a legislative analyst for Marijuana Policy Project, and now the director of
federal policies. He prefers limiting cultivation by square footage
instead of plant numbers. "Even if we can agree on what a ma-

ture plant is—a flowering plant—my plant might be three feet tall and your plant might be five feet tall," Riffle said. "How do you delineate what's mature versus what's a seedling versus what's a cutting versus what's a clone? It's really hard to define a plant."

If Dan Riffle were to meet Catherine Cobb, she'd likely have two words for him: no kidding. As initiatives and bills were molded after approval, the labyrinthine task of determining a law's intention was bequeathed to local officials, like Cobb.

When Cobb arrived to work in Augusta, Maine, on a cold early November morning in 2009, she read an e-mail from her boss. He expressed his surprise that voters had passed an initiative to allow medical cannabis dispensaries in the state. Cobb, then director of the division of licensing and regulatory services for Maine's Department of Health and Human Services, had voted against it. The language was "too loosey goosey," and she didn't think it had a chance of passing. Little did she know that she would be responsible for implementing the law; overnight, Cobb's position had expanded from the regulation of hospitals and nursing homes to include the creation of the infrastructure for medical cannabis storefronts throughout the state. Maine's dispensaries would be the first to be licensed in New England, so she would help set the regional example. The learning curve was steep. "This has been almost all-consuming," Cobb said nine months into her effort, surrounded by piled boxes of dispensary applications that cluttered her otherwise neat office decorated with photos of her horses on the walls.

As the face of Maine's medical cannabis program, Cobb's job perks were one of a kind. A college student called her at 6:30 A.M. to say he was losing weight and asked if his condition was severe enough to qualify for medial cannabis. ("You need to talk to your doctor.") A man called to ask what would happen if he got pulled over by police and cannabis smoke wafted out of his windows, but he showed the cop his medical cannabis card. ("You can't break the laws about driving while impaired.") One woman who wasn't selected to run a dispensary called Cobb, insulted her with every name in the book, hung up, then left a message the next day to apologize for ruining her day and to explain that she was set off because she needed a job. Cobb eventually got used to being strangers' temporary informant, therapist, or worst enemy.

Cobb's one and only jaunt down cannabis lane was short-lived. She had a puff in college and didn't like it. "I got too giggly, out of control," she said. "And if you knew me, the regulatory area is very much suited to me because I don't like to be out of control." But Cobb spent many hours and days trying to stay true to what Maine voters wanted while providing enough structure to ensure the medical cannabis program wouldn't transform the state's lobsters and lighthouses image into bros with bongs. The state was as far from California as the Lower 48 could get, and she wanted the program to reflect that distance. As an experienced regulator, Cobb understood that specific was synonymous with smooth. She called New Mexico, the first state with a law that allowed for licensed dispensaries, and asked for advice. People overseeing the state medical cannabis program told her to take it slow.

First, Cobb said, she immersed herself in the language of the initiative. Cobb decided to limit the number of dispensary licenses in the first round to eight. With the help of a task force, she deleted the line "a nonprofit dispensary is a primary caregiver" from the initiative.[26] Cobb wanted caregivers to be people who cared for a few patients and dispensaries to be the brick-and-mortar storefronts that provided for many—a distinction that California struggled to make. She specified that hospice or nursing home staff could serve as caregivers, a clarification she felt necessary after her years of working with these facilities. She changed "qualifying" patient to "registered," lest a debate begin about what it takes to be "qualifying."[27]

Once the regulations were finalized, legislators approached Cobb to express their sympathy. She laughed and told them, "I can regulate the hell out of anything." The regulation of this complicated industry was an opportunity to learn something new, and Cobb joked that she'd be in trouble if anyone looked through the Internet searches that had her immersed in the wide world of cannabis for weeks on end. Patients, such as a woman with cancer who wilted below eighty pounds and a teenager who suffered migraines after losing a part of her brain in a skiing accident, also helped Cobb embrace her role in the new program. A woman with months to live told Cobb at an event that she needed the dispensaries to open because she couldn't find a caregiver. Cobb knew that she shouldn't intervene in this woman's personal situation, but she introduced her to a man in attendance who had identified himself as a caregiver. At first, it was easy for Cobb to focus on the criminal aspects of cannabis use. But after talking to patients, she said, "Listening to the benefits of medical marijuana and how it's improved their quality of life and their functioning in this society, I think that people really need to start being open-minded about it. It's not always about what's legal and not legal." The experience was, in many ways, transformative. Cobb likely never thought, in her decades of traditional work, that she'd have the opportunity to respond, when asked her job title, "Besides Weed Queen?"

While Cobb's goal in Maine was to clarify the rules of the game, New Jersey tried to overhaul the game. But, after a series of questionable moves, New Jersey officials invited the ire of frustrated and impatient residents. First, Governor Chris Christie proclaimed he did not support the medical cannabis law signed in the eleventh hour of former governor Jon Corzine's term.[28] Christie had inherited an unwelcome responsibility, and the activists figured he'd be as friendly to the law as that wicked stepmother was to Cinderella. Christie then attempted to designate

Rutgers University as the state cannabis grower and restrict cannabis distribution to teaching hospitals, despite the legislation's call for six nonprofit dispensaries.[29] Rutgers rejected the idea because doing so would put roughly $500 million in annual federal funding on the line (the federal and state disagreement at play once again). Finally, New Jersey's more than one hundred pages of rules became known as the nation's strictest.[30] The state did not allow homegrown cannabis and decreed that none of the distributed cannabis could have over 10 percent THC—both firsts in the country. The 10 percent limit required time and money for repeated trial and error in the garden, and then even more money for testing. The rule that prohibited home cultivation would eventually force some patients to drive more than 150 miles round-trip to visit a dispensary. Patients and activists, who saw better medical cannabis options elsewhere in the country, began to refer to New Jersey as the No Garden State.[31]

Officials sometimes struggle to reconcile the desire for strict regulation with the needs of constituents when it comes to medical cannabis, but it became clear that the New Jersey Department of Health and Senior Services wouldn't budge on these provisions. Anyone who wanted to participate in the program needed to get used to it. During an informational session set up by the department on the state's medical cannabis program in October 2010, nine months after the law passed, the auditorium in Trenton's War Memorial building felt like a battleground. Early in the public comment period, Chris Goldstein, a cannabis advocate affiliated with NORML, took the microphone. He was particularly perturbed by the 10 percent THC cap and reminded Deputy Commissioner Susan Walsh, who helped draft the rules, that the pharmaceutical anti-emetic drug Marinol contains 100 percent THC.

"That's not what the legislation told me to do. The legislation did not tell me to give you all a pill to take for nausea," Walsh said, sitting onstage.

Goldstein replied, to applause, "It didn't say to regulate the cannabinoid content of New Jersey medical marijuana either."

One man who came up to ask a question said, "It's hard to imagine a more hostile interpretation of the law than the one proposed by the department."

"Hostile?" Walsh asked.

"Yes, hostile. Absolutely."

"I guess we'll disagree about that bit," Walsh said before the man continued.

Up to the microphone came Anne Davis, a lawyer and executive director of NORML New Jersey, who often worked with Goldstein. "What I've been seeing," Davis said, "is that the level of cannabinoids varies within strains greatly and it also varies within the plant. So, question: how are you going to take that into consideration and enable a grow operation which won't have to be destroying plants because . . . they don't know how to grow at a limit of 10 percent THC?"

Walsh eventually replied with an expert nonanswer answer and said, "There's a minimum and maximum so that within that range of 3 to 10 percent a plant can grow. If a plant is 12 percent or 15 percent or 20 percent, it would have to be destroyed. And that's just part of the regulations."

At one point a woman in a plaid shirt angrily waved a piece of paper and insinuated that the Department of Health and Senior Services already had its final rules set because the rulemaking deadline had passed (it hadn't) and that it had no plans to incorporate the public comment. This was a clear misunderstanding, but the department's distance from the medical cannabis community seemed to breed mistrust. "It's all a big freaking smoke and mirrors act up there and it's got me so frustrated," she yelled.

Perhaps the tenth person to bring up the THC cap issue was a man who began, "I don't mean to harp on the issue on the 10 percent THC—"

Walsh interrupted sarcastically, "Feel free, feel free."

Another man, upset that growers and dispensers required separate licenses, asked, "Could you please explain again why you have made this program seemingly uneconomically viable by splitting the functions of production *and* distribution when the law wasn't written that way? It seems like you put several barriers into the process."

Walsh told him that the legislation allowed a licensed facility to operate as either a cannabis producer or a distributer: "Remember the word is 'or.' It's not 'and.' It's 'or.' The legislature and the advocates could have pushed for 'and.'"

Shortly before this remarkable hairsplitting, a woman said slowly and righteously, "There's a patient belief that the Christie administration is trying to set up this program to fail."

Walsh seemed fed up. The forum had begun to feel like an inquisition. She replied to the woman in a deliberate tone, "I'm going to take that as a question because I want to answer it, so thank you. This program came to my department, to me personally, to my desk. Absolutely at no time did the governor or his staff reach out to me and say, 'Sue, make this restrictive, make this not work, we got a plan.' . . . [No one] told me to do anything except to implement this law. And that's what my staff and I have been doing from January 1 on without a break. And my staff is here, you could recognize them because they're exhausted, and I'm tired myself. But I'm glad you stated it because I know the thought is out there that there's something going on here that's not out in the open. If it is, it's beyond me and I was the one who was told to do this."

This quarreling was not solely the by-product of disagreement among the regulators, patients, activists, and wannabe dispensary owners. Unacknowledged was a shared frustration as they tried to bring cannabis out of the black market and into the hands of patients in the shadow of an adversarial federal government.

Toward the end of the public comment period, one man asked what would happen if the federal government decided to re-schedule cannabis and recognize it as a medicine. Walsh thought for a moment, and then leaned into the microphone. "If medical marijuana was rescheduled to a Schedule II drug, then it will certainly be a lot of work we did for a long time that we wouldn't have needed to do," she said. "Is that a good way of saying it?"

On the West Coast, where medical cannabis laws have been on the books for nearly two decades and cannabis communities are well established, change has proven especially difficult to bring about after the fact. Washington State's medical cannabis law, for example, was passed in 1998, only two years after California's, as part of Nadelmann's sweep of six states. It allowed patients to grow their own cannabis or designate someone to do so for them. Patients were protected only with an affirmative defense, an option to present their case in court, but they could still be ar-rested and hauled off to jail. Senator Jeanne Kohl-Welles, a petite blond twenty-year veteran of the legislature, molded much of the original Initiative 692. But Kohl-Welles knew that the law was problematic and that she eventually would have to draft what she called "the Big Bill" to fix it.[32]

Kohl-Welles and the ACLU of Washington worked together for months on a list of goals for the draft bill introduced in early 2011. They wanted, among other things, to license dispensaries and growers; to allow collectives of twenty-five patients to grow up to ninety-nine plants; explicit arrest protection for patients found within their possession limits who chose to register with the Department of Health (with only affirmative defense for the non-registered); and an option for owners of illegal dispensaries (there are usually some) to comply with the new rules and apply to be-come licensed the following year. Along with some proposed re-strictions, Kohl-Welles and the ACLU of Washington also sought

custody, workplace, and eviction protections. Without such protections, for example, a woman with cancer could lose her child,
job, and apartment if a pesky neighbor who disapproved of her
medical cannabis use were to summon a prohibitionist cop. This
draft bill was a proactive piece of legislation that patients elsewhere would have celebrated. Certainly, not all of these provisions would survive the legislative process, but, at the time, few
politicians were willing to ask for so many reforms on behalf of
the cannabis community. Kohl-Welles saw where the community
was headed, but rather than prohibit collectives or punish the
illegal dispensaries, she offered a forgiving option to cooperate.

By the time Washington's lawmakers and law enforcement
officials added their two cents, however, the draft bill forbade
doctors from seeing patients solely to recommend cannabis and
limited collectives to three patients and forty-five plants. While
intended to prevent recommendation mills, the doctor rule was
problematic because many patients' primary care physicians refused to recommend cannabis, and those patients would turn
to willing doctors; however, those physicians could not take on
every patient for whom they had recommended cannabis. Kohl-
Welles did not like the idea of three-person collectives. "When
we think of sixty thousand—seventy or eighty thousand people
in the state, [imagine] how many collective gardens there would
be. It's ridiculous, but that's all that they want," she said, referring
to law enforcement. Kohl-Welles also wanted a registry because
it offered a definitive way for a patient to prove to police that he
had a right to the cannabis he possessed, but the activists and
the ACLU were opposed for privacy reasons. So they agreed on a
voluntary registry. Unfortunately, medical cannabis patients often have to choose between privacy and protections from law
enforcement when they are owed the right to both.

Kohl-Welles acknowledged then that the draft had become
"more problematic and less ideal" with these changes, but that it

was still much better than the law in place at the time. Indeed, the Big Bill was better than what was offered in most medical cannabis states at the time. People in New Jersey were so busy trying to combat the arbitrary THC cap that they never even got to privacy rights. (There was barely a shrug in New Jersey when, in late 2012, as the first dispensary in the state prepared to open, N.J. Department of Health and Senior Services accidentally sent an e-mail to more than 450 patients that included all e-mail addresses and some names of medical cannabis patients.)[33]

While activists in other states often rally behind pro-cannabis legislators, many Washington State activists opposed Kohl-Welles's effort because of the changes to the Big Bill. After championing the polarizing issue for over a decade on their behalf, she had somehow become the enemy. Their misgivings began in 2007 when Kohl-Welles wrote another bill, Senate Bill 6032, the first clarification to the medical cannabis law since its passage in 1998. SB 6032 was supposed to allow cooperative growing but, by the time it got through the legislature, all that was left was the opportunity to define a vague term in the law that allowed patients a "sixty-day supply" of cannabis. The possession limits Kohl-Welles helped determine—1.5 pounds prepared cannabis and fifteen plants—were unseen in most other medical cannabis states. But some Washington activists seethed when SB 6032 passed because they wanted to be allowed to form collectives and viewed the possession limit as unwelcome regulation where there previously was none. "We ended up with the amounts for usable marijuana and plants that are the highest in the whole country by far, but it was like the end of the world when the rules came out," Kohl-Welles recalled, palms down on a stack of papers in her Olympia office, seeming annoyed by, yet resigned to, the tug-of-war. "I was vilified, the Department of Health, the governor were vilified. And they got the best thing imaginable. They fought it and fought it and fought it because it was not the ideal bill that *we* wanted—I mean, *I* introduced it."

The Big Bill of 2011 proposed the most regulation that Washington activists had faced in years, so many again demanded the status quo. As the bill worked its way through the legislature nearly one hundred members of the Seattle-area cannabis community gathered at the Cannabis Defense Coalition (CDC) headquarters. Holiday lights lined the windows of the otherwise plain building, where a stop sign read: STOP ARRESTING MEDICAL MARIJUANA PATIENTS. Just inside the door were pamphlets, magazines, stickers, and a Ping-Pong table; a sign with Dennis Peron's name on it and an "Herb is Superb" poster were displayed nearby. From the high ceilings hung green and purple cutout cannabis leaves and a disco ball. Participants sat in a circle of chairs in front of a whiteboard with the following discussion topics: ADOPT-A-HIGHWAY, COUNTY FAIR PROJECT, BULK RECYCLING, CANNABIS COLLEGE, and DRUG CZAR.

Steve Sarich spoke most often, to no one's surprise. Sarich, who looks like a roughed-up Al Pacino, had become a customary interloper at the state capital around the cannabis issue. A *Seattle Weekly* writer described him as a "gun-toting provocateur." He claimed, for example, that Kohl-Welles had offered a state senate seat to Alison Holcomb, then director of drug policy at the ACLU of Washington, who advised on the bill, "for selling out the patients." (It's worth noting that Holcomb, with Kohl-Welles's support, led the successful effort to legalize cannabis for adult general use in 2012; once again, Sarich was one of the major opponents.) Sarich had a knack for sounding remarkably convincing while exclaiming falsities. The bill clearly stated that dispensaries would be licensed by July 1, 2012, but Sarich said to the group that the true date was years later, part of a master plan to trick people into supporting something that would potentially never take effect. Standing up, Sarich added, "We can't wait that long. But that's what it's going to take. We won't have any dispensaries until then. We won't have any licensed grows until then. All they're doing is they're pushing the ball down the field to not have to deal with this."

A guy named Phil, who sat to Sarich's right, corrected him, "The plain language in the bill says they're legal on July 1, 2012."

"No, no. You know what, Phil, I wish you'd read the bill before you say things like that," Sarich said. "That's not what the bill says. The bill actually says that we've got some kind of ambiguous affirmative defense provided we don't violate any of the other sections of the law. . . . There won't be any dispensaries because there's no provision for it after July 1, 2012."

Phil smirked at Sarich. This sort of infighting was common in Seattle. The activists disagreed among themselves as often as they disagreed with the legislators.

"I've got it here, don't laugh at me or I'll make an ass out of you. I mean, I came prepared," Sarich said. Then he got to his point, "What does anybody want to keep in this bill? Because I don't see much I want to keep."

"What *do* you want to keep?" asked Ben Livingston, a CDC member about half Sarich's age.

"I can't see much of anything that I would want to keep," Sarich repeated.

"There's not one thing in there?" Livingston asked. "What about parental rights?"

The conversation in the room bounced among various topics of concern. Livingston later reiterated the agreed-upon "demands" of the group: provide arrest protection for those not registered, return collectives to former limits, and remove all language that restricted doctors. Ezra Eickmeyer, a towering lobbyist for the Washington Cannabis Association, insisted that they needed "a good bill or no bill." The conversation again turned worst-case scenario as one guy, who looked like Santa in a black zip-up sweater, offered his take on the no-cannabis-doctors part of the bill. "As far as I'm concerned, it's a Trojan horse," the man said, pointing for emphasis. "No doctor is going to do it. No nurse practitioner is going to do it because they are going to be under scrutiny through the professional ethics committee. . . . If that gets through, we have just lost medical marijuana in the state."

Eickmeyer smoothed his black pea coat and, in a reassuring tone, said that they should wait to see what came out of the House Health Care & Wellness committee. As a liaison between this group and the state legislature, he knew how to tell both groups what they wanted to hear. And some in this crew worried that they were up against a repeat of what happened with SB 6032, which passed in a form they disapproved of before they could kill it. "I think we still want to be in the phase of trying to fix the words on the chalkboard. But if push comes to shove and you have to shoot the chalkboard in the skull, then . . . " Eickmeyer trailed off. Earlier, he recalled the SB 6032 experience. "I felt like somebody was ripping my testicles off, man," he said. "I cut my fucking hair to get that through the Ways and Means committee—" applause drowned him out, "and here they are, all these people who just want to cause harm just screwed the bill up. And our friends didn't fight that hard to protect us."

But it appeared Kohl-Welles and Holcomb understood and supported the activists as wholeheartedly as politics would allow. Holcomb said, "I think, rightfully so, grassroots activists, especially those who are actually patients dealing with this law that has not been working for them for twelve years now, are very skeptical of government looking out for them."

Holcomb, Kohl-Welles, and the majority of activists ultimately wanted the same thing: reliable access to medical cannabis and protections from arrest. That should have been enough to unite them, but some in the Seattle cannabis community had what Holcomb called an "expectations management issue" when it came to the difficult process of watching an ideal bill go through a legislative sausage maker. "We put in everything we thought we could possibly reasonably ask for with a straight face, know- ing . . . that it's a huge lift," Holcomb said. "There's a lot of asks, and the likelihood of us getting all of those things is really, re- ally minimal. So for people who aren't used to that, it's really frustrating when you see something that looks like a great bill that you support get introduced and things start getting stripped out. And a lot of activists have their expectations at a certain place and they think that 'oh, you're just giving up on us.'"

As these battles over medical cannabis resolved themselves state by state, a patchwork of medical cannabis laws developed across the country.[34] This process has its consequences—but it's necessitated by the federal rejection of medical cannabis. Complex medical decisions are left to legislators, regulators, and voters. They are forced to decide, for example, which medical conditions qualify a person to use cannabis. While New Mexico, Delaware, Connecticut, Oregon, and Maine permit medical cannabis use for post-traumatic stress disorder, for example, the rest of the medical cannabis states do not. Eight states allow Alzheimer's patients access; the rest do not. Patients cease to be considered patients once they cross into a nonmedical cannabis state or one that does not recognize their condition. So, if one of thousands of patients using medical cannabis for PTSD in New Mexico moved to a state that didn't accept cannabis for PTSD, that patient would be forced to leave the medicine behind or face arrest.

There are also discrepancies over what would typically be con- sidered a refill, in this case referred to as possession limits. Alaska allows one ounce, while Washington State allows twenty-four. In New Jersey, D.C., and Delaware, patients may not grow their own cannabis, while in Alaska and Hawaii patients have no choice but homegrown. Neither extreme is ideal. If the cannabis must

be homegrown and a disabled patient cannot find a willing caregiver, the person who stands to benefit the most from this plant
cannot benefit at all. Conversely, mandating that patients obtain
cannabis from a dispensary could require a patient to travel long
distances for a supply that a skilled caregiver could provide them
more affordably near home. Limits on dispensaries are also assigned arbitrarily. New Jersey permits six licenses, while the less
populated Massachusetts allows up to thirty-five.

State laws aside, the inconsistencies and uncertainties around
medical cannabis extend to where the various state programs
are housed. In Hawaii it's the Narcotics Enforcement Division;
D.C. tried to stick it (to the delight of many cannabis legalization
advocates) under the Alcoholic Beverage Regulation Administration; Connecticut chose the Department of Consumer
Protection; in Vermont the registry is overseen by the Criminal
Information Center, alongside the state's sex offender registry;
and most others are under health. The requirement that patients
in Vermont contact the police and register like sex offenders, and
share the name of their caregiver, was such a turnoff that few
caregivers were willing to put that uncomfortable target on their
backs. As a result, for seven years before dispensaries were approved in 2011, many patients who did register with the state had
to procure their cannabis on the black market and what was supposed to be a medical cannabis program functioned as little more
than a registry. And as if the state-to-state and state-to-federal
disagreements aren't enough, towns and cities within states often
have the option to implement moratoriums.

Ill patients ought to be the focus of this conversation. After all,
the medical cannabis movement is based on the desire to present a therapeutic option to those who need it. Ironically, the
very patients who provided the initial impetus for these laws are
oftentimes lost in a complicated process dominated by activists'

desires, legislators' fears, relentless taboos, and the looming pos-sibility of federal intervention.

Every day, millions of people across the country wake up in pain that could be alleviated with cannabis. Some of the diag-noses have become household names, like cancer; others, like Ehlers-Danlos syndrome or Crohn's disease, require patients and their families to do endless research. Their lives often do not follow the nine to five, TGIF routine. They have pill bottles in place of spice racks. These are people for whom a staircase is a challenge, a meal is intolerable, and carrying the groceries is impossible. The last question on these patients' minds should be how to safely and easily access cannabis as a medicine. Politics should not deprive these sick Americans of the right to feel relief.

The lists of qualifying conditions for medical cannabis are of-ten imperfect and some patients are inevitably excluded, and yet the process to add a condition to the law can take years. Tristan Thayer, who double-majored in botany and molecular genet-ics at the University of Vermont, was diagnosed with leukemia in 2002. The Vermont medical cannabis law wouldn't pass for another two years, but as he underwent chemotherapy Tristan decided to grow and consume cannabis to alleviate his nausea. Before he died in 2005, he urged his teenage brother, Max, who struggled with nausea and wasting as a result of chronic renal failure, to try cannabis.

In the fall of 2010, twenty-two-year-old Max walked near Tristan's grave behind his family's home, built by his father up in the tree-covered hills of southern Vermont. Max and his mother, Sue, knew the Latin names of each of the plants that grew on their property. Perfect heads of cabbage sat in their garden, and small, bright peppers hung from vines. Max had fine blond hair and a pronounced Adam's apple, and he moved like a mario-nette. His lanky appearance was further exaggerated by his wast-ing, a side effect of his condition. Though cannabis helped Max,

Max and Sue Thayer talk near Tristan Thayer's grave on the property of their rural Vermont home. ALYSON MARTIN

his condition was not included in the new law at the time his brother suggested he use it in 2005. Sue said she did what any mother would do and maintained a cannabis garden for Max even though he couldn't yet legally participate in the program. In August 2007, Sue was sitting in her rustic living room as she finished a cross-stitch that read "Don't Panic"; then she went to shower. Max's condition was added to the law the previous month, but he hadn't yet applied. As he sat on the porch, at the end of a long, winding driveway from their property to the main road, state police showed up. Max ran to alert his mother. The police raided their garden, and Sue was arrested and charged with felony cultivation.

Three years after the arrest, as Sue's case lingered in the courts, Max sat at his dining room table while the setting sun shone through the windows. "It bothers me that the state has labeled my mother as a felon because all she's ever done is try to provide me with the best medicine. It bothers me that the state viewed my brother as a criminal when all he was trying to do was alleviate the severe symptoms from his disease," Max said. "And being a political symbol of this law that was in flux and is still in flux is very difficult for us. We have a life to lead." The Thayers came to medical cannabis advocacy, like many others, due to circumstances. Before Sue's arrest, she and Max were content with limiting their community involvement to the library board and other local activities. But soon they were in the news, speaking up on behalf of patients' rights and telling the story of how cannabis helped Tristan and Max. Ultimately, though, their public support for medical cannabis was more about defending the family than the plant.

The Thayers are one of many families who have had to break laws to access cannabis. The plant allowed Essie DeBonet, who weighed eighty-three pounds, to eat and keep her pills down. In her Albuquerque living room on a spring 2010 morning, DeBonet credited cannabis as the reason she is still alive in her late sixties. The former nurse was diagnosed with AIDS in 1994 and began using cannabis from the black market in 2000 because New Mexico did not yet have a law. "We're being forced to choose between an archaic and inhumane law and staying alive. And what would you do? What choice would you make? What choice would anybody make? Rot slowly and die a horrible death or die with some dignity?" she asked in a forced whisper, sitting on a brown leather couch. Her walls were covered with photos of children and grandchildren and painted landscapes.

DeBonet vividly remembered the struggle to get New Mexico's medical cannabis law passed. For years, she faithfully made the trip to the state capital to offer her testimony during hearings on the proposed bill. When members of the Agriculture and Water Resources Committee voted to table the bill in 2006, one year before it was finally signed, DeBonet remembered that she mustered all of her strength and screamed, "Why are you trying to

Essie DeBonet shows the gun she keeps under her bed for protection from those she fears may want to steal her medical cannabis. ALYSON MARTIN

kill us? Why are you trying to kill us?"[35] As legislators debated the issue, she felt like they existed in a world so removed from hers. "They talk about getting high. There is no more high. That does not exist anymore," DeBonet said, looking over the glasses pushed down on her long nose, her face thin and sunken, blue veins visible down her cheeks. Her dogs remained faithfully by her feet; otherwise she lived alone. Just above her bed, she displayed pictures of Christ that reminded her that "the fight isn't mine, it's his. I tell him that the fight may be his, but I'm the one that's living with it. And it's tough."

DeBonet sleeps with an Ultra-Lite handgun under her mattress in case anyone attempts to steal her cannabis plants or supply. So much energy is spent scrutinizing patients and their caregivers that legislators often forget that these people are in a vulnerable position. They have access to a plant that remains lucrative on the black market as a result of prohibition. One burglary of a patient's home could net thousands of dollars in cannabis, an amount that weighs no more than a pound and could be easily transported in a backpack. Ellen Smith, of Rhode Island, was burglarized twice. The first time, a man delivering oil began to behave suspiciously when he smelled cannabis and came back later that night to steal her harvest. The following year, four neighborhood teenagers broke in and stole Smith's supply. After both thefts, Smith had to restart her crop.

In 2004, Smith was diagnosed with Ehlers-Danlos syndrome, a connective tissue disorder that caused her tendons to work like overstretched, brittle rubber bands. To prevent breathing interruptions, she sleeps with her head, neck, and chest fastened in a hospital-style bed that is pushed up against a twin bed on which her husband, Stu, sleeps. Smith's service dog, Maggie, is often tucked between them. When his wife is hurting, Stu wants nothing more than to hold her, but that would only hurt her worse because a tight hug could displace a rib or, worse, her sternum. As a result, Smith has undergone more than twenty operations after dislocations throughout her body. These operations required travel to out-of-state hospitals and left her wheelchair-bound for months at a time during recovery. The retired schoolteacher was reluctant to try cannabis until she learned that her body was intolerant of nearly all painkillers. Cannabis was her best option. She eventually overcame her internal stigma and felt ready to confront anybody else's. "I'm not a bad person. I'm not a dirty person. I'm a person with a medical condition and I need help," she said from her country home, next to a window that faced a barn and farm animals. With her husband's help, Smith turns cannabis into oil that she mixes with homemade applesauce to eat. But when she is required to travel out of Rhode Island for surgery, to states where she is no longer qualified for medical cannabis, she is left without pain relief when she needs it most.

"When I have a really horrible day, I'll cry and I'll wonder how many more days I can do it. And then I have a decent day; once

Ellen Smith stands in her basement, where her young cannabis plants grow. ALYSON MARTIN

in a while, I'll have a good day. And I'll say to my husband—what do I say to you?"

"Hold on to this day," her husband said.

"Just remind me that I had the good day because you know in your heart it's not going to be there tomorrow," Smith finished.

4

GREEN DIGGERS

When faced with a new frontier or a promise of untapped riches, Americans rush forth in hordes. This happened during the Gold Rush, and history will remember the founding of the medical cannabis industry as the Green Rush. There is money to be made, from the farmer who thumbs a seed into dirt to the vendor who sells specialty rice papers for joints.

Yet for all of the opportunities this new commodity presents, medical cannabis is one of the most complicated industries in the United States. Just as some gold seekers emerged from the rush with generations of wealth and others returned home with only stories of struggle, this industry promises nothing. Those who have been lured by the possibility of money know that, for now, the bulk of the profits rests in the manufacture (growing) and sale (dispensing) of cannabis—two endeavors that are illegal under federal law. The fate of any entrepreneur who handles this plant is therefore hazy. The future could be a lifetime in prison or a secure spot at the ground level of the American cannabis market.

Of course, many Americans happen to be willing to take the great risk for the great reward. This was most evident when the rush first peaked and attracted national attention between 2009 and 2011, due in part to the recession. A report by the trade

publication *Medical Marijuana Business Daily* estimated that, after just fifteen years, the sales for medical cannabis in 2012 were
$1.3 billion—and growing.[1]

Ironically, one woman who helped make this industry possible
is exceptionally anti-industry. Valerie Corral has been called the
Mother Teresa of Pot. The matriarch of the Wo/Men's Alliance
for Medical Marijuana (WAMM) in Santa Cruz, California, pad-
dled far in front of the medical cannabis wave when she formed
the collective in the early nineties. Before Corral helped draft
Prop 215, California's original medical cannabis law, she worked
with the city of Santa Cruz to enact a local measure that permitted medical cannabis and encouraged law enforcement to leave
ill patients alone. Although Corral helped pour the foundation
for the legalization of medical cannabis, a bourgeoning industry
is not what she had in mind.

"If we look at the dispensaries, how do we see them serving
people? They sell pot," Corral said. "We move farther and farther
away from service, serving people, when we move farther away
from knowing who we serve."

Corral packs a whole lot of fire in her slight frame at five feet
tall and just over a hundred pounds. She is commanding, but
rarely raises her voice. Corral's Santa Cruz home is a moun-
taintop cocoon that peeks between towering trees at the Pacific
Ocean. The homestead is where WAMM members grow cannabis, and it also serves as a rotating shelter for members who need
company or a place to sleep. True collectives, like Corral's, are
now rare, but represent what much of California's medical cannabis community looked like when voters approved the state's
medical cannabis law in 1996. On a busy day of trimming plants
during harvest season 2010, Corral wore a black tank top screen-
printed with the words "No Enemy" and a pink bandana wrapped
around her long, wavy auburn hair. Gold earrings tracked up her
left ear. As Corral sat on the armrest of a couch in her sunlit

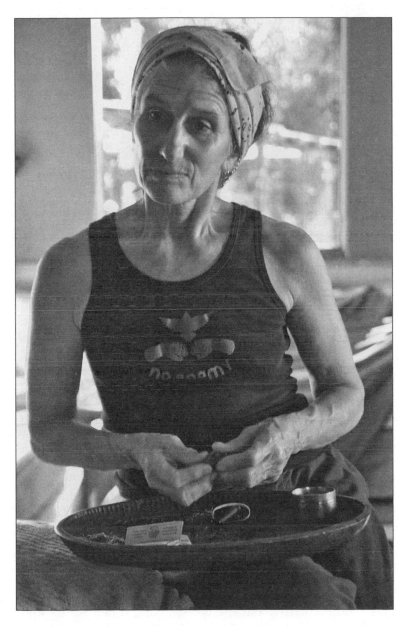

Valerie Corral rolls a joint in her home in Santa Cruz, California. She uses cannabis to help control seizures. ALYSON MARTIN

living room, she methodically rolled a joint on a wooden tray upon her lap. She placed it to her mouth, lit the end, and slowly inhaled.

In 1973, at the age of twenty, Corral was riding in her friend's VW Beetle in Nevada when a small World War II–era fighter plane plunged down and almost hit the car, causing a near-fatal accident.[2] Corral was thrown from the car, and, after severe head trauma, she was left with grand mal seizures and migraines that were never controlled by pharmaceuticals. After realizing how much cannabis helped her condition, Corral began to advocate for medical cannabis in California in the 1990s and became one of the state's first patients.

A nurturer above all else, Corral describes her role as using cannabis to help seriously ill and dying WAMM members make the transition from life to death. She calls patients who have died "masters" or "teachers" because they have endured the end of life and gone to a place the living have not. A bright yellow wall at the WAMM headquarters, also in Santa Cruz, displays photographs of collective members who have died. In Corral's office, she keeps a Victor Hugo quote on one wall, "As the purse is emptied, the heart is filled," and a poem on another, "This is the end/of the tunnel/and guess what/there is/a little/light."

"In all honesty, you want me by your bedside if you're dying or if you're sick. To be with people is much more important to me. So how do you build an important and useful organization? You build it from the people up," Corral said of the WAMM model. "And if you build it from the people up, it'll serve the people. It's really probably the most obvious answer and that's how come WAMM is a bit different."

Harvest season is work season for able-bodied WAMM members. Corral buzzed about the office, asking if new shears were needed as the sticky resin gummed up the ones in use. All four strains of WAMM cannabis are grown down the hill from

Members of the Wo/Men's Alliance for Medical Marijuana trim cannabis during harvest season. ALYSON MARTIN

Corral's home, in a large garden. These trimming parties are necessary to prepare massive crops of cannabis for the collective in a short period of time. At one table long enough for a formal Thanksgiving dinner, seven WAMM members cut off the extra fan leaves from the tight cannabis buds. A bald man with a gray goatee sat at the helm, wearing a white cutoff shirt inscribed with "Humboldt." Two silver-haired women, wearing pastels and glasses low on their noses, leaned in close and chatted across the table about errands they needed to run together later that day. If knitting needles and yarn had replaced the ceramic bowls and cannabis, this group could have been in a coffee klatch.

WAMM's business model has more to do with caregiving than fund-raising, so the office is constantly in danger of closing—all while many dispensaries pull in six and seven figures per year, benefiting from the law Corral helped write. Although Corral still hopes that cannabis activists will follow WAMM's lead away from the bottom line, her model is atypical for medical cannabis businesses; WAMM is one of the last of its kind, endangered but not extinct.

In the absence of strict, explicit regulation, Californians have opened dispensaries everywhere, from the lush northern mountains to the southern sandy beaches, and particularly in Los Angeles and the Bay Area. In the 1990s, when California's medical cannabis industry was in its infancy, it was more difficult to open a bakery than a store to dispense cannabis. It's hardly surprising that Proposition 215, the Compassionate Use Act of 1996, didn't remain purely about compassion, and that those with monetary goals took up the cause and opened up shop. Still, few could have predicted that, fifteen years after the passage of Proposition 215, a rowdy crowd would huddle over a long row of bongs at a smoky Medical Kush Beach Club hash bar in Venice Beach. Young men waited for busty women to serve them the cannabis equivalent of liquor shots in the Hooter's-like atmosphere. With a view of Muscle Beach, customers stood by for wrestler Rob Van Dam to host the Hash World Cup. A visiting Brazilian "patient" wearing sunglasses and a tan fedora smeared his lips over a microphone and crooned "Riooooo de Janeiro" until an employee joked, "All right, don't give this guy anymore hash."

When state medical cannabis laws are passed, officials often declare they want to steer clear of that Golden State mess. Some state programs forbid dispensaries, for example, without realizing that California's law never even mentioned dispensaries. Indeed, few medical cannabis laws can be so airtight as to withstand the wild-eyed scramble toward fertile ground. As of 2012, ten states permitted cannabis dispensaries, but dispensary-like storefronts appeared in an additional six. In those non-dispensary states, enterprising types studied the laws to decipher how they could strike big money while getting medical cannabis to ill—and, sometimes, perfectly healthy—people.

On the commercial strip that leads to the palatial state capitol in Lansing, Michigan, Compassionate Apothecary was one of the more tasteful cannabis shops. With its tree-shaded residential exterior, plain carpeting, and wood-paneled walls, it still resembled the insurance agency it had replaced in early 2010. Jars filled with cannabis lined the tops and interiors of glass display cases. Whenever a patient wanted to inspect a particular bud, owner Ken Van Every gingerly reached into a jar with engraved chopsticks. A back table recalled a school bake sale, piled high with cannabis-infused snack mix, double chocolate chip muffins, and gummies. A selection of loosely branded Sweet Leaf Gardens candy had the label, "Hard Candy. Watermelon. Max Potency"; another read, "Soothing Throat Lozenges. Menthol. Max Potency." (All estimates, of course, because "max" could mean a panicked high for some or an indiscernible buzz for others.) Van Every said his dispensary served between thirty and sixty of its five hundred members each day.

Van Every was an unexpected member of the otherwise youngish cannabis industry. The retirement-aged fly-fishing enthusiast looks more the part of small-town board member. In his office, he kept a framed photograph of his kids posed in ascending order of height. Copious NASCAR memorabilia told the story of his years managing professional motor sports programs for General Motors.

While dispensaries are not allowed under Michigan law, Van Every felt emboldened by a sense of safety in numbers: similar shops had opened, like creeping ivy, all along East Michigan Avenue, without harassment from law enforcement. By 2011, the city had roughly a dozen within view of that state capitol building. But there were canyons between Michigan's medical cannabis law and the inferences necessary to justify any of these shops. Michigan caregivers could legally grow twelve cannabis plants in an "enclosed, locked facility" for five patients, or four patients if the caregiver was also a patient (a total of sixty plants). Caregivers were permitted to possess two and a half ounces of cannabis per patient (a total of 12.5 ounces). The law stated that "medical use" by a patient included "transfer, or transportation of marihuana or paraphernalia relating to the administration of marihuana to treat or alleviate a registered qualifying patient's debilitating medical condition."[3] Dispensary owners interpreted this to mean that the law allowed patients to "transfer" their cannabis to other patients and, further, that "transfer" implied "sell."

The Apothecary acted as a middleman between these patients, who paid $5 a month for membership dues. Van Every provided lockers (the "enclosed, locked facility") that patients could rent for $50 a month to store excess cannabis, either their own or, if they were also caregivers, amounts that their patients determined they did not need. The Apothecary kept 20 percent of the proceeds from the "transfer" (sale) of cannabis from patients who grew to patients who did not.

"Each one of those patients has to sign a patient attestation form saying they're willing to do this, to keep their medical marijuana in a locker and do patient-to-patient transfers," Van Every said. "It's a unique business model formed around the law in Michigan. It's been tested in the courts of Isabella County. The prosecutor wanted to put a cease and desist on our location up there and the judge ruled in our favor that our model and the patient-to-patient transfer falls within the guidelines of the law."

Another court would later rule that "transfer" does not mean "sell," and that any sale is illegal. As the case rose to the state supreme court, the attorney for the Apothecary—which had three locations, one being Van Every's—argued, according to the *Lansing City Pulse*, that "unless conduct is prohibited by law, it is not unlawful."[4] The attorney for the state replied, "If it was

[legal], the statute would say so." If it were held that only conduct not prohibited by law was permitted, legislators would spend
all of their days drafting lists of no-no's that could get as silly
as "do not sell cannabis-infused snow cones during adult softball leagues" or "no holding cannabis-infused soup supper fund-
raisers." Compassionate Apothecary and other dispensaries had
to close when the state supreme court ruled in February 2013
that Michigan's medical cannabis law "does not contemplate
patient-to-patient sales of marijuana for medical use and that, by
facilitating such sales, defendants' business constituted a public
nuisance."[5]

While the artistic interpretation of cannabis laws in Michigan
was an anomaly east of the Mississippi, entrepreneurs in some
western states took their cue from California and created an
industry where none was yet permitted. A clever workaround
arose in neighboring Nevada. The state's original medical cannabis law was so explicit that it forbade caregivers from receiving any kind of compensation. And yet there was Jacob Lill's
Completely Legal nonprofit cooperative in Las Vegas—its sign-
age so bold that passersby could not continue to a Pilates class
or to Groomingdales, in the same plaza, without noticing it.
Inside, the green lights, black-and-silver patterned wallpaper, and
black leather loveseats were suited for a showy casino lounge.
Framed photos of cannabis buds bunched into heart shapes hung
throughout. When Lill sat on one of the couches, his arm atop
the back cushion, he grinned eagerly, as if he had just remembered that all this was his.

Lill, very much in his mid-twenties, insisted that Completely
Legal was not a dispensary. Registered medical cannabis patients
could come in, donate money, and, in return, receive cannabis.
The name of this charitable establishment was the result of a
brainstorming session between Lill, a perennial entrepreneur,
and a friend. "What do we want people to think of when they

think of us? And 'Completely Legal.' It just kind of—we said it and, 'Wait, that's the best name I think I've ever heard of,'" Lill said, smiling again.

Completely Legal was one of the first businesses of its kind to reappear after sweeping raids by federal and state law enforcement in late 2010 shut down nearly every establishment in Las Vegas with any link to medical cannabis.[6] It's a day spoken about solemnly. Before the donation model, many of those raided in Las Vegas had obtained medical cannabis consultation licenses, set up shop, charged consultation fees, and gave patients free medical cannabis.[7] The consultation included anything from an overview of the law to a brief growing lesson.

Nevada's image is decidedly not wholesome, so it was surprising that such a hard line was taken against cannabis. Las Vegas openly welcomes prostitution and gambling, both of which often go hand-in-hand with the consumption of large amounts of alcohol (not to mention all those buffets). But the city of excess has taken its time to work through the stigma surrounding medical cannabis. Shortly after Lill opened his doors, there was another set of raids by state law enforcement; Completely Legal did not survive. Lill, his mother, and five colleagues were charged with a heap of felonies. Between a residence and four businesses, all connected to Lill, police seized 454 plants, roughly $100,000 cash, and an exorbitant amount of dried cannabis and hash, among other items.[8]

Today, it's not uncommon for Las Vegas police to find cannabis plants packed into homes in and surrounding Sin City. The area's desert climate requires cannabis cultivation to happen indoors. So cannabis growers—those supplying the pop-up shops, and especially those supplying the black market—profited from the recent surge of foreclosures in Las Vegas. During a five-year period when Nevada was, according to *Realtor Mag*, the country's "foreclosure capital," inconspicuous suburban homes became available for as little as $80,000.[9] Beginning in 2007, as the economy tanked, these locations were hollowed out and filled with illegal grow operations.[10] Since then, there's been a constant climb in the number of grow-house busts.[11] The Southern Nevada Cannabis Operation and Regional Enforcement (SCORE) team seized 8,579 cannabis plants from 142 grow houses in the Las Vegas area in 2012; they also found 195 firearms during those busts. In early 2013, Las Vegas police reported that grow houses remained a problem: in two January raids, police seized about 2,000 cannabis plants from one house and 1,481 from another home. "We run into this all the time," said Las Vegas Metropolitan Police spokesperson Officer Bill Cassell in 2011, emphasizing that they did not pursue caregivers or patients following state law. "There has been an increase in the number of illegal marijuana grow operations that has come to our attention in the last year."

The economy played a role in the growth of the cannabis industry in nearly every medical cannabis state; as stores were emptied and jobs lost, medical cannabis businesses moved in and hired employees. But the Las Vegas case was distinct. If the value of houses hadn't plummeted when unemployment was high, inexpensive sites for cannabis grows likely wouldn't have looked as lucrative—nor would they have been available. With cheap real estate, and therefore cheaply grown cannabis and a cheap storefront to sell the buds from, it is no wonder people were so tempted to open ephemeral operations.

In these states, it became clear that some cannabis business owners preferred to forge ahead and apologize later, rather than wait for permission. Washington, especially Seattle, had been lenient toward medical cannabis for years, but its law did not have a provision for dispensaries in the spring of 2011. Steve Sarich invented a uniquely evasive model, and this was why he stood out as one of the most outspoken against the changes promised by the Big Bill. For Sarich, it seemed, competition, rules, and scrutiny were undesirable—and change was synonymous with worsening business.

Under Sarich's system, a medical cannabis patient entered his dispensary, CannaCare, and immediately filled out the Designated Provider Agreement, which named Sarich or an employee as his or her caregiver for several minutes. In those minutes, the caregiver would sell cannabis to the patient. Other patients would come, one by one, and do the same. The agreement text referred to the document as a "legally binding contract" and required that a patient be of "sound mind" at the time of agreement. So Sarich was particularly miffed when Senator Jeanne Kohl-Welles, a well-known medical cannabis supporter, tried to close this loophole with SB 5073, the Big Bill. Under the proposed rules, a caregiver would be required to wait fifteen days before changing patients.[12]

But like a pro basketball player, Sarich anticipated a block and pivoted first. "Well, no one could run a dispensary if you could only see two patients a month," he said, seething but dismissive of the reality that, at this time, no one was permitted to run a dispensary of any kind. "Now, because I've got such a large organization, I've got a way to fuck 'em on that. Because I've got enough patients that if you're one of our patients, you have to come in and volunteer for ten minutes twice a month. And you're going to be a designated provider for someone else who's got an appointment and comes in. And we'll just keep rotating people. There's more than one way to skin 'em, but most of the other dispensaries won't be able to do it," Sarich said, of his then competition in Seattle. "Is it practical? Is it a logistical nightmare? Yeah, it's really a logistical nightmare. I'd do it just to fuck with them though. Just to prove to them that they think they're one step smarter than they really are."

Such unabashedly defiant members of the pro-cannabis community sometimes set the movement back, irritate their peers, and invite law enforcement backlash. But those who operate cannabis businesses outside the law have also contributed to a broader dialogue about the shortcomings of medical cannabis legislation. If attention is drawn to the fact that a medical cannabis law is poorly worded or, as Michigan attorney general Bill Schuette put it when discussing his state's law, has more holes than "Swiss cheese," more legislative efforts will be prompted to fill in what the law lacks.[13] The spread of dispensaries in Michigan led to the state supreme court ruling that the stores were not allowed, which then compelled lawmakers to draft legislation to create dispensaries.[14] In Washington, though parts of the Big Bill aimed to stop caregiver quickies like Sarich's, the bill also aimed to allow licensed dispensaries in their place. Even in Nevada, where tolerance for the medical cannabis industry was low, there has been progress. Nevada's law was particularly unrealistic in its expectation that every patient too ill to grow for him- or herself could find a caregiver willing to labor over cannabis plants solely out of the kindness of his or her heart (other states allow caregivers to receive some kind of compensations). In March 2012, a district court judge, Donald Mosley, used the dismissal of a drug trafficking case against medical cannabis providers to express his thoughts about Nevada's law: "It is apparent to the Court that the statutory scheme set out for the lawful distribution of medical marijuana is either poorly contemplated or purposely constructed to frustrate the implementation of constitutionally mandated access to the substance."[15] In early 2013, the Nevada ACLU called the law unconstitutional for the same reasons and, as in Michigan, state lawmakers introduced a bill to allow dispensaries.[16] The Nevada bill became law in June 2013.

No matter how carefully worded a law is, the way in which it ultimately manifests in a state is due to a unique mix of elements—from the number and brazenness of activists to the attitudes of law enforcement and from the language of the law to legislator support. Even in states with nearly identical laws, the outcomes can be completely different. Both Oregon and Nevada industries, for example, originally opted for a donation model; neither cannabis businesses nor compensation for cannabis was legally permitted.[17] A short walk from the Las Vegas casino strip, the Blue Bird Café, where patients could consume cannabis, was immediately shut down. But in Portland, Oregon, law enforcement and locals alike tolerate the World Famous Cannabis Café, one of the first of its kind in the country.

A converted wine bar located in the basement of a plaza unit, the World Famous Cannabis Café feels a lot like Cheers. The tables are lined with people who might wait in line for Simon and Garfunkel tickets. Rafael Martinez Jr., the general manager, greets every patron the same way: with hands clasped and head bowed. "Welcome home," he says.

Martinez is tall and burly, with sleeve tattoos down to his hands, gauged plugs in his ears, and a thick gray goatee. His manner was serious and calm as he described the café. "We have this place for a social gathering," he said, "for us medical lepers to get down here and be the real people we are."

A piano stands at the entrance of the 4,000-square-foot café, and the long, low ceiling seems to go on forever. Electric fireplaces warm the dim and smoky room. Martinez took a puff and then placed the joint in an ashtray. Under the glass tabletop, a piece of paper gives the Wi-Fi password: Always420. The number 420 now means many things. April 20 is the unofficial national Cannabis Day, the day when dispensaries have their own holiday rush; 4:20 P.M. is when cannabis enthusiasts either chuckle, announce the time, or feel it imperative that they take a hit; and 420 is a code used in texts, e-mails, or on Craigslist when people discuss having or wanting cannabis.

The writers of Oregon's law could not have foreseen something like the World Famous Cannabis Café when they shaped the legislation. But, through crafty interpretation and an ideal location, the café is able to exist; the basement property is not for use by the general public and is out of public view. Madeline Martinez, Rafael Martinez's mother and the executive director of Oregon NORML, opened the café in 2009. On an average day, fifty to one hundred people unwind in the café, which is run by volunteers. Admission is $5 a day with a $20 monthly member-ship fee, or $10 a day without the membership. The cannabis is free. A bell hangs near the bar to acknowledge cannabis dona-tions by members, and its ring is the cue for everyone in the café to applaud. Next to the donation bell is a sign that reads, in all capital letters, PARKING FOR HIPPIES ONLY. ALL OTHERS WILL BE STONED. CITY ORD 420. Another sign gives the phone number for the main switchboard to reach Congress to urge support for cannabis reform. Jars filled with money, from pennies to twenty-dollar bills, are labeled, "March for Babies donations. Show the world cannabis consumers care." Behind the bar, a refrigerator cools non-alcoholic drinks and a shelf is stocked with snacks. A whiteboard listed the day's menu— a ham or turkey sandwich with Swiss or provolone cheese and, for dessert, homemade white cake with chocolate frosting.

Once a week, the World Famous Cannabis Café hosts a ka-raoke night. On this particular night, a man who called himself the Reverend Cole took the stage and grabbed the rim of his fedora as Prince's "Kiss" played. He swayed and closed his eyes as he aimed for the high notes, his gold front tooth reflecting the light as his mouth opened wide. During the funky musi-cal interlude he stomped on the ground, grabbed and pulled up his brown slacks, and twirled in his long black leather jacket as the audience clapped and shouted encouragement. One woman looked up at the stage and laughed, a faux cannabis leaf lei on her graying hair like a crown and a nearly finished joint in her hand. After the Reverend exhausted himself and his vocal cords at the end of the song, the emcee patted his back. Before the Reverend jumped off stage, he leaned into the microphone and said, "Note to self: don't sing Prince after smoking a vapor bag."

As states with prepubescent industries endure their many growing pains, states with more than a decade of experience have slowly matured. Even in California, while many miscreants still take advantage of the state's faulty law, more and more reformers strive to create interim standards and regulations. Part of the impetus to evolve comes, as it would in any industry, from growing competition and increasingly sophisticated market demands. It's one thing to own a clothing store in a small town, and another to own one in Manhattan. The days of filling jars with the lowest common denominator of medical cannabis and dodging the authorities are phasing out.

The sign hanging in the window of the Farmacy reads: VERY OPEN. The blinds and the front door are almost always open, too. On a typically warm California day in the spring of 2011, curious pedestrians on the busy Santa Monica Boulevard poked their heads into the airy, yellow building. No one bought anything, but they looked around the lobby where a receptionist awaited patients. The owner, JoAnna LaForce, was a founder of two other Farmacy locations in southern California. She is a pharmacist-turned-herbalist, a woman seriously Santa Barbara who calls the coastal city home even though it's nearly a hundred miles away. That day, her wispy blond hair showed just a hint of white and she wore a turquoise shirt and stone earrings.

The Farmacy opened in 2004 in West Hollywood, a tiny city within greater Los Angeles that accepted and, in 2005, regulated its medical cannabis industry earlier and better than most.[18] When other municipalities didn't cap dispensaries, West Hollywood did. Hours of operation are limited and, to avoid crime, no cash in excess of $200 can be kept overnight. No doctors can make recommendations inside of dispensaries (a practice that would call into question the integrity of their "recommendations"). And a staff member is required to give law enforcement and all neighbors within one hundred feet the company's contact information.

The Farmacy goes above and beyond local and state expectations for medical cannabis. Out of respect for community members, nothing on the building's exterior indicates what is stocked inside. No parents walking by with their kids need to worry about probing cannabis questions. By contrast, across the street, a dispensary has a neon-lit green cannabis leaf. Its windows are gated. The sign reads ALTERNATIVE HERBAL HEALTH SERVICES, with a smiley face in the background, and every single letter of the establishment's name includes a cannabis leaf.

The "farm" in Farmacy is intentional. LaForce scrutinizes the medical cannabis she distributes and says she accepts buds only from conscientious farmers. That cannabis is used to create oil for some interesting items, including bath bombs, soaps, and lotions similar to those sold in body shops (many patients swear by the benefits of topical cannabis products for conditions like psoriasis, though research is limited). For $10, cannabis-infused butternut squash, tomato soups, or macaroni and cheese appeal to patients who don't want sweets like brownies or cookies, which are also for sale. An eight-pack of coconut cookies costs $15. One of the more popular genres of edibles is the cannabis-infused drink in a soda bottle, with flavors like lemonade and pomegranate juice (buy five, get the sixth free). A sign on the cooler reads, 1 DRINK = 3 DOSES. All of these items are packaged and refrigerated as if destined for a prepared foods section at any nearby supermarket.

LaForce and her staff were in the process of improving the Farmacy's edible dosage labels that spring, which were then mostly 1X, 2X, 3X (meaning one, two, or three doses). Of course, the complication with any kind of cannabis consumption comes from each individual's understanding of what constitutes a dose. A typical dose for Jane could be the same dose that does Johnny in for a twelve-hour siesta. Who would take Tylenol without instructions that clearly stated the milligrams in each capsule? Cannabis edibles should have similarly clear dosage indications, and LaForce had begun to state the amount of cannabis in each product. While this is helpful, different strains have different potencies; whether 1 gram contains 8 percent or 16 percent THC is significant. An overdose from a cannabis edible is never fatal but can be anxiety-inducing and uncomfortable before fatigue sets in. It's surprising that only a few state medical cannabis laws regulate edibles when most patients want to anticipate what will happen to their minds and bodies after consuming the products. Knowing this, LaForce wants to eventually take the edible labels a step further to include the amount of THC and CBD in every product.

The other reason staff began to change the dose labels was, in some ways, more urgent for their patients. When Farmacy patients were stopped by police and found with medical cannabis edibles such as dense, fudgy brownies, officers sometimes placed those items directly on a scale; if the scale read two pounds, the police could charge the patient with possession of two pounds of cannabis, LaForce said. Not true, of course—a couple of ounces of cannabis oil might go into the batter, along with sugar, cocoa, and eggs, which all contribute to the hefty dessert—but attempts to explain the complexities of cannabis and cannabis-infused oil to busy police officers aren't likely to be effective. LaForce pointed to a cookie with the amount of cannabis on the label. "[Police] like that because that helps them see," LaForce said. "This has 1.75 grams of cannabis."

While LaForce has been able to self-govern to some extent, she faced a regulatory hurdle in her effort to adhere to food safety standards. She struggled to retain access to a commercial kitchen.

"We had a kitchen for the last . . . three years. And, wanting to be upfront and everything, last year, we had it certified by the Department of Health. At the time the guy knew what we were doing," she said. "Well, we went for our yearly reinspection and it was a different guy. . . . Two days later, the Los Angeles Police task force came in and took everything and closed us down. So, that's the problem. We try to do it right and unfortunately, with the way things are now, especially in Los Angeles, it's really forcing people to go under the radar, underground. And then you don't have those standards and consistent quality."

This maturing industry increasingly demands sensible oversight. The Farmacy and about forty other dispensaries are affiliated with or accredited by the Greater Los Angeles Collective Alliance (GLACA), an organization devoted to providing safe access to medical cannabis while meticulously following state and local guidelines.[19] In surrounding L.A., there are innumerable disreputable shops: small, dingy cannabis storefronts with menacing armed security just past the front door, some with blackened or reflective windows. These places would and could never join GLACA. Unfortunately, the two types of storefronts often get lumped into the same group. The Los Angeles city government frustrated the cannabis community when, in an attempt to rein in the number of cannabis stores, it passed a hasty ban on all dispensaries in 2012. Then, adding to the confusion, it reversed the ban a few months later. Taking initiative where the city would not, in January 2013, three different organizations—Americans for Safe Access (the only national advocacy group solely for *medical* cannabis), the United Food and Commercial Workers International Union (the industry in California has begun to unionize under UFCW, another shot at legitimacy), and GLACA—joined to advocate for reform. They introduced a measure that banned the hundreds of dispensaries that opened after 2007, which was when the city placed a

JoAnna LaForce in her Farmacy in West Hollywood, California. ALYSON
MARTIN

moratorium on all new dispensaries and planned to regulate the
135 in existence. These three groups dropped their own ballot measure in support of a similar one later proposed by the
L.A. city council, Measure D. There was, of course, an oppos-
ing measure supported by the unauthorized post-moratorium
storefronts. In May 2013, Measure D overwhelmingly passed.[20]

It's important to reiterate that the federal government does
have a set of standards for research-grade cannabis that could
be of great use to industry members, like LaForce, in states that
lack regulations. While the federal government doesn't consider
the cannabis grown at the farm in Mississippi under contract
with NIDA "medical cannabis," it is research-grade. The farm's
growing, drying, trimming, storing, packaging, and potency- and
purity-testing methods are established and could be applied to
state medical cannabis. For example, workers at the University
of Mississippi farm freeze the cannabis that is used for research
and for the remaining federal patients because, they say, it re-

mains fresh longer. Cannabis is produce, after all. No state law addresses cannabis freshness in its rules or regulations. Federal patients are told the percentage of cannabinoids in their cannabis cigarettes, but the majority of states don't mandate that their patients be given the same comprehensive information. Without federal—and with little state—guidance, the industry has no choice but to take on the challenge.

From the outside, the Steep Hill Lab building is nondescript, much like those that house LabCorps or Quest Diagnostics, where employees are sent for mandatory drug screenings. Inside, tubes fit snugly into red trays, but they are partially filled with a translucent light green liquid instead of blood. Lab workers wear white lab coats and the same purple latex gloves that phlebotomists prefer. A refrigerator note reminds employees that a lab cooler is not to be used for storing refreshments.

Steep Hill, the first medical cannabis lab in the country, opened in 2008 to offer laboratory-grade quality control and cannabis analysis to California dispensaries. A client could bring a sample of cannabis, a cannabis lotion, or even cannabis-infused cotton candy and find out its cannabinoid profile. The lab also flags cannabis grown in hazardous conditions. Steep Hill's owners take into consideration cannabis degradation, so they have developed customized bags for samples and invested in a nitrogen-sealing machine to create a food-grade seal that removes oxygen from the packaging. Simply put, Steep Hill exists to try to ensure that Californians don't get any undesirables in their cannabis.

Cannabis patients nationwide could benefit from the type of testing conducted at Steep Hill. Many storefronts make some effort to visually inspect the cannabis they sell or allow patients to look at their cannabis under a magnifying glass and light. But a magnifying glass cannot tell the whole story of how a plant was grown. Lab tests, on the other hand, can screen for microbiological contaminants and identify mold, funguses, and pesticides within the cannabis buds.

AnnaRae Grabstein, the Steep Hill operations director between 2009 and 2012, insisted that cannabis is a book that cannot be judged by its cover. "In terms of mold analysis, it is amazing to look at a bud that just looks beautiful, has great bag appeal, it doesn't look contaminated in any way. You think it's just going to come back clean and perfect and then see that it has unsafe levels of mold in it after you do the plate count and grow out the mold," Grabstein said. "Right now, we're a self-regulated industry. Nobody in California is telling collectives that they need to be doing quality control and safety testing on their products."

Still, not every dispensary gets its cannabis tested. Because it's not mandatory, those that are comfortable with the bare minimum—usually to get maximum profit—are unlikely to go out of their way for patient safety. Some medical cannabis clients order all of the analyses, but most are interested only in potency. A low-range THC potency is 8 to 10 percent, but lab workers have seen as high as 22; the average is between 13 and 14 percent. Those dispensaries that inquire only about potency may be more concerned with a customer's high than her health. But when dealing with medicinal-grade cannabis—and immunosuppressed patients—mold and fungus testing should be more important than potency because of the potentially serious health effects. Inevitably, some of the thousands of batches of cannabis samples that pass through Steep Hill test positive for pesticides, molds, or funguses. The lab's protocol is the same for those cannabis samples that are clean as it is for those that are dirty: they inform their clients of the test results. There is no accountability required by California's medical cannabis law, so Steep Hill cannot enforce what is ultimately done with an unsafe batch of cannabis. "We're not police," Grabstein said of dispensary owners who may ignore Steep Hill's findings about contaminated cannabis. "We give the people their results . . . and hopefully they're going to be responsible with the information that they get from us. It's up to them. Who knows what happens to that cannabis after they find out that it's moldy. I mean, it might still end up with patients. I certainly hope that isn't the case."

The Steep Hill laboratory deals mostly with dispensary owners, but Grabstein said testing would be more efficient if they could go straight to the source—the growers. This would prevent the redundancy that occurs when dispensaries individually bring product they all obtained from the same grower. Unsurprisingly, given cannabis's huge business potential, someone in the industry had already taken on that part of the market, contaminant-wise.

Chris Van Hook's utility-sized van is a rolling office and home away from home that works well for someone who spends two-thirds of his year cruising up and down the Pacific Coast to inspect cannabis grows. A light blue surfboard hung from the ceiling of the van and a tan board from the side. Clothes were hanging on a bar in the back. A pragmatic mesh canopy hovered above a narrow cot, holding an apple and toilet paper. The van is the size of several chest freezers, but because every item is multipurpose, it makes for a comfortable-enough meeting place.

"Everybody wants to walk into a cherry-paneled law office and see the degree on the wall. That's sort of your standard law office I figure, isn't it," Van Hook said as he gestured toward his own degree and cherry-paneled van wall. Van Hook was dressed in a navy zip-up hooded sweatshirt, navy sweatpants, and a pair of rugged sneakers. After spending the first part of his adulthood as an abalone farmer, he reinvented himself midlife as a USDA-accredited organic inspector—until one day in 2004, when an older woman in Pasadena called and asked him if he could inspect her cannabis garden. Van Hook couldn't believe someone somewhere wasn't already doing this. "If we are going to have massive retail distribution, which we clearly have, then it does need to be . . . regulated. I mean, it's obscene to have a multi-billion dollar unregulated, untaxed industry, you know, operating in the state," he said.

Upon receiving that request, Van Hook called the USDA for advice, and he said the department suggested he treat canna-bis like any other crop. As a branch of the federal government, the USDA cannot officially recognize any cannabis plant as or-ganic—only illegal. Still, Van Hook's inspections hold merit. For his Clean Green certificate, the same USDA organic guidelines apply to cannabis plants, and this approval means a grower can charge more for his or her vetted crop. Some collectives and co-operatives in California will dispense only "organic" cannabis, meaning no pesticides or unnatural solutions were used while growing the plant. With so much competition among growers in California, every distinguishing factor counts. "Now we're in an oversupplied market so you need to start differentiating your product," Van Hook said. "What I'm doing really is just sort of applying standard agricultural economics and agricultural tech-niques and agricultural work to an agricultural industry that doesn't have any of that infrastructure already."

As an inspector, Van Hook coordinates his trips so he's on the coast during surfing season and near Oregon during backpacking season. By the time he arrives to a cannabis garden, the process has already started with an initial questionnaire. If Van Hook feels the cannabis gardener is serious about becoming certified, he goes for a basic inspection. He examines the plants for dust, molds, mildews, and any unwanted pests. Van Hook wants to get as close to the USDA organic certification process as pos-sible; since he can't send the cannabis leaves to federally licensed standard agriculture labs to determine growing conditions, such as pesticides used, he sends soil samples instead. Ideally, he would be able to conduct the more accurate leaf analysis. (Steep Hill can test leaves, though it is obviously not federally licensed.)

The Clean Green certification requires a grower to use sustainable practices that address soil erosion and recycling. Every farmer also has to have a plan to reduce his or her carbon footprint every year. Irresponsible and unethical farming operations—some supplying patients and others the black market—have scarred the mountains of northern California. A February 2013 *Mother Jones* video narrated by Anthony Silvaggio, an environmental sociologist with the Institute for Interdisciplinary Marijuana Research at Humboldt State University, explored the ecological ruin wrought by more than six hundred cannabis grow sites.[21] The otherwise lush green mountains looked skinned in places; tan blotches suggested deforestation, excessive water use, and waterway diversion. Silvaggio noted that, as long as cannabis is federally prohibited, regulations to prevent these practices will be tough to put in place. "I think the fact that it's unregulated is a real problem and it makes a problem when dealing with agencies also," Silvaggio said in the voice-over. "Talking with agricultural commissioners of different counties, they report to me that it's difficult for them to help growers that want to do the right thing because they can't talk about it because it's federally prohibited and they get federal dollars."

Over the course of his travels, Van Hook has met farmers who have tried to mask some shady practices. One tried to hide some growing aids—synthetic fertilizers and the like—and another had used a bug bomb. Yet another grower didn't pass because of her fertilizer. Van Hook remembers the phone call. She said, "We're so organic, you hardly even need to come by. My only question is can we use human manure as fertilizer?" The answer? "No," Van Hook said.

In his work as a USDA-accredited organic inspector, Van Hook sometimes felt about as welcome as a Fish and Game warden. But, "in the weed business, they're actually really happy to have you. They've wanted you to come, for one thing. They want the verification or the legal compliance work," Van Hook said.

For over a decade after Proposition 215 passed, mention of the medical cannabis industry generally turned conversations toward California because there was no other comparable industry. Although the state did not have detailed regulations, it had far more dispensaries than any of its peers.

There was a moment in early 2010, however, when Colorado, a state that also didn't allow dispensaries, stole the spotlight. That year, NORML referred to Denver as America's Cannabis Capital because the city had more dispensaries per capita than Los Angeles.[22] But Colorado didn't just maintain this title because of Denver's dispensary saturation. The state is respected because it went where California never ventured: in 2010, ten years after the state's original medical cannabis law, the governor signed two regulatory bills so strict that dozens of noncompliant dispensaries closed and the remaining thousand or so shops were forced to track their product from seed to sale.[23] These regulations were, at the time, the most comprehensive in the country. Colorado became known as the leader of the medical cannabis industry, in both innovation and regulation.

The senate bill required patients to have a "bona fide" relationship with the doctor providing a medical cannabis recommendation, and doctors were required to perform a "full assessment" of the patient's medical history, along with a physical exam.[24] Further, physicians who recommended medical cannabis to patients were forbidden from any "economic interest in an enterprise that provides or distributes medical marijuana."

The house bill ruffled more feathers.[25] It required that dispensaries be regulated by both the state of Colorado and local municipalities; allowed those municipalities to implement bans or moratoriums on both dispensaries and cannabis grows; and required that dispensaries grow 70 percent of the cannabis they sell, forcing a quick restructuring of their business models. The bill also refined labeling. Under the new regulations, Colorado dispensaries were required to label their products with "a list of all chemical additives, including but not limited to nonorganic pesticides, herbicides, and fertilizers, that were used in the cultivation and the production" of the plant.

In conjunction with these bills, rules were drafted to cover everything from sanitation to storage.[26] Those who created cannabis-infused products were licensed separately from those who sold them. Inventory requirements forced growers to separate and indicate where plants were sprouting, growing but not flowering, and flowering. Every crop was to be tagged and weighed and, as the batch moved from one place to another, weighed again. In addition to specific alarm and lock requirements, one subsequent rule required that all dispensaries have twenty-four-hour video surveillance that could be connected to the Internet.

Where California didn't go far enough, Colorado, in some ways, went a little too far.[27] First, the hundreds of dispensary applications—even those already operating illegally had to apply for a license—overwhelmed the state, which did not have the staff to process them quickly enough. Additionally, the regulations were overly ambitious. With a limited budget, the Medical Marijuana Enforcement Division never implemented the seed-to-sale or surveillance systems—hallmark features of its regulation. The combination of unrealistic requirements and insufficient resources for oversight meant that the rules eventually needed loosening. A state task force worked to hammer out more feasible regulations in early 2013.[28]

While some aspects of Colorado's strict rules weren't enforced, their existence held much of the state's industry accountable and forced it to become more responsible. By 2012, Colorado had nearly 700 licensed dispensaries—a decline from the 1,130 or so that existed in 2010, early in the Green Rush—and earned $5.4 million in sales taxes in the previous year.[29] Medical cannabis businesses often close in Colorado because meeting the bare minimum doesn't cut it; they have to truly innovate to beat the competition. And to be taken seriously as a medical industry, Colorado dispensary owners feel they need to continue to push for purer and more consistent plants and products.

Evergreen Apothecary is a telling example of the cannabis dispensaries that have thrived in Denver, where the shops blend into the downtown urban landscape. The front room could be a cannabis museum gift shop, with tasteful displays of books and T-shirts. Only when a patient ventures toward the back of the store does she see cannabis displayed on wood-trimmed cases. The branded items are particularly noteworthy. For example, the Mad Hatter Coffee and Tea Company creates cannabis-infused tea bags and coffee grounds; from afar, the colorful and whimsical packaging looks fit for a hipster coffee shop. A rainbow of Dixie Elixirs & Edibles brand cannabis drinks are even sleeker than those in California. A body "budder" made of cannabis oil and shea butter and a pain cream made with cannabis oil resemble pharmacy-packaged versions. Every item label indicates just how much THC and CBD are inside.

These products are so advanced because owner Ralph Morgan and many of his colleagues in the state's medical cannabis industry now consider their competitors to be not the farmers or the other mom-and-pop dispensaries, but established companies like GW Pharmaceuticals and its cannabis-based product Sativex. Morgan sees the pharmaceutical industry as a giant ship and the dispensaries as tiny sailboats. He wondered if they would stay afloat. "Our next step is to create products that are unique, something that's patentable," Morgan said in the spring of 2011. "Because we feel like we've got this big monster coming in that's going to try to squash everyone in the space. And they've got the political clout to do it and they'll have the [backing] of the government. . . . We're a cottage industry, so we don't have the attention of a lot of politicians, a lot of the movers and shakers. So what are we going to do to survive?"

That's just it. To survive the changing atmosphere, entrepreneurs will need to think outside the joint. Never-before-seen products, like milligram-specific sublingual cannabis oil tablets or futuristic cannabis oil e-joints that come packaged as if they were iPhones, are entering the market. OrganaLabs, which Morgan also owns, turns raw cannabis into the goop that goes into these products.

The tablets and the e-joint were featured prominently on tables at the fortieth National Organization for the Reform of Marijuana Laws conference in April 2011. (At a table just across the way, one vendor sold colorful ceramic coffee mugs that doubled as pipes for those who wanted to truly wake and bake.) Several attendees took advantage of the Astro, which was the brand name of the aforementioned and rather discreet cannabis oil vaporizer that resembled a pen. It was smooth, like breathing fruit-flavored air at a tacky oxygen bar—except that with the touch of citrus came a rush of cannabinoids. This interesting widget represented the forward thinking of the industry. Morgan eventually reinvented the Astro as an O.pen, pitched on the OrganaLabs website in 2013 like this: "It's what's inside that counts. Your O.pen cartridge is filled with strain specific™ CO2 extracted Honey Oil, with a new atomizer in every cartridge. Its [sic] simple and discreet, with no buttons, dials, or odor. The O.pen is automatic and shuts off in 8 seconds for the 'Perfect Puff,' and comes with a lifetime warranty."[30] The days of Saran-wrapped brownies and Max Potency labels are fast fading.

The 2011 NORML conference was appropriately called Coming of Age. The big event was a debate, moderated by talk show host Montel Williams, during which Denver mayoral candidates took positions on medical cannabis in an attempt to garner support from an audience that was once dismissed. Inside the downtown Grand Hyatt Denver, the hotel staff looked the other way when they passed a sign that read, "Need to medicate during the conference? Visit the WeedMaps Medication Lounge Room 501." The lounge, which was really a room on the fifth floor, was open 8 A.M. until 6 P.M. to "Patients Only." No one was checking Colorado identifications, so the room became a place where attendees from across the country went to relax, smoke, and chat between events. The fate of cannabis in Colorado was clear: it was only a matter of time before full legalization.

The more ubiquitous, profitable, and developed the national medical cannabis industry becomes, due in part to regulatory advancements in Colorado and California, the more clever entrepreneurs across the country are when carving out their niches. Increasingly, legal and medical offices embrace the opportunity to serve a new client base and wrap their practices around the cannabis plant. Allison Margolin, a Harvard Law School graduate in Los Angeles, represents cannabis cases and calls herself L.A.'s Dopest Attorney. For those who want to learn more about growing cannabis or opening a dispensary, a cannabis college called Oaksterdam University in Oakland, California, attracts students from across the country. The school offers semester-long programs, weekend seminars, and electives with titles like Advanced Extracts or Cooking with Aunt Sandy! Cannabis Infused Sweet and Savory Recipes. For the thousands of cannabis storefronts nationwide, a website called WeedMaps locates dispensaries and offers customer reviews. The *Medical Marijuana Business Daily* hosts seminars, publishes industry guides, and offers a directory that lists medical cannabis-related accountants, bankers, and security, among others; wholesalers of hydroponic equipment or headshop specialties are listed, too. The D.C.-based National Cannabis Industry Association refers to itself as "the national voice for the cannabis industry," with a membership that includes WeedMaps, Steep Hill Lab, the Farmacy, Dixie Elixirs & Edibles, and Oaksterdam University.

The cannabis industry is changing, and playing this game now requires money—a lot of it. Wealthy entrepreneurs often move into states that fail to stipulate that medical cannabis business owners must be residents. The Northeast Patients Group, a branch of the California-based Berkeley Patients Group, for example, took four of eight dispensary slots in Maine (the four later changed their name to Wellness Connection of Maine and cut ties to the Berkeley dispensary).[31] As soon as Massachusetts passed its medical cannabis law, Denver-based Vicente Sederberg LLC announced that a branch of its law office would move in.

So strong was the interest in Arizona, the first state to pass a medical cannabis law after the national Green Rush kicked into full force, that lawmakers proposed a residency requirement in 2011 to block out-of-state entrepreneurs.[32] With 126 dispensary slots up for grabs, Arizona was slated to come closest to the profitability of Colorado; no other state offered that number of dispensary licenses. The House of Hydro, Mr. Nice Guy Mobile Meds, contractors, a realty team, a neuropathic physician, scores of consultants, and a place called the Paraphernalia Boutique were advertised in local glossy cannabis magazines before the program launched.

Arizona put an additional filter in place for those who wanted a shot at this new American dream: an applicant is required to have $150,000 in start-up capital to apply for a dispensary and needs to be prepared to pay $5,000 in annual fees.[33] Over time, the bar has risen higher. Connecticut, which passed its law in 2012, requires a $2 million in-state escrow from growers in case a production facility goes belly-up.[34] And now, aspiring entrepreneurs with ideas but no money can just pitch investor networks like the ArcView Group, which appeared after 2011, for start-up capital—a safe way for investors with deep pockets to be indirectly involved in a risky but profitable world.

This is one reason medical cannabis is turning into an elite business. It isn't just because capitalism is running its course. State regulators helped make it that way. In this time of un-funded mandates and fiscal constraints, some state leaders look at cannabis and see dollar signs. State regulators want to charge fees every way they can and transfer surplus monies from medical cannabis programs to help bridge budget gaps. In 2012, Michigan spent $3.6 million to oversee its program, but the state brought in just under $10 million.[35] Between 2011 and 2012, Arizona made just over $9 million in fees, while the program cost the state only $2.5 million.[36]

A more buttoned-up medical cannabis industry is visible in the Northeast, where laws most recently passed. The dispen-sary and licensing application processes are an entirely different proposition than in the bygone days of the Wild West, where a couple of friends could band together and scrape up enough money for rent. While the only requirement to enter the busi-ness was once a knack for risk taking, the modern dispensary in-volves long-term planning, hefty investments, and connections. The demands placed by states allow only the dispensaries willing to blend in and behave. New Jersey law requires that a medical advisory board that includes at least one physician be part of the dispensary team, while Connecticut allows only pharmacists to apply for a dispensary license. Regulators scrutinize applicants' bank accounts, as well as their financial and personal histories.

The greatest virtue for someone considering the pursuit of a dispensary in such a climate is patience. As states adjust to the growing industry, rules and regulations constantly change and there are endless stops and starts, sometimes for years, between application and being chosen or rejected. In Rhode Island, the application process was restarted the week that dispensary teams were to be notified because one group used an appendix to write far over the twenty-five-page limit. Just like that, they were all back to the drawing board despite the tens of thousands of dollars, months of effort, hours of attorney fees, and rented storefronts. On the other hand, the limited number of dispensaries in northeastern states—ranging from three to three dozen or so—means guaranteed foot traffic and business. It's about as close to a sure bet as exists in an industry loaded with legal and economic uncertainties and complexities.

Year after year, the number of storefronts, products, businesses, states, and profits involved in the medical cannabis industry continues to grow, despite the looming federal threat. Medical cannabis is a costly investment, but thousands of Americans are willing to pay the price.

5

THE CLASH

The first dispensary to be licensed on the East Coast is owned by Leo Trudel, an assistant business professor at the University of Maine at Fort Kent and a former cop. In the fall of 2010, Trudel began construction on an empty shell of a house in Frenchville, Maine, on the southern bank of the Saint John River, which marks the Canadian border. This humble building would eventually become Safe Alternatives.

Flags are permanent trim for the houses in this extremity of Maine. One home's sign reads, "In this country, you are allowed to burn our flag. I am allowed to shoot you if you try to burn my flag. Semper Fidelis." The route to Safe Alternatives clings closely to the border, but the pride is all American.

Trudel chose Frenchville for Safe Alternatives because he was familiar with the area and secured the land at a reasonable price. But his small plot turned out to be one of the most complicated in the country: Safe Alternatives, only a few hundred feet from Canada, is on property that is technically both state (Maine) and federal (Border Patrol) land. Border Patrol can stop anyone, for any reason, within one hundred miles of the border—and its agents do, so often that in 2006 the ACLU dubbed this area a "Constitution-Free Zone."[1] This alone, Trudel said, is enough to "make me wake up in the middle of the night with cold sweats." He fretted about potential federal arrest, asset seizure, and jail time because, as Trudel knows all too well, even the most legal medical cannabis dispensary can still be illegal.

The website for Trudel's dispensary looked more suited to a local tourism bureau than a medical cannabis business, with its image of huddled towering trees surrounding a body of water.[2] After a series of zoning disagreements, Trudel still hadn't opened Safe Alternatives as a storefront in the spring of 2013 and, on the website, listed delivery as the only available service.[3] Regarding the logistics of delivery, "it's a nightmare," Trudel said. If any employee were to be stopped with a medical cannabis delivery at a Department of Homeland Security border checkpoint, he or she could be arrested for felony drug possession and trafficking and face time in federal prison. All dispensary owners are aware of federal law, but they can try to lay low; Trudel and his colleagues are exceptionally vulnerable because they regularly encounter federal agents. "If you're a Border Patrol agent or a police officer, it's easy to pop a couple of kids with weed—or dispensaries with weed—in order to make your quota," Trudel said.

Part of the quandary for Trudel was that he understood the relationship between supply and demand and, as one of the first dispensaries on the East Coast, he faced a significant remunerative opportunity. If caught in the federal net, however, he would fall hard. Trudel stood to lose all he had earned. "I own a fair amount of property and have a fair amount of assets," he said. "If they seize this, they can seize everything. They could wipe me out."

When Trudel received his license in 2010, he sought advice about how to safeguard himself from federal arrest from Catherine Cobb, who was the program's regulator at the time. Unfortunately, she didn't have much to offer Trudel. "It'd be very possible that they could be stopped and subject to federal arrest.

And he asked me what my advice was and I said 'don't keep it within 200 miles of the border,'" Cobb said. "He's decided that he wants to do this. He's a citizen of the state of Maine. It's legal in the state of Maine." Part of Cobb's responsibility was to bring order to the cannabis program and, as someone who seemed born to regulate, the fact that state and federal law disagreed so fundamentally didn't sit well with her. Even in the early stages of drafting program rules, long before Trudel's predicament and the dispensary licensing process, one central question raised by the state-federal legal dissonance bothered Cobb.

"You also have the chicken and the egg situation here where, you know, where do I buy my seeds? Well, buying seeds in the mail is illegal," Cobb said. "This was like the original sin. You're going to be selected to do this, you can be a caregiver, you can be a dispensary, but don't tell me where your stuff is coming from." Without cannabis seeds, medical cannabis programs cannot exist, yet no state law in nearly two decades has addressed the issue of seed origin. This is because seeds must come from one of two places when launching a medical cannabis program: if from within the United States, they likely are obtained from another medical cannabis state—illegally crossing state borders—or from someone local who was already growing illegally; otherwise, the seeds often arrive from seed banks in Canada or Amsterdam through the mail, which is also illegal. (Cannabis plants can also be grown using cuttings from a mother plant, but the original plant still requires a seed.) Rather than waste time wrestling with an impossible situation, legislators, lobbyists, and regulators have decided that cannabis seeds are a conversation best kept under the rug, where they are swept. So the dance begins.

Such legal no-man's-lands are created the moment a state passes a medical cannabis law, when dual sovereignty comes into play.[4] The federal government may always enforce its own cannabis laws within individual states, but it cannot force those states to use their own resources to enforce those laws. Still, the most fundamental places on a town map where both the state and federal governments play a role—hospital, bank, home—force uncomfortable choices upon citizens caught in the middle of the legal grind.

Norma Winkler is a woman in her eighties who carries herself with the confidence and style of Lucille Bluth.[5] At the age of fifteen, Winkler was in a car accident that fractured her skull and spine. The injuries never healed correctly. At home one autumn evening in 2010, Winkler pored over research her assistant had compiled about medical cannabis and talked about an oil recipe she received from a Rhode Island Patient Advocacy Coalition member. She pulled out a palm-sized ceramic bowl and a mini-spoon from her medicine cabinet with which to mix her cannabis oil and applesauce. "It's really been a lifesaver for me," Winkler said of the cannabis oil during an interview for a *New York Times* story we wrote on cannabis and nursing homes. Winkler's peers were generally active like her, but some were also bound by in-home aid or nursing care. Winkler never wanted to slow down. She vacationed abroad regularly with a group of lady friends and worked long hours in her jewelry factory that supplied stores like Chico's. Still, aware of the realities that came with her age, she fretted over her long-term care options, partly because she knew that she would be forbidden from consuming her medicine of choice.

"I wouldn't go if they didn't allow me to take it," Winkler concluded in the same interview. Why wouldn't "they"—the directors of a nursing home—allow medical cannabis? Because most nursing homes receive some kind of federal funding and therefore cannot allow cannabis use on their premises. But Winkler is one of many who face (or will face) this dilemma. In October 2010, Fred Miles, a Colorado lawyer who focuses his work on health law, presented at an American Health Care Association conference program called Medical Marijuana—Are Nursing Homes Going to Pot? "What do these health care facilities do? Adopt a 'don't ask, don't tell' policy? Somebody is using medical marijuana in the residence and you just close your eyes to it? I don't think that's going to work very well," Miles said in an interview for the same story.

Hospitals are another battlefield for medical cannabis patients. Norman Smith was in his early sixties and had liver cancer when he was placed on the list for a transplant in 2010 at Cedars-Sinai Medical Center in Los Angeles.[6] Soon after, he was pulled from the list because he'd used the medical cannabis his oncologist had recommended he consume.[7] The hospital's transplant center policy is that patients on transplant lists may not use illicit substances, and the policy went with the federal interpretation of cannabis, despite its approval as a medicine in California.[8] Similar scenarios unfolded for medical cannabis patients in at least four other states, and also for another patient at Cedars in 2012.[9]

"We do not make a moral or ethical judgment about people who are smoking medical marijuana," Sally Stewart, a spokesperson for Cedars-Sinai, told the Los Angeles Times.[10] "Our concern is strictly for the health and safety of our patients." Stewart noted that smoking improperly harvested, moldy cannabis could be fatal for a patient with a suppressed immune system; one leukemia patient died in 1988 from pulmonary aspergillosis believed to be linked to unsafe cannabis. But this concern neglects the fact that Smith could have just had his cannabis tested.[11] Smith was required by hospital rules to abstain from medical cannabis use for six months to be reconsidered for the transplant list.[12] After fighting the hospital's order, Smith stopped using cannabis in August of 2011 for six months, but he never received the transplant and died in July 2012.

Similarly, universities cannot maintain millions in Title IV funding while accommodating enrolled students who are also medical cannabis patients. University of Maine student Robyn Smith was a legal patient under the state's law.[13] The twenty-five-year-old veteran survived a tour in Afghanistan, but suffered from a number of ailments, including anxiety, migraines, and a joint disorder. Under the Drug-Free Schools and Communities Act Amendment of 1989, he was not permitted to smoke cannabis on campus. When he needed to medicate, he told NPR, he smoked in his parked vehicle off campus or went home.

Even at home, some patients are forbidden from consuming their medicine. The U.S. Department of Housing and Urban Development determined in 2011 that public housing "must deny *admission*" to medical cannabis patients, but left it up to individual agencies to determine what to do about existing tenants.[14] San Francisco's housing authority employs private contractors to oversee city properties, such as Hunters View, a Section 8 unit.[15] Tenants grew angry when, in late 2012, a host of new rules included one that "strictly prohibited" medical cannabis. On the East Coast, in what was referred to as "a war upon the poor" by a local legislator in 2012, the Maine State Housing Authority banned medical cannabis from all Section 8 low-income housing.[16] Maine representative Deborah Sanderson told the *Bangor Daily News*, "Any other person who's a medical marijuana patient and not in need of Section 8 housing cannot by law be discriminated against and be denied housing because of their status." She later added, "You have instilled fear of homelessness upon people who are ill." The Housing Authority eventually placed a moratorium on the policy that banned medical cannabis, allowing more time to research the probability of losing federal funds.

If the threat isn't loss of housing for medical cannabis patients, it might be loss of income. The most well-known employee dispute over medical cannabis was with the largest private employer in the United States: Walmart. Joseph Casias had worked for a Walmart in Battle Creek, Michigan, for about five years when he was fired for testing positive for cannabis. According to court documents, Casias was diagnosed with a brain tumor and sinus cancer a decade earlier when he was seventeen.[17] At his oncologist's recommendation, Casias became a card-carrying member of Michigan's medical cannabis program, using the cannabis for nausea relief and appetite stimulation. Casias medicated only during his time off. Urine tests used by employers, though, can't distinguish between use on the job or use from days or weeks prior. After Casias twisted his knee, his manager offered a ride to the emergency room for treatment, but once Casias arrived he was given a drug test because the injury occurred while at work. Casias told his manager he was a patient and then tested positive because he regularly medicated. He was fired. As long as the federal government didn't consider cannabis medicine, neither did Walmart.

The American Civil Liberties Union and the law firm of Daniel W. Grow, PLLC, represented Casias, contending that "no patient should be forced to choose between adequate pain relief and gainful employment, and no employer should be allowed to intrude upon private medical choices made by employees in consultation with their doctors." In a 2010 ACLU press release, Casias wrote, "I came to Wal-Mart for a better opportunity for my family and I worked hard and proved myself. I just want the opportunity to continue my work."[18] Ultimately, a district judge held, in 2011, "Nowhere does the [Michigan Medical Marihuana Act] state that the statute regulates private employment, that private employees are protected from disciplinary action should they use medical marijuana, or that private employers must accommodate the use of medical marijuana outside of the workplace."[19] Casias appealed, but lost.

Military members, some returning from Afghanistan and Iraq, are an emerging demographic of medical cannabis patients caught in murky legal terrain. Some use medical cannabis for visible injuries, while others do so to soothe the invisible ones. Over the last decade, while these men and women were serving, many states legalized medical cannabis, and the number of Americans exposed to its therapeutic benefits skyrocketed. States permitted the plant for conditions from persistent pain and nausea to PTSD, all of which often plague men and women in the military. In New Mexico, approximately 3,900 of the 9,200 patients registered in the medical cannabis program as of May 2013 have PTSD, and many of them are veterans.

Jay Waldroup's life was craggy after he returned home from service in the marines. Waldroup was injured during training at the end of 1998. He spent another year in the military before he was medically discharged in early 2000 and headed to Chicago. After a traditional pain pill regimen for degenerative back injuries, including a constant stream of Vicodin and Demerol for five years, he described his insides as "destroyed." Then he spiraled. His personality changed; his friends intervened. Waldroup confronted the effects of the pills and cut back with the help of cannabis. "I started denying [the pills from the Veterans Affairs] and then they started asking questions: 'Why? How are you surviving? What are you doing without these pain medications?'" Waldroup said. "That's when shit hit the fan."

Despite warnings from Veterans Affairs (VA) that he would be cut off from his pain medications, Waldroup continued to use cannabis. "I'm a disabled veteran and the VA was coming down on me hard," he said. "They said I had to check into rehab in fifteen days or start losing my benefits." When confronted with the choice between cannabis and the VA pain management program that included pills, only one option felt possible. No matter what, Waldroup needed pain relief—but he'd felt ruined by overreliance on the legal option once before, so he stuck with the cannabis.

In July 2010, the Department of Veterans Affairs changed its policy forbidding cannabis use.[20] While VA doctors still couldn't recommend medical cannabis, veterans in medical cannabis states would not lose access to services if they joined a state program. "Although patients participating in state medical marijuana programs must not be denied VHA [Veterans Health Administration] services, modifications may need to be made in their treatment plans. Decisions to modify treatment plans in those situations are best made by individual providers in partnership with their patients," wrote Dr. Robert Petzel, undersecretary of health for the VA. "VHA endorses a step-care model for the treatment of patients with chronic pain: any prescription(s) for chronic pain should be managed under the auspices of such programs described in VHA policy regarding Pain Management."

Waldroup eventually moved from Illinois, where medical cannabis was not yet legal, to Michigan, where he is a medical cannabis patient and caregiver. His medical conditions have escalated; he had a stroke in his early thirties. But he rests easier knowing that, for now, his access to pain management through the VA in Michigan will stay put. "If you have a medical marijuana card, which they don't offer in Illinois, the VA can't punish you for your use of cannabis as long as it doesn't seem to be recreational or abusive," Waldroup said. "If it's true medicine to you, they can't take away my other prescriptions, they can't deny me my benefits that I already have via contract, which they were doing over there."

Medical cannabis patients tend to be keenly aware of their rights because they've become accustomed to losing many the moment they choose to participate in a state program. Americans for Safe Access, the national medical cannabis organization with more than thirty thousand members, provides legal resources by region so patients may stay current on what's considered lawful.[21] One recent change that cost medical cannabis patients a constitutional right was made in September 2011, when the Bureau of Alcohol, Tobacco, Firearms and Explosives (ATF) released an open letter to those issuing firearms licenses.[22] The ATF letter concluded: "Therefore, any person who uses or is addicted to marijuana, regardless of whether his or her State has passed legislation authorizing marijuana use for medicinal purposes, is an unlawful user of or addicted to a controlled substance, and is prohibited by Federal law from possessing firearms or ammunition." Drinkers—even those who show up at the bar at the same time every day for most of the day—are permitted their guns. On the other hand, all medical cannabis patients are considered addicted and are therefore prohibited from exercising a constitutional right.

In the nearly two decades of medical cannabis laws, the community has seen, it can be argued, violations of members' constitutional rights: First (doctor-patient recommendations challenged after Prop 215), Second (forbidden from gun ownership), Fourth (lost privacy with patient registries), Fifth (asset forfeiture during raids), and Tenth (ignored states' rights) Amendments.

The clash between the federal government and state residents is most visible during raids. These are the front-page stories people read over breakfast or see on the news during dinner. In the years of medical cannabis, because it was such a small industry, there were fewer raid targets. One of the highest-profile early federal raids occurred in 2002 when Drug Enforcement Administration (DEA) agents raided the Wo/Men's Alliance for Medical Marijuana in Santa Cruz, where Valerie Corral takes care of seriously ill patients. Valerie and Mike Corral were arrested but not charged, and they were released the same night. WAMM's crop was destroyed and more than one hundred nearly mature plants were seized. After the raid, then California attorney general Bill Lockyer wrote to then U.S. attorney general John Ashcroft and then DEA director Asa Hutchinson, "A medicinal marijuana provider such as the Santa Cruz collective represents little danger

to the public and is certainly not a concern which would warrant diverting scarce federal resources."[23] The city council allowed
WAMM members to distribute medical cannabis in public, on the
steps of city hall. "It's just absolutely loathsome to me that federal
money, energy and staff time would be used to harass people like
this," Santa Cruz vice mayor Emily Reilly said to USA Today.[24]

Of the nearly 250 WAMM members at the time, more than
three-quarters were considered terminal.[25] The cannabis destroyed by the DEA was solely intended to treat symptoms of
these patients' conditions. But WAMM eventually bounced
back. Ten years later, an old photo in the WAMM office depicts
the Corrals as they pat down the dirt and smile on each side of a
cannabis seedling replanted after the raid.

These federal confrontations continued to splatter the medical cannabis canvas throughout the 2000s, but they appeared
largely unconnected. JoAnna LaForce, owner of the Farmacy in
West Hollywood, remembers January 17, 2007. It was her birthday, she said, and she was on her way to the Farmacy when DEA
agents stormed in, pointing their guns at patients and staff.

"We had a patient who was in the waiting area with forearm
crutches and another guy who was in a wheelchair and they
made both of them lie flat on the ground. It was just horrify-
ing," LaForce said. She recalled a strange dynamic between the
DEA agents and the Farmacy patients. Many of the agents were
young, LaForce said, and behaved as if they were entering cartel
territory. "And so when they came rushing around the corner,
they thought, I guess, they were going to have to pound down
the door. And they realized the door was open and they just kind
of didn't know what to do," she said. "Some of the guys actually apologized for their over dress and said, 'We don't know why
we're doing this, you know, this isn't right.'"

LaForce said the agents took all of the cash and cannabis
in the store. The Farmacy reopened two days later with non-

cannabis products until collective members brought in new cannabis. In recounting the raid, LaForce expressed a frustration that was shared repeatedly during interviews for this book: when law enforcement intervened, there were sometimes no follow-up charges, but cannabis was still destroyed and money and property were not returned. Under the asset forfeiture laws in the war on drugs, that property didn't have to be returned in most cases—charges or no charges.[26] The Department of Justice Assets Forfeiture Fund "increased from $500 million in 2003 to $1.8 billion in 2011," according to its website.[27] Most of that money goes straight back to the DOJ and to compliant state and local law enforcement. "We have a really, really good inventory system and we've always been aboveboard," LaForce said. "So we knew exactly how much cash—and we had over $60,000 in cash and they sent us a receipt for $44,000. And took all of our cannabis inventory." LaForce knew how much cash she had because no employee had made it to the bank since before the Martin Luther King Jr. Day long weekend (and she had on hand more than West Hollywood rules allow). But it was her word—a criminal's, according to the federal government—against the DEA's.

No one was safe from these raids—not even the Mother Teresa of Pot or the Farmacy employees who later developed a personalized plan to nurse an L.A. city councilman with neuropathy and cancer back to health.[28] (Now retired councilman Bill Rosendahl was so overjoyed with the results that he wrote a blog for the *Huffington Post* in May 2013 to encourage others to come "out of the cannabis closet.")[29] Both Corral and LaForce helped push for local regulations, and both followed the law like a gymnast follows a balance beam. As more states passed medical cannabis laws, those who ventured into the new territory feared these sporadic but calamitous raids.

Then, a smooth-faced Illinois senator started talking about medical cannabis. And when he spoke, people listened. Barack

Obama had called the war on drugs an "utter failure" in 2004, while campaigning for his U.S. Senate seat, so even before he mentioned medical cannabis, advocates were hopeful.[30] At an August 2007 event in New Hampshire, on the presidential campaign trail, Obama expressed what seemed like a true commitment to protect medical cannabis patients from federal intervention. "I would not have the Justice Department prosecuting and raiding medical marijuana users," he said. "It's not a good use of our resources."[31] If he would be friendly to patients, many hoped he would be to those who supplied them, too.

Voters often interpret these statements as promises, but they're visions of what a politician would like to accomplish under the most utopian of circumstances. The reality is that these ideas start as thick sheets of aluminum. Then supporters and opponents start pounding. When the sheets return, they're more like foil. Still, Obama discussed medical cannabis enough times, and with enough consistency, that it seemed like he could be trusted to see reform through.

During a 2008 interview with the Jackson County, Oregon, *Mail Tribune*, Obama took it to a new level when he almost but not quite acknowledged the cannabis *plant's*—not just its cannabinoids'—therapeutic potential, which the federal government had never done.[32] "My attitude is that if it's an issue of doctors prescribing medical marijuana as a treatment for glaucoma or as a cancer treatment, I think that should be appropriate because there really is no difference between that and a doctor prescribing morphine or anything else," he said, later reiterating, "What I'm not going to be doing is using justice department resources to try to circumvent state laws on this issue."

When Obama was elected in 2008, those in the medical cannabis industry genuinely felt more at peace. The first sign of follow-through came during a February 2009 press conference, when attorney general Eric Holder said, "What the president said during the campaign, you'll be surprised to know, will be consistent with what we will be doing here in law enforcement. (Laughs) He was my boss during the campaign. He is formally and technically and by law my boss now. And so what he said during the campaign is now American policy."[33]

On October 19, 2009, then deputy attorney general David Ogden released a follow-up memo to U.S attorneys that indicated a gentler view of medical cannabis:

> As a general matter, pursuit of these priorities should not focus federal resources in your States on individuals whose actions are in clear and unambiguous compliance with existing state laws providing for the medical use of marijuana. For example, prosecution of individuals with cancer or other serious illnesses who use marijuana as part of a recommended treatment regimen consistent with applicable state law, or those caregivers in clear and unambiguous compliance with existing state law who provide such individuals with marijuana, is unlikely to be an efficient use of limited federal resources.[34]

This much was clear: the sickest of the sick—those in hospice care, the AIDS and cancer patients, the Susan Sarandon character in *Stepmom*—should not be the targets of federal raids. The reason, as noble as the memo sounded, was likely because these people weren't making millions off of medical cannabis, so they just weren't worth the resources.

Two oversights happened at this point, though. First, when the Department of Justice said the focus shouldn't be on patients "or those caregivers," it clearly did not realize how many dispensaries called, or would call, themselves caregivers. As a result, many assumed dispensaries to be safe. Second, some very excited people just stopped reading the memo right there. Even the *New York*

Times ran this headline: "Obama Administration to Stop Raids on Medical Marijuana Dispensers."[35]

Further down, the Ogden memo read,

> On the other hand, prosecution of commercial enterprises that unlawfully market and sell marijuana for profit continues to be an enforcement priority of the Department. To be sure, claims of compliance with state or local law may mask operations inconsistent with the terms, conditions, or purposes of those laws, and federal law enforcement should not be deterred by such assertions when otherwise pursuing the Department's core enforcement priorities.[36]

The memo reiterated that those working with medical cannabis could be investigated for any reason, at any time, and prosecuted if necessary: "Nor does this guidance preclude investigation or prosecution, even when there is clear and unambiguous compliance with existing state law, in particular circumstances where investigation or prosecution otherwise serves important federal interests."[37]

Sometimes, believing is seeing. The stern lines above were as clear as the encouraging ones—but they got much less play in the medical cannabis community. Those who wanted to believe that the Ogden memo offered reason to exhale did just that. Bursts of medical cannabis activity—the flurry described in the previous chapter—cropped up in cities across America. Entrepreneurs who participated in the rapid development of the industry said they felt much less at risk after the memo than before.

With the release of the memo, economic desperation intersected with a novel and supposedly safe economic opportunity, and thus began the great Green Rush. But soon, the rising wave would break over immovable rocks.

—✻—

Montana Cannabis, co-owned by Chris Williams and three others, was one of the many caregiver organizations that swelled after the Ogden memo. In February 2011, its cannabis plants could be seen beside Highway 12 between Helena and Missoula. Even a speeding driver could easily spot, inside a greenhouse the size of an indoor soccer field, rows of tall, bushy plants stretching toward the lights above. Out back, cannabis lay in piles like oak leaves in the fall.

Inside, Montana Cannabis was a compound of rooms that seemed to never end, some small and others cavernous. An employee corkboard displayed two perfect cannabis leaves, pressed and laminated as neatly as dried flowers. A sheet of paper from Montana Botanical Analysis, dated February 7, 2011, revealed the latest batch of test results. Two stickers read, "No More Drug War" and "Stop Arresting Medical Marijuana Patients." In a back room painted a candy apple green, volunteers methodically clipped buds from stems while Lynyrd Skynyrd's "Freebird" blared in the background. Sunlight streamed in.

Williams examined a drying room where cannabis was fastened to wood-framed crisscrossed wires the size of screen doors. The frames swung like department store poster racks. Another room was dedicated to drying cannabis in an earlier stage, where the stalks hung on red ropes. A main walkway of the facility had weights for lifting.

Standing in the 12,000-square-foot greenhouse, Chris Williams wore a black zip-up hooded sweatshirt with the words "Montana Cannabis" written in white; he also wore a pin with a cannabis leaf in front of a red cross. Tall with a flinty stare, he resembled a salt-and-pepper bearded Brawny man. Williams started growing cannabis when it was one of his childhood chores on a thirty-acre farm in northern Arkansas. His family had rabbits, ducks, horses, and cattle. Williams bailed water from their well to give to the animals and the cannabis plants that grew indoors in the winter and outdoors in the summer. "It really sucked," he said.

In step with family tradition, Williams later encouraged his son, fourteen in 2011, to grow strawberries, basil, and pineapple, among other herbs, fruits, and vegetables, in a small corner patch—but not cannabis. "It's pretty fun, we get to play a little bit," Williams said. While some parents choose to hide their personal or professional connection to medical cannabis from their children, afraid they may say something to friends or parents who are opposed, Williams took a more honest route with his son and allowed him to spend a great deal of time at Montana Cannabis. It was surprising just how open everything was at the greenhouse. "We had curtains up over those windows for the first nine months. And then we got all of our fencing up and stuff, and then we dropped curtains," Williams said of the windows that faced Highway 12. "It was a marketing thing, for one. I know a lot of caregivers are importing medicine"—which is both illegal and lazy—"and I want people to know ours is all grown right here. We can prove it. You can look at it. The other thing of it was we lose 20 percent of our sunlight having that window covered."

By the time Williams was interviewed for this book, Montana Cannabis was one of the largest and most visible cannabis cultivators in Montana, if not the country. Despite the Ogden memo and Holder's announcement, though, Williams and his employees were still fish in a barrel that the federal government was just waiting to shoot. "We try not to own much. We don't own any property. We own a few vehicles. On purpose, we lease and rent everything. And then none of my other managing partners, none of our members hold large assets," Williams said. "All of this started pretty small and actually, it's because the federal government only seems to be attracted to money. . . . We try to make sure that if they come in here, all they're going to have to do is burn some plants down. They can't get anything from us."

Cannabis plants grew inside Montana Cannabis, once located on the side of Highway 12 in Helena, Montana. ALYSON MARTIN

Montana Cannabis did supply a lot of patients with medicine. The caregivers earned $1.3 million gross in 2010, Williams said, about a half million of that going toward payroll. "We didn't start the company to get rich. . . . Our goal was to serve our patients better. . . . By grouping together and starting to staff, now we're caring for well over four hundred people." Montana Cannabis had outlets in Helena, Billings, and Miles City, as well as two delivery drivers.

The Helena outlet was nondescript and looked like it could have housed anything from a shipping store to a rural café. Underneath a clock face nestled in mushrooms, a white dry-erase board displayed a menu handwritten in green, black, and red marker. "Montana Cannabis," it read. "Check out our special $190/oz. jars." Cannabis-infused edibles were for sale: lollipops, brownies, and muffins ($5); rice "crispy's" ($7); three-packs of oatmeal raisin, chocolate chip, or ginger snap cookies ($15). The bottom of the sign read, "Bring your friends and tour our greenhouse facility. $15 per person. All proceeds go to the

Helena Food Bank." There was also a poster that quoted Dr. Lester Grinspoon, the well-known associate professor emeritus of psychiatry at Harvard Medical School who wrote *Marihuana Reconsidered* in 1971: "[Marijuana is] safer than most medicines prescribed every day. If marijuana were a new discovery rather than a well-known substance carrying cultural and political baggage, it would be hailed as a wonder drug."

Montana Cannabis started as a small operation and then expanded—due in part to Montana troublemaker Jason Christ. He was infamous and disliked in the local and national cannabis communities because of his unruly behavior, like repeatedly smoking cannabis on the steps of the state capitol and threatening to bomb a Verizon store. Christ's office reeked of cannabis as he explained how he helped increase the number of patients in Montana from 3,921 before the Ogden memo to just under 30,000 one and a half years later, in early 2011.[38] He slowly rolled a blunt and proudly described his business model, which involved traveling around the state with a doctor—not always the same one—who would indiscriminately sign hundreds of cannabis recommendations back to back. Sometimes, the doctor would examine patients through a video chat. Christ was profiting handsomely from the post-memo increased interest and demand; one recommendation cost $150, and he boasted that he and the doctor could make thousands, if not tens of thousands, of dollars in one day.[39] And the more recommendations he gave out, the more patients Montana Cannabis and other caregivers served.

Another reason Williams's Montana Cannabis became such a large operation is because the state's medical cannabis law placed no limit on the number of patients for which a caregiver could provide. In the Big Sky State, land became currency; the more land a caregiver had, the more cannabis was grown for more patients, and at lower prices. State lawmakers did not notice this loophole in the law because no one was bold enough to test it before the federal memo. So it was perfectly legal under Montana law that Williams grew for so many patients. Colorado had a similar reaction when it removed its caregiver/patient cap in 2007. In the first eight years of the program, up to January 2009, only 5,051 people had been approved for medical cannabis cards.[40] One year later, after the memo, more than 53,000 were participating in the state's program and the caregivers began to look more like dispensaries. Colorado handled this transition gracefully and developed regulations for an industry that its citizens clearly wanted. In Montana, the spurt that resulted from those familiar unintended legislative omissions would have serious consequences.

On a cold March 2011 morning, three weeks after Williams referred to himself as "not that high-profile," the feds showed up. Montana Cannabis was raided. "Guns blazing. Doors were unlocked," Williams said, speaking that day to *The Lowdown*, a blog run by the Montana correspondent for *USA Today*, about the multiagency federal raid.[41] "They came in with, you know, guns out. They actually did use flash bang. To the agents' credit, they've been respectful of me and my staff through this process. They're just doing the king's deed for the king's dime, it seems to me." Williams spoke to the blogger while the raid was under way and plants and property were being taken; his staff members were being detained and questioned by police, he said. At this time, only one of his employees was arrested because he had an outstanding warrant for a speeding violation. But Williams wasn't the only target; a broader coordinated coup was under way. That day federal agents from the DEA, FBI, and ATF raided twenty-six caregivers and dispensaries throughout Montana that had been under surveillance for eighteen months.[42] "Any judge that signed these search warrants, that's a judge here in Montana, they shouldn't be in their position anymore. This is really clear that this is a state issue, not a federal issue and there shouldn't be federal agents on my ground when we've done everything we can to be legal and do what's right," Williams said to the *Lowdown* reporter.[43] "They've told me they're not going to be arresting any of my staff. They're just going to be detaining them. And they told me that they're here because marijuana's federally illegal."

Williams said the caregivers' computers and some staff cell phones were seized, along with cars belonging to Williams's partner and an employee, according to the *Helena Independent Record*. Williams also told the paper that DEA agents had asked "where I had all of the money hidden." The agents severed and hauled off the cannabis plants. Later, $1.68 million from business bank accounts was also seized.[44] When another reporter asked Williams what his next step would be, he told her that he had retained an attorney.[45]

Then, Williams was arrested. Because guns were found during the raid, and federal law mandates increased penalties when guns are present during a felony drug arrest, the combination of firearm and trafficking offenses added up to more than eighty years.[46] For the then thirty-eight-year-old, it seemed his freedom would come sooner from death than release.

Within minutes of speaking to Williams, it becomes obvious that he's a constitutionalist and libertarian. He seems to be a fair man, and one who wants that same fairness for himself. Williams adamantly refused plea deals when his colleagues at Montana Cannabis snatched them up and testified against him.[47] Williams was convicted in September 2012. An olive branch was extended: if Williams waived his right to appeal, his sentence would be reduced, likely closer to ten years. Williams refused, emphasizing that he had done nothing wrong. "I have decided to fight the federal government because for me, not defending the things that I know are right is dishonorable," Williams wrote to the *Helena Independent Record*.[48] "Every citizen has a responsibility to fight for what is right, even if it seems like the struggle will be lost."

Ultimately, one person proved more important than a fight for justice. When a final offer came with a further reduced sentence of a minimum of five years, Williams conceded.[49] His son was then sixteen and Williams wanted a chance to attend his college graduation.

A short drive away from Montana Cannabis, at the state capitol, one man detested that medical cannabis had become so available. Mike Milburn, then speaker of the Montana House of Representatives, was austere but at times warm. In the corner of his spacious office, a sign read, "Politicians! Scrape shit from boots before entering." Otherwise, Milburn was the epitome of a wholesome, conservative politician in his crisp red tie, white shirt, and navy blue blazer.

The former speaker launched a medical cannabis law repeal effort that was well under way when the Montana Cannabis raid happened. The push to rid the state of medical cannabis resulted from what he described as an onslaught of negative correspondence from Montanans. He received e-mails, phone calls, and plenty of snail mail—mostly from law enforcement and "concerned parents"—about the post-memo prevalence of medical cannabis, unforeseen when voters approved the law in 2004. Some Montana residents took issue with medical cannabis, which they felt was a veil for illegal activity. They argued that medical cannabis at this scale was a wolf in sheep's clothing, a planned course for cannabis legalization. Milburn was particularly disturbed that his state had been singled out as an example of booming medical cannabis. "I'm a Montanan and I love my state and the image of our state is not marijuana," he said. "And that's not what I want to be known as."

The magnitude of the problem—evidenced, according to Milburn, by these complaints—eventually pushed him to demand repeal. "You know, people are still saying, 'Well, it's an initiative put in place by the people. We're going against the will of the people.' My argument is no we're not. . . . The medical marijuana part now is a very infinitesimal itty-bitty piece of this situation. Now we're dealing with a free drug trade problem that's going on in Montana. So that's where I'm focusing my attention," Milburn said. "The people that really voted for it for the medicinal purposes felt that it was going to be very, very restrictive. Didn't read the law, didn't read the initiative, you know. And so, here it comes to us. And it really wasn't a problem until the Obama administration said that they're not going to enforce [laws against] marijuana use at all. And so when that happened then, the growing operations started."

Someone identified only as a sixteen-year-old sophomore at Helena High School wrote passionately to Milburn to share her thoughts about his "great bill," and how medical cannabis had crept into her school and camped out on the breath and minds of students. "Kids come in every day after lunch smelling of pot," she wrote, then shared a personal story about one of her close friends. "He's been smoking weed for a while now, and his girlfriend does it with him from time to time. One night, him and his girlfriend were hanging out. He left her to go buy something. That something, was a Bong. So he could smoke more weed. He talked about how cool it was. Later on, his girlfriend broke up with him. Why? Because he had neglected hanging out with her, so he could go buy a bong. Yes, this is what our teens are doing today." The e-mail expressed how easy it was to get a "green card" (doctor's recommendation) and how those who supported the medical cannabis law in Montana were "addicted." "Stop this madness, this utter take over of my highschool," the panicked e-mail continued. "If you must repeal this law AND start over to provide those who are sick then so be it. But you CANNOT legalize it. You CANNOT make it any easier to get then it already is . . . There is only a small amount of people who need it medically, and the rest are just money hungry druggies trying to sale it and make a profit off of our vulnerable, missguided, mani-luplated youth. They took advange of our ignorance, and now we are hooked and trapped in the lies of Mary J."

Milburn often referenced the risk medical cannabis poses to Montana youth, and even alluded to its role in the prosti-tution of girls. When pressed, though, Milburn was vague. A letter from Roger Nasset, the chief of police in Kalispell, who shared his experiences dealing with cannabis "on the streets," reinforced Milburn's claim. On the date the letter was written, February 7, 2011, "Just today I took a report of a nineteen-year-old 'card holder' who is utilizing his right to possess marijuana to lure underage girls from the high school for sex in exchange for marijuana." No other state had attempted a repeal effort, and no other state legislature reported underage teenage girls prostitut-ing for cannabis. Whether or not these incidents actually hap-pened, a fever all too reminiscent of reefer madness was rising in Montana.

All of this feedback was, in Milburn's mind, a consensus and evidence that he needed to act. "You have to shut it down. And so I'm getting that from DEA, I'm getting that from everyone around the country that has dealt with this in other states," Milburn said. He added, "It's not a black and white issue, is it? Am I making a black and white issue? Pretty much. I have to. I'm selling this. I'm selling a product, okay? Is it the right thing to do? Yes, I think what I'm doing is the right thing to do. Do these other states have suffering people, too, and they don't have medi-cal marijuana? You bet. And they're doing it without it."

Milburn could have instead added some teeth to the law and closed the loophole that allowed limitless cannabis grows. But he pushed for repeal and, in April 2011, one month after the Montana Cannabis raid, the medical cannabis repeal bill passed. Then Montana governor Brian Schweitzer vetoed the bill, saying it went against the will of the people.[50]

—〰—

After the Montana raids it was unclear whether this federal attack was isolated or the launch of a longer, widespread fight.
In retrospect, this was only the beginning of a crackdown that
would rattle the industry from coast to coast. By late 2010, there
were certainly signs that tension with the federal government was
brewing, as far as the big players in this industry were concerned.

One of those players, Steve DeAngelo, is an outspoken and devoted medical cannabis advocate who owns Harborside Health
Center, one of the country's largest dispensaries, in Oakland,
California. He also owns another, much smaller dispensary by
the same name in San Jose. In late 2010, the Internal Revenue
Service audited Harborside to determine whether the dispensaries had adhered to a federal tax code called 280E.[51] In general
terms, 280E prohibits any business involved with "trafficking
in controlled substances" from writing off expenses, including
basics like insurance, salaries, and rent. This strange tax code
intended for black-market kingpins was written in 1982 when
Ronald Reagan reignited the war on drugs; it now creates financial strain for those who run state legal medical cannabis
businesses. DeAngelo was not adhering to the tax code because
he—and many other dispensary owners in states with medical
cannabis laws—did not believe it applied.

"What we may be seeing is that the IRS is collecting data, is
trying to understand the industry, so that they can figure out an
equitable way of taxing us," DeAngelo said as he relaxed after a
panel at the annual NORML conference in April 2011. "What I
fear is happening is that the IRS or persons within the IRS have
decided to use the 280E provision as a way to accomplish through
the backdoor what the Obama administration has promised not
to do through the front door, i.e., close down medical cannabis
dispensaries. I don't think that we know the direction that the

IRS is going right now, but certainly, if they choose to enforce the 280E provision bluntly, without sensitivity, it has the potential of closing down the entire legal cannabis industry in this country." By November 2011, DeAngelo, who kept meticulous books and prided himself on setting the bar in northern California and throughout the nation, was in danger of closing his shops, thanks to $2.5 million in back taxes owed by the Oakland location (in addition to the more than $3 million he already paid in state and local taxes).[52]

This was only one of many ways to pummel medical cannabis without raids. The feds were purposely targeting the fractures that exist between state and federal law, and the investigations into Williams and DeAngelo represented the launch of a national, coordinated federal crackdown on state-legal dispensaries.

Another early notice that the feds meant business came in February 2011, when then Oakland city attorney John Russo received a response to his inquiry about four industrial-sized cannabis grows the city planned to license. In the letter, northern California's U.S. attorney Melinda Haag wrote in a heavy-handed tone:

> The Department is concerned about the Oakland Ordinance's creation of a licensing scheme that permits large-scale industrial marijuana cultivation and manufacturing as it authorizes conduct contrary to federal law and threatens the federal government's efforts to regulate the possession, manufacturing, and trafficking of controlled substances. Accordingly, the Department is carefully considering civil and criminal legal remedies regarding those who seek to set up industrial marijuana growing warehouses in Oakland pursuant to licenses issued by the City of Oakland. Individuals who elect to operate "industrial cannabis cultivation and manufacturing facilities" will be doing so in violation of federal law.[53]

With this letter, Oakland's grow plan had to go, along with the dream that the facilities would help bridge the city's budget deficit, projected to be $58 million for fiscal years 2011–13.[54] Oakland was somewhat foolish to believe that its locally approved plan would be federally forgiven, but it had proposed it in mid-2010, when everyone was flying high from Holder's announcement.

It was soon clear that the Department of Justice, not just individual U.S. attorneys, realized that Holder's words and Obama's campaign trail promises had indirectly led to the growth of medical cannabis into a billion-dollar industry. Now they needed to backtrack and clean up. In June 2011, another memo, written by deputy attorney general James Cole, expressed disapproval toward medical cannabis and the original interpretation of the Ogden memo. But the DOJ should have promptly clarified the original memo or Holder's speech when, for well over a year, everybody seemed to think cannabis businesses were safe. For a moment, their silence indicated the DOJ might back off of the budding industry and understand that support among Americans for medical cannabis remained over 70 percent. Instead, they were preparing to strike.

Cole's letter reiterated that it was "likely not an efficient use" of resources to target seriously ill patients or their caregivers (not the Montana Cannabis kind of caregiver, but someone who might maintain, out of compassion and with little to no compensation, a closet-sized garden for an elderly neighbor).[55] All moneymaking ventures, however, would still be investigated and possibly prosecuted:

> The Ogden Memorandum was never intended to shield such activities from federal enforcement action and prosecution, even where those activities purport to comply with state law. Persons who are in the business of cultivating, selling or distributing marijuana, and those who

knowingly facilitate such activities, are in violation of
the Controlled Substances Act, regardless of state law.
Consistent with resource constraints and the discretion
you may exercise in your district, such persons are subject
to federal enforcement action, including potential prosecution. State laws or local ordinances are not a defense to
civil or criminal enforcement of federal law with respect
to such conduct, including enforcement of the CSA.
Those who engage in transactions involving the proceeds
of such activity may also be in violation of federal money
laundering statutes and other federal financial laws.[56]

In the first half of 2011, just before this new memo and following Haag's response to Oakland, nine states received similar
letters from their U.S. attorneys. As a result of these letters, in
which the U.S. attorneys made it clear they were ready to enforce
federal law, hundreds of dispensaries would drop over the next
year and a half, through either threat or force. The letters were
like the cough that came before the plague.[57]

Many of these letters were sent to dispensary landlords. In
Haag's letter to Oakland city attorney John Russo, she cited laws
that would be used to coerce landlords into forcing out medical
cannabis businesses: "Title 21 Section 856 making it unlawful
to knowingly open, lease, rent, maintain, or use property for the
manufacturing, storing, or distribution of controlled substances;
and Title 21 Section 846 making it illegal to conspire to commit
any of the crimes set forth in the CSA."[58]

In the case of Harborside, Haag filed a civil forfeiture complaint
against both landlords in addition to the ongoing IRS audit struggle, a double blow. The Oakland landlord then asked Harborside to
vacate in July 2012, but Harborside took the issue to court. Three
months later, the city of Oakland got involved and sued the federal
government because of the "irreparable harm" that would result

from the closure of Harborside.[59] Tens of thousands of Harborside patients would have to turn elsewhere for cannabis—until wherever they turned was shut down, too—and the city stood to lose over $1 million in taxes they received from the dispensary. When clarifying the purpose of targeting Harborside, which was in full compliance with state law, Haag said in a statement, "The larger the operation, the greater the likelihood that there will be abuse of the state's medical marijuana laws, and marijuana in the hands of individuals who do not have a demonstrated medical need."[60] In other words, it was just too big.

It did seem odd that the feds went after Harborside due in part to its size. The dispensary was so up front that it had even opened its doors to the Discovery Channel for the show *Weed Wars*. Viewers from around the world tuned in to experience what life was like inside the walls of a California medical cannabis store. The financial books were no secret, either, and Harborside staff often talked publicly and to the media about the state and local taxes they paid.

Harborside has been allowed to remain open while the case is resolved, but its targeting overwhelmed the medical cannabis community with trepidation. If the DOJ would target one of the leading dispensaries in the country, then it would target anybody. Worse, the rationale behind and direction of its potential moves were unclear.

Just a few months before Haag set her sights on a civil forfeiture complaint against Harborside, she'd indicated that she was primarily interested in dispensaries located within one thousand feet of places children frequent. "I simply don't have the resources to take action with respect to every dispensary in the northern district, so I've had to make some decisions about how to best use my resources. So I've decided to focus on dispensaries that are near kids," Haag said to KQED News, northern California's NPR affiliate, in March 2012.[61] Harborside was nowhere near a "drug-free school zone." But Berkeley Patients Group, another large northern California dispensary, was located within one thousand feet of the French American school Ecole Bilingue de Berkeley over on Heinz Avenue. This distance became the basis of a dispute between the Berkeley Patients Group, the group's landlord, and the feds. The dispensary, a pillar in the medical cannabis community for more than a decade, was forced to close in April 2012 by its landlord.[62] (It has since reopened but is again fighting closure as of mid-2013.) "There were no instances of violence, they were excellent neighbors, they had good security, they contributed to the economy, and helped local nonprofits by making contributions," Berkeley mayor Tom Bates said to KQED.[63] "The voters of this city voted unanimously that they wanted to have four dispensaries in Berkeley and that was it. We grandfathered them in. But evidently we get trumped by the federal government."

The one-thousand-foot rule became a basis for federal intervention in Colorado, as well. Dozens of dispensaries closed throughout the state in 2012 in response to letters from state U.S. attorney John Walsh that noted their distance to schools and told them they had to close "within 45 days."[64] Other dispensaries in the state faced a new dearth of banking options. For banks, medical cannabis is off-limits; dealing with dispensaries essentially means accepting money that is illegal in the eyes of the federal government, which could in turn mean loss of Federal Deposit Insurance Corporation (FDIC) protection.[65] Banks who were willing to work with this industry pulled away as federal intervention swept across the country; for example, the Colorado Springs State Bank, according to the *Denver Post*, became the only remaining bank to allow dispensary accounts—until the crackdown.[66] Dispensaries have to hoard cash, either in their shops or at home; many dispensaries across the country are cash-only for customers because the outlets are cash-only for the owners. They may as well advertise to thieves that their shops would make a lucrative hit. Some dispensary owners, unwilling to be cash boxes, chose to lie to banks, saying that they served as a yoga studio, for example, so they could have access to credit lines and savings accounts.

The conflict over medical cannabis took a puzzling turn when federal law enforcement started going after local law enforcement, a group one would think immune from such scrutiny. Mendocino County's 9.31 program demonstrated that law enforcement and outdoor medical cannabis growers could have a mutually beneficial relationship, despite confusion over state and federal law. Having understood that medical cannabis played an integral role in the local economy, the county and the sheriff's department worked to bring the gardeners out of the shadows and, in exchange for their trust, offer legitimacy. The purpose of the 9.31 program was clear. According to a Mendocino County Ordinance on the sheriff's website, the county and its sheriff's department wanted to meet "(1) the needs of medical patients and their caregivers for enhanced access to medical marijuana; (2) the needs of neighbors and communities to be protected from public safety and nuisance impacts; and (3) the need to limit harmful environmental impacts that are sometimes associated with marijuana cultivation."[67]

For $25 apiece, local growers could buy zip ties to wrap around the base of their cannabis plants.[68] With this small nod of approval, these growers could prove their compliance with local law enforcement, and both parties could rest easier. In 2008, when this program began, county law had allowed twenty-five plants per grower; when expanded in May 2010, the program allowed growers to cultivate the large gardens many likely already had, up to ninety-nine plants. Zipties cost $50 apiece for the larger gardens, and the application and inspection fee was $1,500. Nearly one hundred growers applied. The sheriff's department reinvested the money generated by this program in training, and it was as close to win-win as one could expect between cops and cannabis growers.[69]

After a threat from the U.S. attorney's office, however, this program was modified on Valentine's Day 2012, when Mendocino

County reduced the number of plants allowed from ninety-nine back to the former twenty-five.[70] That should have been the end of it. But in October 2012, it became obvious that the 9.31 program was headed for more trouble. The federal government issued a subpoena for records from January 1, 2010, to the moment the letter was received, pertaining to those who were part of the 9.31 cannabis grower program (including "emails, letters, and any other communication" related to the program; "any and all financial institution account numbers" used by Mendocino County and its sheriff's and district attorney's offices; and "record of inspections, applications," which would reveal names of growers and their farm locations). Mendocino County fought back on behalf of the sheriffs and program participants with a motion to quash that cited confidentiality, calling the subpoena "unreasonable" and "overbroad," and saying that it "chills protected First Amendment conduct." (Mendocino County eventually reached a deal in April 2013 and agreed to release the records, but not applicants' identities.)[71]

One form of intimidation affected entire state bureaucracies: threats to state employees who worked with medical cannabis programs. U.S. attorney's letters indicated that these employees risked federal prosecution for doing their jobs—or, conversely, they could quit and dive into a dry pool of job openings. State governments were reluctant to enact legislation or create programs to protect the rights of medical cannabis patients if state employees were left vulnerable as a result. In response to a question by then Washington governor Christine Gregoire regarding federal reaction to her state's Big Bill, U.S. attorneys wrote that "state employees who conducted activities mandated by the Washington legislative proposals would not be immune from liability under the CSA."[72] Gregoire, concerned for state employees, vetoed major parts of Kohl-Welles's Senate Bill 5703. While the legislature supported the bill, which had been months in the making, Gregoire was not comfortable with the federal government's potential involvement.

The notion that state regulators and leaders could be responsible for the prosecution of their employees created a chilling effect in medical cannabis states across the country. Delaware shut down its dispensary program within a year of passing a medical cannabis law, rendering the entire program ineffective because patients were not allowed to grow their own.[73] New Jersey governor Chris Christie delayed the implementation of the state's medical cannabis program for weeks.[74] Jan Brewer, governor of Arizona, took government employees' fears and ran with them, suing the Department of Justice for definitive clarification as to whether the state law was preempted by federal law. Paradoxically, the DOJ wanted the case dismissed because Brewer had no evidence, according to court documents, of a "genuine threat that any state employee will face imminent prosecution under federal law."[75] The court sided with the DOJ and so the program moved forward. But the threat had been real, even if the department never intended to act upon it. Six months later, Brewer received a letter from the state U.S. attorney that reiterated "state employees who conduct activities authorized by the AMMA [Arizona Medical Marijuana Act] are not immune from liability under the CSA."[76]

The amorphous nature of the medical cannabis industry makes the exact economic costs of this nationwide showdown difficult to quantify. Americans for Safe Access released a report in 2013 titled "What's the Co$t? The Federal War on Patients." The report determined that of the 528 raids known to the organization that have been conducted since the passage of the first medical cannabis law in California in 1996, 270 occurred in Obama's first four and a half years in office. ASA estimates that this administration's enforcement has cost nearly $300 million, which is already $100 million more than George W. Bush spent over the whole of his two terms.[77] There are some more clues in one state's lost jobs and evaporated tax dollars. A November 2011 article in the *San Francisco Chronicle* revealed that, at that time, 2,500 California residents had lost their jobs at shuttered dispensaries; with salaries between $17 and $20 an hour, plus benefits, these were considered "breadwinner" jobs, Dan Rush, United Food and Commercial Workers International Union national medical cannabis and hemp division director, said to the paper.[78] California collects annual sales tax revenues estimated by the state Board of Equalization to be between $58 million and $105 million. Each business that closed in 2011 and 2012 diminished that revenue, sometimes by hundreds of thousands of dollars, and increased unemployment.[79]

A major flaw in the federal strike against the medical cannabis industry was that the DOJ went after the big dogs instead of the bad guys—producing a disquieting, rather than lasting, effect. When the feds target those they deem too large versus those who flagrantly break state law, they reveal that their priority is to prevent the legitimization of a growing industry. The crackdown tried to maintain a stigma, because familiarity was already breeding comfort. By pursuing landlords and bank accounts and sheriff-distributed zip ties—which offer transparent locations, financial records, and regulations—the federal government further indicated that it prefers to force cannabis back underground.

The misguided nature of the federal blitz was not lost on the states. Even with Montana's repeal effort, Delaware's pause, Arizona's lawsuit, and New Jersey's delay, no state overturned its medical cannabis law. Oakland and Mendocino loudly and confidently fought back in court. In a climax of frustration, Rhode Island governor Lincoln Chafee and then Washington governor Christine Gregoire petitioned the federal government to move cannabis from Schedule I to Schedule II and acknowledge its medical properties. "What we have out here on the ground is chaos," Gregoire told the *New York Times* in an interview.[80] "And in the midst of all the chaos we have patients who really either feel like they're criminals or may be engaged in some criminal activity, and really are legitimate patients who want medicinal marijuana." (All along, of course, the national epidemic of arrests over minor non-medical cannabis possession was proceeding apace.)

In the end, the federal efforts proved unpopular across the country, even in states without medical cannabis. In May 2012, Mason-Dixon Polling and Research reported that 74 percent of Americans polled said they wanted the federal government to "respect state laws."[81] A House bill was introduced in Congress to withhold funding from the DOJ that would be used to meddle in medical cannabis states.[82] Even late-night talk show host Jimmy Kimmel used his time at the 2012 White House Correspondents' Dinner to ask Obama, "What's with the marijuana crackdown? I mean, seriously, what is the concern? We will deplete the nation's Funyun supply? You know, pot smokers vote too. Sometimes a week after the election, but they vote."[83]

The Obama administration's response to cannabis has drawn plenty of criticism, with *Reason* calling the president "just another drug warrior."[84] *Rolling Stone* slammed Obama's "war on pot" and Rob Kampia, executive director of the Marijuana Policy Project, said in the same feature, "There's no question that Obama's the worst president on medical marijuana."[85] While it's true that Obama has dealt with the most widespread presence of cannabis seen since prohibition began, he dismissed an opportunity to evolve on the issue alongside Americans. And after all the evidence of the crackdown's failures, nothing signals more powerfully than the opening, in July 2013, of the first dispensary in Washington, D.C, within view of the U.S. Capitol dome.[86]

6

PHOENIX

Outside Oakland City Hall on the brisk, bright autumn morning of November 2, 2010, a group of cannabis legalization advocates believed they were making history. A dozen men and women in blazers and windbreakers stood between two towering white columns and held signs that read, CONTROL & TAX CANNABIS, YES ON 19. That evening Californians would decide whether to support the taxation and regulation of cannabis for general use by adults twenty-one and older. People nationwide were watching and reckoning with the implications of a win. Before the *Los Angeles Times* named Proposition 19 the "most talked-about ballot initiative in the country," political satirist Stephen Colbert had joked that "if Prop. 19 were a human, it would be the most popular candidate in California."[1] Proposition 19 was the potential dark horse of the 2010 election year.

Stephen Gutwillig, then California's director of the Drug Policy Alliance, spoke at the podium below the steps of Oakland's One City Hall Plaza. "Today is the day that we end the chaos and begin to bring this enormous, unregulated, underground marijuana economy into the light of day, and under the rule of law, once and for all. Today is that day," he said.

Speaking before Gutwillig that morning, then Oakland city attorney John Russo had compared cannabis prohibition to alcohol prohibition: neither stopped unauthorized sale or use, he said, and both put lucrative markets into criminal hands. Dan Rush, of the United Food and Commercial Workers Union Local 5, who is now national director of the medical cannabis and hemp division he helped create, talked about the thousands of Californians who had lost their jobs in the recession, and the new ones that would be created with the passage of Proposition 19.

The speakers called the proposition "the first step in repairing our economy." It was for the sake of "jobs and education." During the most severe recession since the Great Depression, the idea to bring aboveground and tax a billion-dollar market was a promise of green in a sea of red. Proposition 19, the speakers said, was also "a civil rights and racial justice priority." A report released by the California NAACP and the Drug Policy Alliance the month before had revealed that blacks used cannabis at similar rates as whites, but were arrested for possession more often—for example, seven times more often than whites in Los Angeles.[2] Over the previous two decades, possession arrests in California had tripled to more than sixty thousand a year. Did the punishment of time, money, and a permanent record truly match the crime? And could cash-strapped states afford such misplaced law enforcement efforts?

Given the rhetoric that day, it was hard to remember at times that the proposition was about cannabis legalization. The Prop 19 campaign wanted to distance voters from the idea of legalization for the sake of legalization. Two national and devastating crises years in the making—a crumbling economy and the financial and human costs of cannabis prohibition—had lent the campaign the spinoff narratives it needed. To further divorce their initiative from the stoner stereotype, the ballot authors did not include the word "legalize" in the text of the Regulate,

Control and Tax Cannabis Act of 2010, which they submitted to the state in July 2009.[3] The word was just as scarce on their website (though it appeared on the voter guide released by the state attorney general's office).[4]

Dale Sky Jones, the spokesperson for the Yes on 19 campaign, stood at the podium and spoke with confidence. "Your vote 'yes' on Prop 19 will be the vote heard 'round the world," she said, her smile uninterrupted. "Make no mistake, the world is watching."

Across from her, a row of news reporters and documentary filmmakers stood behind video cameras on tripods, their shadows cast before them on the ground.

A white-haired woman named Ann Lee dressed in a bright red, purple, and blue blazer charged up to the podium among cheers. A silver cross rested on her chest. She began to speak loudly before she reached the microphone. Her friends back in her childhood home of Louisiana, all in their eighties, she said, had "prayed for us on this." "This is striking many people across the country because it is just right," she continued, with conviction and a Texan timbre. "It is not just the young; there's some of us, too, who have learned the good lesson." Whenever Lee got passionate, she hit her multicolored cane on the ground and took a preacher's emphasis. That day, the devoted Tea Party supporter had educated nearly every passerby about the racist enforcement of drug laws that reminded her of the Jim Crow laws of her youth. She was particularly unnerved because she'd recently read Michelle Alexander's *The New Jim Crow*, which had confirmed the connections that she'd begun to piece together. Throughout the day, she reiterated, "the drug war is a racist war."

From the steps, Richard Lee looked on, proud of his mother. For more than a decade, he had worked to advance both the medical cannabis industry and the politics around it; without him, there would be no Proposition 19. The then forty-seven-year-old wore a deep green jacket and aviator-style sunglasses and sat quietly in his wheelchair throughout the rally; he was paralyzed below the waist in the early nineties, when he fell on his back while working as a lighting technician for an Aerosmith tour. Lee arrived in California from Texas in 1997, one year after medical cannabis became legal. He owned a warehouse where he grew cannabis to supply dispensaries and, by 1999, he was also supplying his own newly opened Bulldog Coffeeshop, a tip of the cap to one of the now famous first coffee shops in Amsterdam that opened in the 1970s. These were the first of many properties he would come to own in Oakland, including a gift shop, a cannabis clone nursery, a glass-blowing studio, and Coffeeshop Blue Sky.

Lee secured his place in the national medical cannabis industry when in 2007 he opened Oaksterdam University, the first trade school in the country devoted to all things cannabis.[5] The school offers classes that cover a range of topics, from cooking with cannabis to understanding state laws. From a distance, the university emblem intentionally resembles a green-and-gold version of Harvard's motto, Veritas; up close, the letters spell Cannabis. When the school opened, the germinating medical cannabis industry had just begun to stir interest, even from those who resided out-of-state. Thousands of devotees traveled hundreds of miles and paid hundreds of dollars for a crash course in the state that brought medical cannabis back to the country.

Oaksterdam also became the unofficial name of the area of Oakland revitalized by Lee-owned businesses—around Broadway between 22nd and 14th Streets. A smoothie shop next to vacant storefronts can't expect too many hungry customers—but a smoothie shop next to a place filled with patrons who may have recently inhaled can rely on a bump at the register. Oakland welcomed Lee, his businesses, and its new nickname. In 2009, the city was the first in the country to tax its medical cannabis, which earned it roughly $500,000 in 2010 (a tax increase would bring revenue the following year to nearly $1.4 million).[6]

In Oaksterdam, residents found steady work, the city earned tax revenue, and landlords rented properties.

Lee invested $1.5 million of his own earnings to draft Proposition 19 and gather nearly twice the required 433,971 signatures necessary to place the proposition on the ballot.[7] At its core, the proposition would allow adults to grow as much cannabis as they could fit in a twenty-five-square-foot space—about the size of a tight walk-in closet.[8] The proposition also enabled adults to purchase up to an ounce of cannabis (possession limit) from a licensed shop. Beyond that, there were too few specifics.

Proposition 19's content (or lack thereof) was not the only fodder for controversy.

Where there were already divisions in the cannabis movement, Proposition 19 placed a widening wedge. NORML, Marijuana Policy Project (MPP), and Drug Policy Alliance (DPA) believed that 2012 would be a wiser election year to introduce legalization. The turnout in a presidential election year, they argued, could be the difference between a loss and a victory. A crushing defeat for cannabis in the 2010 midterm election would take resources from 2012 and cause voters in other states to ask: if California didn't want legalization, who would? MPP immediately told the Prop 19 team that it wouldn't contribute any funding in 2010; it was unwilling to ask for money and endorsements for an initiative its members didn't believe could pass. Some argued that this would amount to a self-fulfilling prophecy, but MPP didn't think more money would make the difference. DPA, at that point, agreed to work with Lee on the draft only.

Despite this lack of support, Lee collected signatures with a sense of urgency. If he could offer an oasis in the financial desert, he figured, it would lure voters to the booths for Prop 19. As he plainly told the *Wall Street Journal* in October 2009, "We're the answer for all of the things on the news."[9] Lee drew a comparison to alcohol prohibition, which was repealed during, and due in part to, the Great Depression.[10] It's not difficult to understand why Lee made the leap. In February 2009, California state assemblyman Tom Ammiano introduced a legalization bill, the Marijuana Control, Regulation and Education Act.[11] His aim was to help reduce California's $41 billion budget deficit from the sale of a product that was already all but legal in the state; the Board of Equalization estimated the act could generate $1.4 billion in annual revenue (through an excise tax of $50 per ounce and state sales taxes).[12] The bill never went anywhere, but it got people thinking. An April 2009 poll conducted by the nonpartisan Field Research Corporation revealed that 56 percent of registered California voters would "legalize marijuana for recreational use and tax its proceeds."[13] While the national cannabis and drug policy organizations were clearing the way to 2012, Lee ran ahead because he saw the potential for voter buy-in. Lee did not have the resources for a masterful campaign, but he was able to place on the ballot his vision of a state revived, as Oakland had been, by the taxation of cannabis.

In addition to a lack of campaign support from national cannabis and drug policy organizations, disagreement over the terms of legalization led to localized infighting leading up to the vote. Some disliked the initiative because it created new restrictions (like the activists in Washington who opposed the Big Bill, despite its clear benefits). For example, Prop 19 would have made it illegal to use cannabis in front of a minor, something previously unaddressed in California. Dennis Peron opposed the initiative because it would criminalize these otherwise law-abiding adults (this one stung Lee because, he said, "he was always a hero of mine"). The tax-and-regulate aim of Prop 19 was also too corporate for the legalization purists, who thought of cannabis more like the potato at the farmer's market than the alcohol in the liquor stores. One group, the Stoners Against the Prop 19 Tax Cannabis Initiative, had a few hundred members.[14] On their website, they wrote "This is not our only chance to vote yes to legalization, but it may be our only chance to VOTE NO to the corporatization of cannabis." The group was so mistrusting of big money (not realizing big money got them their beloved Proposition 215) that they pushed the conspiracy theory that George Soros supported cannabis law reform because he owned major shares of Monsanto and wanted it to patent the plant to increase his profits. A blogger wrote on the site that "if Prop 19 passes, buying marijuana will only be legal if you buy it from Richard Lee and a handful of select others."

Fueling the hysteria was Oakland's plan, approved in July 2010 but later terminated during the crackdown, to allow "industrial cannabis cultivation and manufacturing facilities."[15] The increasingly broke city seemed willing to try anything to relieve its 17 percent unemployment rate, especially at a time when it looked like Holder and Obama were in hands-off mode.[16] The bulk of cannabis consumed in California had always originated from the gardens of reclusive growers in the Emerald Triangle, which included Humboldt, Mendocino, and Trinity counties. Nowhere else in the United States were so many farmers willing to bear the risks of cultivating dozens of cannabis plants outdoors, nor communities willing to accept them. Oakland's plan—city-sanctioned large-scale grows—and legalization would encroach on these growers' long-held market share.

The city's plan also snubbed anyone who didn't have access to six or more figures in spare capital necessary to imagine and implement such a business.[17] Unlike growers in northern California, whose ingenuity and resilience had supported them through decades of risk, this new crop would require wealth and maybe a smidge of corporate sense. In another Prohibition-era link, one of the applicants was Ben Bronfman, great-grandson of Samuel Bronfman, who began what would become the Seagram Company as a bootlegger just north of the U.S.-Canada border in the early 1900s.[18]

The pro-legalization but anti-corporatization crowd was especially vocal in the weeks before the election. On Election Day, a block away from the Prop 19 campaign office and in front of Oaksterdam University, a small group of unruly men donned white "No on Prop 19" T-shirts and jeered at supporters. "We're just trying to bring some awareness to the situation that money is going to leave the state," a tubby, scruffy protester said to Jeff Jones, husband of Dale Sky Jones and then Los Angeles chancellor of Oaksterdam University.[19] Jeff Jones shook his head in denial and laughed, his arms crossed over his light dress shirt and tie. Of all the protesters, a guy in an Ezekiel T-shirt and San Francisco Giants cap was loudest. "They're going to make all the money!" he desperately yelled at an Oaksterdam employee walking past with a couple of other Yes on 19 supporters, pointing at Oaksterdam. "Nobody's going to make nothing. They're not going to pay y'all nothing."

"It's not about the money for us, man. It's about freedom," the Oaksterdam employee said.

"This is the building of a corporation," the man answered, his arms thrust upward toward the university. "They don't care about Oakland."

The situation escalated as the group heckled Jeff Jones about the profits he's made from cannabis over the years. Jones began his career in medical cannabis in his early twenties and, in 1995, co-founded the Oakland Cannabis Buyers' Cooperative.[20] The federal government moved to shut down the club in 1998 because it defied federal law, even though Oakland had come to Jones's defense.[21] "You're right, I completely got rich off of this," he said sarcastically, shaking his head again and laughing.

As the protesters dispersed, a Ford Model T Depot Hack decorated with a YES ON 19 sign drove past Oaksterdam and toward the campaign office during one of its many rounds up and down Broadway that day. Prop 19 headquarters was located at 1776 Broadway in downtown Oakland. The address, referencing the

year of this country's independence, was no mistake. Just inside
the campaign headquarters, an exhibit titled Human Rights and
the Drug War displayed, under the text "Why We Fight," photos
of people who either had been arrested or had died as a result of
the American drug war. Three rows of phone bankers sat at old
desktop computers with phone receivers stuck to their ears. The
whole room was covered with banners and signs for Oaksterdam
and for the campaign. Maps of California and hand-drawn
charts documented the campaign's progress. In the back room, a
whiteboard laid out the day's schedule. As afternoon turned into
evening, the scrawls grew more urgent. "6 P.M., switch to rapid
fire, switch to only ID'd 'yes' voters." "No party until after we win.
Until then, we make calls."

Jodie Emery, wife of Marc Emery, who was sentenced to five years
in prison for selling cannabis seeds to U.S. growers, live streamed
the events for their popular Canadian online magazine, Cannabis
Culture. The site had trouble handling the thousands who visited
to watch what was happening in California. Despite signs that reminded people inside to "please be quiet, our phone bankers appreciate it," the room was anything but. As the countdown neared,
the buzz intensified. One woman shouted, "There's so much love
in this room. That's what this community is about. L-O-V-E!"
Another chanted one of the Prop 19 mottoes, "Yes we cannabis!" a
play on Barack Obama's 2008 presidential campaign slogan.

There were reasons to be hopeful. Poll results had remained
close for months. And in a July 2010 post, Nate Silver, the well-
known statistician and writer behind the FiveThirtyEight blog, reported that support for Proposition 19 was higher in automated
polls than in those with a live operator.[22] He proposed that this
was a reverse of the Bradley Effect, named after the 1982 election
in which black Los Angeles mayor Tom Bradley seemed to be
winning the race for governor based on polls but ended up losing
to a white candidate.[23] The theory was that people respond to

live operators less honestly than to automated polls, and some voters may not have wanted to admit their choice would be motivated by race. With Proposition 19, Silver theorized that voters were more cannabis-friendly than they were willing to publicly admit because of the stigma. He named this the Broadus Effect (Broadus is Snoop Dogg's last name).

The Prop 19 effort had also unearthed unexpected and diverse support.[24] It got a nod from the Democratic parties of San Francisco and Los Angeles County; former New Mexico governor Gary Johnson and former U.S. surgeon general Joycelyn Elders; California's largest labor union, the Service Employees International Union, which endorsed the proposition as an engine for job creation; the ACLU's California affiliates, along with national black and Latino police officer associations and the state NAACP; and the Libertarian Party of the United States. Eventually, the proposition also received endorsements from all the national cannabis organizations except Americans for Safe Access, a group that focuses solely on medical cannabis, which remained neutral. And it wouldn't be California without some celebrity endorsements, in this case from musician Melissa Etheridge and actor Danny Glover.

Supporter Alice Huffman, president of the California NAACP, was among the first African American leaders to successfully spread the message that drug laws, not drugs, tear apart black communities. Lee said that when Huffman contacted him to schedule a meeting at the campaign headquarters, he expected to have to pitch her for support. Much to the contrary, according to Lee, Huffman said she had had an epiphany and began to include legalization in many of her speeches. She expected tomatoes to be thrown her way, but she got rounds of applause instead.

Including Lee's $1.5 million contribution, the Prop 19 campaign raised a total of $4,041,431.[25] While MPP and DPA originally intended not to fund the campaign, once polls reflected the

possibility that Prop 19 could pass, they herded the wealthy phi-
lanthropist donors who made Prop 215 a reality to chip in: more
than $70,000 from George Zimmer of Men's Wearhouse, nearly
$210,000 from Peter B. Lewis of Progressive Insurance, and, only
a week before the vote, $1 million from George Soros. There was
also a notable thread of support from the start-up world: $105,000
from a Facebook engineer, $70,000 from Facebook co-founder
Dustin Moskovitz, and $100,000 from Sean Parker, of Napster
fame. When Reddit's parent company, Condé Nast, said it could
not agree to ads in support of Proposition 19 because, "As a corporation, Condé Nast does not want to benefit financially from this
particular issue," Reddit cleverly interpreted that as permission to
post the ads for free.[26] The campaign also received $75,000 from
David Bronner of Dr. Bronner's Magic Soaps (made from hemp).

The anti–Prop 19 side raised only $125,687, and mostly from the
usual anti-cannabis suspects: $49,999 from the California Police
Chiefs Association, $20,500 from the California Narcotic Officers'
Association, $10,000 from the San Mateo County Deputy Sheriff's
Association PAC, $10,000 from Greg Munks for Sheriff 2010, and
$7,500 from the California Correctional Supervisors Organization,
Inc. More than $100,000 combined came from dozens of construc-
tion companies and contractors who were likely concerned about
stoned workers on the job, a warning repeatedly trumpeted by the
California Chamber of Commerce.[27] In response to the question
"Will pot smoking be allowed in the workplace if Proposition 19
becomes law?" the chamber wrote, "Under Proposition 19, that
door certainly would be opened. Because Proposition 19 creates
a new protected class of workers, employers would very likely be
required to allow marijuana smoking at work because Proposition
19 would prohibit denial of any right or privilege granted by the
act, without defining what that means."[28]

Similar arguments about the workforce were reiterated by
Kamala Harris and Steve Cooley, both running for state attorney

general. The vagueness surrounding stoned driving got Mothers
Against Drunk Driving to loudly oppose the initiative. MADD
teamed up with Senator Dianne Feinstein to warn that no action
could be taken against high drivers or employees until after an accident had occured. They wrote in the voter information guide,
"Employers who permit employees to sell cosmetics or school candy
bars to co-workers in the office, may now also be required to allow
any employee with a 'license' to sell marijuana in the office."[29]

These concerns were exaggerated. If a forklift driver were rolling
a blunt while on a break, or if an office worker were to hold a can-
nabake sale in the lunchroom, common sense would likely prevail.
But those who drafted Proposition 19 should have thought ahead
and written more specific rules in these areas to counter the opposition. Proposition 19 did not define impairment limits for driving after cannabis use and wrote that employers could "address
consumption that *actually* impairs job performance"[30] (emphasis
added). Who was to determine who was "actually" impaired, and
how? In a way so typical of trailblazing cannabis legislation, like
Proposition 215, these gaps damaged the initiative.

Beyond establishing the baseline that Californians could consume in a "non-public place,"[31] possess up to an ounce of cannabis, and cultivate in up to twenty-five square feet on private
property, Proposition 19 left it to localities to decide their own
possession and cultivation limits, and whether to allow commercial growing and sales. Additionally, cities and counties would
regulate cannabis retailers to determine, for example, location
and hours of operation. The idea of localized legal cannabis in
a state with 482 cities and 58 counties was a hard sell to voters
who had experienced disarray over medical cannabis for nearly
fifteen years.[32] And for all of its emphasis on tax revenue, Prop 19
left the tax structure to localities, including the option to have
no tax, so accurate revenue projections for the state were all but
impossible to make.

The debate around Prop 19 was therefore not always about legalization versus prohibition; it was also about defective legalization or no legalization. Every major newspaper's editorial board opposed Prop 19. "The experience of Proposition 215, the 1996 initiative that legalized the use of medical marijuana, illustrates the danger of voting for a concept instead of the language of a ballot measure," the editorial board of the *San Francisco Chronicle* wrote.[33] "The loosely drawn Prop 215 continues to be a nightmare for many communities." The *Los Angeles Times* was more scathing. "Whether marijuana should be legal is a valid subject for discussion. Californians ought to welcome a debate about whether marijuana is any more dangerous than alcohol, whether legalization would or would not increase consumption, and whether crime would go down as a result of decriminalization," the editorial board wrote.[34] "But Proposition 19 is so poorly thought out, badly crafted and replete with loopholes and contradictions that it offers an unstable platform on which to base such a weighty conversation."

One week after the *Los Angeles Times* op-ed and one month before the vote, then governor Arnold Schwarzenegger reduced the punishment for one ounce of cannabis or less to an infraction that carried a $100 fine.[35] This was by no means legalization, but some saw it as an attempt to dampen support for Prop 19 by removing criminal penalties for minor cannabis possession. For those remaining undecided voters, U.S. attorney general Eric Holder wrote in his response to former DEA directors who publicly insisted he oppose the proposition, "The Department of Justice strongly opposes Proposition 19," and "the Department is considering all available legal and policy options in the event Proposition 19 is enacted."[36] In other words, don't even think about it.

After these blows, polls began to slide, with many showing the proposition facing defeat.[37] In October, the campaign released its first and only television ad, in which former San Jose police chief

Joseph McNamara said, with the husky-voiced determination of Clint Eastwood, "Let's be honest: The war against marijuana has failed. I know from thirty-five years in law enforcement. Today, it's easier for a teenager to buy pot than beer. Proposition 19 will tax and control marijuana just like alcohol. It will generate billions of dollars for local communities, allow police to focus on violent crimes, and put drug cartels out of business. Join me and many others in law enforcement. Vote YES on Proposition 19."[38] The ad was effective, but the Prop 19 campaign would need a whole lot of the Broadus Effect to celebrate a victory.

Just after 7 P.M. on election night, people began trickling onto the parking lot adjacent to Oaksterdam University, which was set up with tables, chairs, and tents as a viewing area for supporters and media. Approximately one hundred people talked and waited for the election results, which would be projected on the side of the white building. A stubby joint on the ground was still lit and burning. One man came dressed as a cannabis leaf.

When 1 percent of all precincts finally reported on Proposition 19, there was a noticeable slump as supporters learned that yes votes were down, with 41 percent voting yes to 59 percent voting no. Initiatives that begin with such a wide margin don't usually pull ahead. The yes side rose as high as 46 percent but eventually flat-lined. There were whispers that the ballot measure had lost. Slowly, the crowd thinned. The campaign was over and many supporters left feeling defeated. But those within the cannabis reform movement understood that Prop 19 revealed something much greater: 4.6 million Californians had voted in favor of broad legalization.[39] Richard Lee released a statement at 10 P.M. that evening:

> The fact that millions of Californians voted to legalize marijuana is a tremendous victory. We have broken the glass ceiling. Prop. 19 has changed the terms of the debate. And that was a major strategic goal. Over the

course of the last year, it has become clear that the legalization of marijuana is no longer a question of *if* but a question of *when*. Because of this campaign, millions now understand it's time to develop an exit strategy for the failed war on marijuana.[40]

The statement reiterated that the return of legalization in 2012 would be "stronger than ever." Lee was right.

In the course of trying to grasp and explain Proposition 19, the national media and millions of voters explored the concept of cannabis legalization, which they had little reason to do in such depth before. A Field Poll in September of 2010 showed that 84 percent of California's likely voters knew about Prop 19.[41] Jon Walker of the collaborative blog *Firedoglake* compared this to the September 2008 Field Poll for California's Prop 8, the nationally debated and discussed same-sex marriage ban, which showed that 70 percent of likely voters were aware of that effort.[42] And once cannabis legalization was propelled into national discourse and came close to reality, it could no longer be cast aside or overlooked. In September 2011, one week after the White House unveiled its "We the People" online petition system, more than 77,000 signatures were gathered for NORML's call to "legalize and regulate marijuana in a manner similar to alcohol," making it the most popular of the early petitions.[43] A Gallup poll in October 2011 confirmed that support for cannabis legalization had risen from 46 percent in 2010 to a record 50 percent the following year.[44] And it would continue to climb.

But a steady end to cannabis prohibition would require a level of public education and legal specificity that Proposition 19 had not offered, which made the effort easier for both supporters and opponents of legalization to abandon. In a major misstep, the Prop 19 campaign had moved forward with less than one year

to sell its message to a public that wasn't yet committed to reforming cannabis laws. There wasn't enough time to chew the
information, let alone digest it. Lee was right when he said 2012
would be "stronger than ever": public education campaigns were
ongoing in Colorado and Washington before Prop 19 was even
a twinkle in the eye of Californians. Those preparing for a push
in the two states knew they needed years to ready their voters.

In the words of Alison Holcomb, then drug policy director of
the ACLU of Washington and soon-to-be head of the state's 2012
campaign to legalize cannabis, "When the *San Francisco Chronicle*
doesn't endorse your marijuana legalization initiative, you've got
to look at what's going on." But, she added, given that the proposition got 46.5 percent of the vote with inadequate funding and
no prior example to offer the clarity of hindsight, Prop 19 had
held its own in a tough-seeded match. "Even though it may have
seemed entirely inadvisable at the time, it completely changed
the conversation about marijuana law reform," Holcomb said. "It
was one of the major contributing factors to making marijuana
law reform a legitimate issue to be debated at the national level."

Holcomb was born in Fort Smith, Oklahoma, and raised in
Tulsa. She moved west to go to Stanford, and north to go to
law school at the University of Washington. After more than
a decade in criminal defense, she made her way to the ACLU
of Washington in 2006. A couple of years earlier, the national
ACLU had taken an increased interest in cannabis law reform and casually requested proposals from state affiliates who
desired grant money to explore policy options. The ACLU of
Washington became a grantee and, through subsequent research,
revealed that voters in the state were unfamiliar with their cannabis laws. Many voters who filled out the questionnaire didn't
know the state had had a medical cannabis law on the books
since 1998, while others thought cannabis was already decriminalized in the state (possession of up to 40 grams was in fact a

misdemeanor that required a minimum of twenty-four hours in jail and a $250 fine). It was clear to Holcomb that no one could fully discuss changing cannabis laws without first educating the public about the laws already in place and their consequences. In February 2008, Holcomb launched the Marijuana: It's Time for a Conversation campaign with local Rick Steves, authority on European travel and member of the NORML board of directors.

The campaign centerpiece was a thirty-minute talk show in which Steves, the host, interviewed experts in front of a studio audience. The panel included Holcomb, retired Whatcom County Superior Court judge David Nichols, and Deborah Small from Break the Chains, a drug policy reform organization. They talked about the history of cannabis laws and their unintended aftermath. Holcomb sent the script to networks with hopes of buying time, but she said many wouldn't participate because of the stigma surrounding cannabis and because they assumed the program advocated for cannabis use. "It was extraordinarily frustrating because the point was to begin to have a conversation about whether our laws should change. We specifically wrote the script for the show not to advocate for any specific reform or law, but only to provide information," Holcomb said. One local NBC affiliate ran the show during a time slot right after *Saturday Night Live*—exactly when most of those still awake turn the television off.

After later releasing the video for download through Comcast, Holcomb realized she was reaching only the existing supporters, those she referred to as "our choir." But if she could intrigue local media, their coverage would reach mainstream voters who weren't already thinking about cannabis laws. So Holcomb planned forums across the state where the video would play and a rotating expert panel would take audience questions.

A forum in November 2009 in the city of Edmonds, north of Seattle on the Puget Sound, did the trick. The panel included Washington representative Mary Helen Roberts, former Nixon official Egil Krogh, and former Western Washington U.S. attorney John McKay. Until then, McKay was known in the cannabis community as the guy who prosecuted Marc Emery, the aforementioned publisher of *Cannabis Culture* magazine and a prominent incarcerated activist. That night, McKay surprised the audience—and captured the attention of the *Seattle Post Intelligencer*—when he said the country's drug laws needed to be changed and reviewed from "top to bottom."[45] Holcomb, who did not expect McKay to unequivocally support reform, realized that she was on to something.

Holcomb spent the next year and a half working with Senator Jeanne Kohl-Welles on the Big Bill, most of which was vetoed by April 2011 as a result of the crackdown. Holcomb knew she wanted to propose cannabis legalization, but wasn't entirely sure when. As the Big Bill was stripped for parts, Holcomb took note of her team from the forums, increasing national support for legalization, and internal polls that showed 54 percent of registered Washington voters would back such a measure. The time was right, she decided, to introduce to voters the opportunity to end cannabis prohibition.

As Holcomb led her forums, groundwork was also under way in Colorado. While the Washington effort was fairly traditional and helmed by a woman in her forties with origins not in cannabis law reform but in criminal defense, one prominent leader of Colorado's law reform, Mason Tvert, embraced techniques he described as "rabble-rousing."

Upon Googling Mason Tvert, one of the first photos to emerge shows him wearing a Drug Enforcement Administration costume, shades, and an amused look on his face. Right after graduation from the University of Richmond, Tvert found a place in the cannabis law reform movement. Born and raised in Scottsdale, Arizona, Tvert moved to Boulder in 2005 at age twenty-three to launch Safer Alternative for Enjoyable Recreation (SAFER), a national organization focused on demonstrating to the public that cannabis is safer than alcohol. According to NIDA and the National Institute on Alcohol Abuse and Alcoholism, one in ten adult users of cannabis or alcohol are at risk of dependence, but that number changes when it comes to teens: one in six teens are at risk with cannabis, while one in two are at risk with alcohol.[46] There are no recorded overdose deaths caused by cannabis, while alcohol overdoses kill twenty thousand each year, according to the Centers for Disease Control and Prevention.[47] Tvert received an MPP grant to steer this program, the vision of MPP's director of government relations Steve Fox. Local media and communities were focused on the issue of binge drinking in college because two students had died the previous fall, one at the University of Colorado–Boulder and another at Colorado State University.[48] SAFER rallied students on these two campuses to pass referendums so that penalties for cannabis use by students wouldn't be higher than those for drinking. They had stickers made with catchy phrases like "Party Organically" and "Equalize It." The SAFER style, fitting for college students, was Reform with Attitude.[49]

In 2005, Tvert wanted to use the SAFER message to push for an initiative in Denver that would remove all penalties for the possession of up to one ounce of cannabis by adults twenty-one and over. He didn't expect Initiative 100 to win, but Tvert had the same goal he had with SAFER: to generate media coverage as part of his "mission of forcing a public debate." A sure way to get media attention, Tvert thought, was to get on the ballot. With a limited budget, Tvert and another SAFER member hustled to get the majority of the signatures necessary while a handful of volunteers gathered the rest. Once I-100 got on the ballot—or, for Tvert, the stage—with thirteen thousand signatures, Tvert said, "We engaged in some shenanigans that really pushed the envelope and got a lot of attention."[50]

In one such scenario, SAFER announced a billboard the organization planned to unveil that October of a beaten woman with her attacker lurking in the background and the text "Reduce family and community violence in Denver. Vote Yes on I-100." Domestic violence experts fumed to the media that the billboards falsely implied the initiative could reduce domestic violence.[51] SAFER instead used a text-only billboard, criticized for the same reasons as the first, that read, "Alcohol use makes domestic violence 8 times more likely. . . . Marijuana use does not. Vote Yes on I-100."[52] The papers covered both billboards—and shared the SAFER message.

When Tvert recalls these strategies, he sounds like a gleeful puppet master, with the media as his perfect puppet. "We had no money," Tvert said, hence the tactic of "earn[ing] media coverage of $3,000 billboards" that the campaign announced but did not always display. Tvert was not afraid to go further. When John Hickenlooper, then mayor of Denver, opposed I-100, Tvert called him a "drug dealer" on the local Fox 31 morning show because Hickenlooper co-founded Wynkoop Brewing Company.[53] "He just happens to be lucky enough," Tvert explained, "that our laws consider his drug legal."

Initiative 100 passed with 54 percent that November and, while other cities had decriminalized cannabis to the point of a nominal ticket and fine, Denver became the first city nationwide to remove all penalties for adult cannabis possession and use.[54] The victory was ultimately symbolic because the city decided to stick with state law. But a twenty-three-year-old's first campaign, using tactics most weathered strategists would advise against, had not only been successful but made national headlines.[55]

Tvert took no time to celebrate. The following year, he placed the similar Amendment 44 on the state ballot to "maintain the narrative." Tvert brought back the billboards for the 2006 campaign. One, resembling a Coors ad, showed a woman in a green bikini reclined beneath: "Marijuana: No hangover. No violence. No carbs! Yes on 44."[56] Tvert again called out Hickenlooper and challenged him to a duel outside the Great American Beer Festival at high noon during which they would each consume their substance of choice and see who was knocked down first.[57] It was a ludicrous suggestion and obviously never transpired, but it attracted attention from the local ABC station.

"We wanted to upset people. We wanted to be funny. We wanted to be controversial," Tvert remembered.

From 2007 through 2010, after Amendment 44 lost, Colorado's budding medical cannabis industry stole the spotlight—and Tvert trained, just as Holcomb did, for a very important day in 2012. Tvert and Brian Vicente of Sensible Colorado, an advocacy group that focuses on medical cannabis, announced in November 2009 that they, along with Steve Fox, MPP's director of government relations who had initially hired Tvert to work on SAFER, would pursue full legalization as a team in 2012.[58] Vicente had moved to Colorado after college to "be a snowboard bum and kind of figure things out" until he was given a full ride to the University of Denver Law School. There, in 2004, he started Sensible Colorado to focus on regulating the medical cannabis industry that had begun to blossom in Colorado.

After Tvert and Vicente's announcement that November, Joel Warner of the *Denver Westword*, a Colorado weekly, wrote, with great foresight, "If Colorado's heady and booming medical-marijuana scene can avoid the pitfalls suffered in California and mature into a respectable and valid industry, that could do wonders for voters considering whether or not pot is worth legalizing."[59]

Holcomb and Tvert, as well as their teams that assembled, were as unalike as could be. The ethos that would drive each campaign to victory began with Holcomb's panels, fit for C-SPAN, and Tvert's provocative billboards.

Both the Washington and Colorado campaigns, however, started out by surveying voters and holding focus groups. They were determined to gain insight into what turned voters on and off before drafting in early 2011. This was a wise move, considering that 11 percent of those who voted against Proposition 19 did support legalization, but just not that particular initiative.[60]

Holcomb, for one, remained in pursuit of the mainstream voter, so the draft of Initiative 502 was conservative and addressed the most popular voter desires, from driving restrictions to no home cultivation and a focus on prevention of youth cannabis use. While the ban on grow-your-own cannabis was met with grumbles from many in Washington, Initiative 502's per se limit for driving under the influence sparked the most controversy within the cannabis community. A test that showed a driver at or above the per se limit was the *only* necessary proof of impaired driving. Many more studies need to be done, and the few that do exist vary, showing an increased risk of a traffic incident with a THC-to-blood ratio anywhere from 2 to 10 nanograms of active THC per milliliter of whole blood (ng/mL).[61] Holcomb balanced studies and settled on 5 ng/mL. This is not the same version of THC (carboxy-THC) that is present in the body for weeks and can show up on employment drug tests. The per se limit in Washington is based on the active THC that should subside within two to four hours after cannabis inhalation. The snag is that there is no official agreement on what constitutes "stoned driving" or how, precisely, the presence of active cannabinoids in the body causes driving impairment—the same ratio could have markedly different effects on different people. The 5 ng/mL limit meant that the regulation could, in theory, punish safe drivers with all of the consequences and embarrassments of a DUI. Holcomb would have to defend this provision to local and national advocates until the very end of the campaign, but she fought for it because a majority of voters she surveyed supported such a limit and she believed the initiative would probably fail in her state without it. "It was absolutely the hardest part of the initiative," Holcomb said. "It is very difficult when people who have been your allies and friends for many years are unable to trust that the reasoning behind including it is at least defensible."

The disapproval of the medical cannabis community, an inconvenience in Washington, would have been a deal breaker in Colorado. While drafting Amendment 64, Fox and Vicente asked first for extensive feedback from the hundreds of thousands of members of the state's medical cannabis community, the most established (read: wealthy and powerful) in the country. The campaign accommodated the medical cannabis community mainly by making a strong recommendation in the draft that they be placed at the front of the line to apply for the new cannabis retail outlets.

The two boldest objectives in Amendment 64, which also pleased the cannabis community, were home cultivation and the reintroduction of hemp farming. Since it was banished in the wake of cannabis prohibition, all hemp has been imported. The amendment called on the state to establish a system for the "cultivation, processing, and sale of industrial hemp." This was quite an economic opportunity, given that the value of imported hemp into the United States in 2009 was nearly $8 million and the Hemp Industries Association put—there is no official estimate— the annual retail sale of hemp products in the States in 2012 at more than $500 million.[62] The logic behind home cultivation was partly self-preservation: the DOJ could swiftly hinder a state-run program by threatening and closing shops and eliminating tax revenues, but it didn't have the resources to go into every single Colorado home.

The Washington team also considered the possibility of DOJ intervention—and in this chess match with the federal government, there was more than one way to play. I-502 took the appeasement route and tried to be as regulated and specific as

possible to protect the initiative from challenges. It would be po-
litically difficult, Holcomb hoped, for the feds to shut down such
a restrictive program.

These differences aside, neither draft altered employers' drug-
free workplace and drug-testing rights. Only adults twenty-one
and older could purchase, possess, and use an ounce of dried
cannabis. (I-502 also allowed for 16 ounces of solid product, like
edibles, and 72 ounces of liquids, like oils, lotions, or tinctures;
Colorado left its possession limit at one ounce of cannabis total.)
Both required licenses for growers to farm, for product manu-
facturers to package the cannabis or turn it into products like
edibles or topicals, and for retailers to sell to the public. More
specific rules would be written after the fact pertaining to, for example, security requirements, hours of operation, bookkeeping,
number of establishments, amount of stock a retailer may have,
packaging, and sanitation.[63]

Voters wanted both initiative drafts to show them the money.
Each state generated revenue estimates by balancing assumptions about how much it would cost the state to run the program
with assumptions about cannabis production costs, consumption
rates, and the number of businesses needed to supply that use.[64]
No place in the world had ever legalized and regulated cannabis, so much of this was guesswork. But research by drug policy
experts did predict the value of cannabis would drop from about
$300 to about $40 an ounce after legalization because there
would no longer be a so-called prohibition tax, the costs a buyer
assumes due to the risk involved for underground-market growers
and distributers.[65] This low estimated post-legalization price per
ounce allowed each initiative to set taxes on cannabis products
that would raise the sticker price of legal cannabis while still
keeping it cheaper than the black market.

Amendment 64 called upon the legislature to later set an excise tax no greater than 15 percent on wholesale cannabis from

growers to processors or to retail outlets, and processors to retail outlets. The initiative dedicated $40 million of the projected $47 million revenue from taxes (which could increase after 2017) toward the state Public School Capital Construction Assistance fund.[66] Meanwhile, I-502 set a steeper, fixed 25 percent excise tax at each stage as the cannabis moved from grower to processor to retailer to consumer, raising the price each step of the way.[67]

Holcomb was much more strategic about where the roughly half a billion in annual revenue would go. She wanted the initiative to signal more than the end of a failed cannabis prohibition. It was also a turn away from the criminalization of cannabis users and toward public health through regulation. Holcomb spent a significant part of the drafting process poring over the Family Smoking Prevention and Tobacco Control Act to borrow language about marketing, labeling, and advertising restrictions. Instead of trying to fix a problem after the fact, as tobacco legislation did, Holcomb wanted to build into the initiative strategies that could discourage underage use before it began. Holcomb gathered intelligence on what programs worked to prevent substance use, especially among youth, and how much tax revenue would ideally be dedicated to those programs. The majority of the revenue, she decided, would go toward research into the effects of cannabis use (including the effects on driving so the DUI law could be modified according to findings), evaluation of areas for improvement in the new law, public health education regarding cannabis, youth and adult drug prevention, and health care services.[68]

By June 2011, both campaigns submitted their drafts and geared up to land them on the ballot.

In Denver's Civic Center Park on July 7, 2011, the Campaign to Regulate Marijuana like Alcohol held a press conference to announce its petition drive.[69] The state required 86,105 signatures,

but the petitioners would need double that to be safe.[70] Tvert and
Vicente, wearing sharp suits, began to gather signatures there and
then. While Fox remained in D.C. most of the time throughout
the campaign, he was particularly involved in the pivotal signature
drive. Vicente referred to Fox as the quarterback who called the
shots for the broader strategy, Tvert as the bulldog who rammed
the message through, and himself as the diplomat who built coalitions and made sure everyone felt ownership of the effort. The
drafters were smart to be so inclusive of the medical cannabis community; at this crucial time, dozens of shops displayed Amendment
64 petitions and encouraged their many customers to sign on.

A dispensary is not the most unexpected place to find a legalization petition, but passersby must have been intrigued, if not
suspicious, as two men who looked like cops toured the front of
the Denver City and County Building on August 3, clipboards
in hand, to talk about wasted law enforcement hours and violence as a result of the cannabis black market.[71] The former
Denver Police lieutenant and a former Lafayette city associate
judge were members of Law Enforcement Against Prohibition,
the organization that endorsed Proposition 19 and would endorse
Amendment 64, as well. Soon, the ACLU of Colorado joined
as part of the campaign's coalition with a similar message about
wasted resources on often race-driven enforcement, citing the
initiative as a "significant step toward dismantling the failed War
on Drugs."[72] These concerns would later also bring on board the
Colorado/Montana/Wyoming NAACP State Conference.

The release of the October 2011 Gallup poll that showed a
landmark 50 percent support across the country energized
the campaign. A poll released by Public Policy Polling a couple months before had shown an equally encouraging 51 percent support among Colorado voters for the amendment.[73] As
Thanksgiving neared, the campaign urged supporters and volunteers to talk to their families about the SAFER message. While

this could have been a polarizing tactic, Tvert wasn't hesitant about new methods of reaching voters. On the campaign website, suggested talking points and counterarguments highlighted, for example, that cannabis legalization shouldn't be thought of as adding a vice but instead adding a choice.[74] The site prompted supporters to bring up the topic through a pop culture reference or, for the brave, a personal experience. And, if relatives drank, comparisons could be drawn between alcohol and cannabis. The resulting Thanksgiving dinner conversations were likely entertaining, but these face-to-face tactics must have worked. After a final tally of more than ninety thousand signatures three months later, on February 27, 2012, Amendment 64 had officially secured a place on the November ballot.[75]

The plan to put I-502 on the Washington ballot unfolded concurrently. At 11 A.M. on June 22, 2011, at the Seattle Public Library, Holcomb announced the campaign name, New Approach Washington, and the signature-gathering effort. She gave an emotion-filled speech about how the war on drugs undermined American values and how this was her attempt to put the country back on the right course. Holcomb would pursue her goal with the help of a convincing team. Among the vocal supporters who took the stage that day were Seattle city attorney Pete Holmes, European travel expert Rick Steves, past president of the Washington State Bar Association Mark Johnson, and former director of the Seattle and King County HIV/AIDS Program of Public Health Robert Wood.[76] By the day of the launch, the *Seattle Times* editorial board members had already decided that they supported "the legalization, regulation and taxation of marijuana for Washington state adults."[77] The editorial, published that day, acknowledged that states needed to lead where the federal government wouldn't and stated, "Prohibition has failed. It fuels criminal gangs. It fills the prisons in America and graveyards in Mexico."

But Holcomb, a perfectionist, wasn't reassured. The campaign wasn't over until it was over, and until then it felt never-ending. The signature-gathering process included Holcomb's "darkest days." As she spent hours doing outreach and trying to convince more legislators, officials, and organizations to endorse Initiative 502, she encountered a lot of hesitation. Some warned that if California couldn't legalize in 2010, Washington certainly couldn't just two years later. Others thought that the campaign wouldn't raise enough money to gain visibility during a presidential election. But Holcomb's outreach started to pay off. In mid-September, Washington State Democrats voted 75–43 to endorse the initiative with a resolution that pointed to wasted law enforcement resources and potential revenues.[78] Still, signature gathering was tedious. Holcomb would sometimes wake up at 2 A.M. and think, If I was standing outside the bars right now, I could probably get more signatures.

Volunteers of all ages, willing to stand in the cold for hours, proved indispensable. By November 2011, they had gathered more than 180,000 of the required 241,153 signatures.[79] Many older adults without roots in the cannabis movement were involved in the campaign, which seemed to especially benefit from its untraditional appeal to this demographic. A late November poll of registered voters by a local news station showed that support was at 56 percent for those aged eighteen to thirty-four—the usual proponents—but increased to 59 percent among those thirty-five to forty-nine, and 69 percent among baby boomers aged fifty to sixty-four.[80]

After Holcomb filed more than 350,000 signatures for Initiative 502, a few days later, in January 2012, Rick Steves held a small private party at his home. Holcomb vividly remembers the drive from the campaign office. As she headed north and looked up at the sky, she realized, "having gotten these signatures filed finally, that we were on the brink of making world history. And literally,

I was thinking everybody is going to be watching to see if the voters of state of Washington will do this."

On January 27, the State Elections Division announced that I-502 qualified for a decision by the legislature. Lawmakers chose not to sign it into law and passed the initiative on to the voters.[81]

By February 2012, with Amendment 64 and Initiative 502 officially on the November ballots, the New York Times and Reuters ran stories about both efforts.[82] The country paused and listened. The two campaigns now had nine months to convince voters in their states of their solutions to cannabis prohibition.

The New Approach Washington campaign appealed to voters by making sure that its message was not that cannabis use was good, but that current cannabis laws were bad. According to the campaign's research the previous year, half of those asked said their feelings toward cannabis were negative and about one-third said their feelings were positive, but about 70 percent agreed that treating cannabis use as a crime had failed. Given cannabis's deeply rooted, emotional connotations, Holcomb felt it would be a challenge to completely reshape feelings about the plant, and she also found the alcohol comparison too risky. So New Approach Washington decided to tug at that 70 percent, focusing on how cannabis prohibition had caused more harm than good.

The campaign's plan demonstrated signs of success over the next six months. In his State of the City address on February 21, 2012, Seattle mayor Mike McGinn backed I-502.[83] "I know every one of the city council members sitting to my left and right believes as I do: it's time for this state to legalize marijuana, and stop the violence, stop the incarceration, stop the erosion of civil liberties, and urge the federal government to stop the failed war on drugs." Then, on April 18, the M.L. King County Labor Council, which represents more than 150 unions, supported the effort. On May 2, sixteen state senators and representatives endorsed I-502, including Jeanne Kohl-Welles, the woman behind Washington's previous Big Bill. On June 13, three high-profile African American reverends came on board, followed by the NAACP Alaska, Oregon and Washington State–Area Conference in August. The Seattle-area women's rights organization Legal Voice also joined that month, citing concern for incarcerated women. It soon became more difficult to rattle off the thirteen Washington newspapers that endorsed I-502 than the handful that didn't.

A thirty-second television advertisement released that August reiterated that voters need not fancy cannabis to support I-502. The ad targeted women, a demographic that did not support legalization in the same numbers as men, and featured a Washington mom dressed in a soft blue cardigan at a café who said, "I don't like it personally, but it's time for a conversation about legalizing marijuana. It's a multimillion-dollar industry in Washington State and we get no benefit." Then she goes on to gently ask the viewer, "What if we regulate it? Have background checks for retailers, stiff penalties for selling to minors. We could tax it to fund schools and health care. Free up police to go after violent crime instead. And we would control the money, not the gangs. Let's talk about a new approach: legalizing and regulating marijuana." Just after the ad ran its course, the ACLU of Washington released a study that showed that cannabis law enforcement cost the state $211 million in the preceding ten years.[84] The study was not part of the New Approach Washington campaign, but its timing was likely no coincidence. The figure gave voters an idea of how much money they could save, in addition to the gained tax revenue, if the law passed.

A successful campaign changes perspectives, and certain occasions particularly stuck with Holcomb. At a League of Women Voters forum in Pasco, a rural community in southeastern Washington, a conservative woman approached her and said,

"I never in a million years would've thought that I might consider marijuana legalization. But you've really got me thinking about this." The Children's Alliance, which includes more than one hundred member organizations such as the Boys and Girls Club of King County, debated for many months about the initiative. Holcomb hoped for their support because she wanted to emphasize to voters that ending cannabis prohibition wouldn't be harmful to youth, a common concern among opponents. The Alliance finally endorsed I-502, stating that the racist enforcement of cannabis possession laws is more of a threat to children, especially black and Latino children, than the cannabis itself.[85] When Holcomb heard of the endorsement, which drew national attention, she cried. "It was these little glimpses where I realized this is happening. . . . That the message that this is not about marijuana, this is about our marijuana laws, is really resonating and the lightbulb is going on and this could happen."

Meanwhile in Colorado, Tvert was adapting his performance for a new audience. He knew he had to temper the hijinks to avoid jeopardizing an otherwise attainable win. "There's a time and a place," he said. "And Colorado in 2006 was a different place and time than 2012." He compared the difference between this campaign and SAFER to that between the Humane Society and the more aggressive PETA.

The campaign's primary message, however, remained that cannabis is safer than alcohol. "If someone thinks marijuana is bad and is going to result in their kid becoming an addict or moving on to heroin, why on earth do they give a shit if there are people who sell it in jail? They think they should be in jail. If you're against marijuana because you think it's harmful then you *do* think it should be a law enforcement priority and you're *not* interested in tax revenue. There's a reason why there isn't an effort to raise taxes from methamphetamine sales," Tvert said. "Once they come to understand that marijuana is relatively benign and is actually safer than alcohol, well, maybe it isn't worth putting people in jail and maybe it is worth generating tax revenue."

In May 2012, three months after Amendment 64 got on the ballot, the campaign pushed the idea of "interpersonal communication" with the launch of a new website, Talk It Up Colorado.[86] Everything, from social media to flyers during the campaign, ended with the same message: Share This. The importance of sharing was emphasized as much as the importance of voting. "I believe strongly that the key to changing marijuana laws is changing the way people think about marijuana. And the key to that is through public discussion, particularly with people you know," Tvert said.

The ads and billboards for Amendment 64, along with Talk It Up, revealed that Tvert and his campaigning style had matured. Through images of a mom, a dad, a son, and a daughter, the campaign raised important questions and talking points and addressed common concerns about cannabis. The first billboard went up above Mile High Liquors across from Sports Authority Field, home of the Denver Broncos. A blond middle-aged woman, arms crossed and dressed as if she had just gone for a morning walk, smiled from above. "For many reasons, I prefer . . . marijuana over alcohol. Does that make me a bad person?" This billboard, with its simple message and conventional-looking messenger, made national news.[87] Just before Mother's Day, the campaign's first TV ad showed a woman in her early twenties, wearing white capris and sitting against a tree in a park.[88] As she typed on her laptop, a voice-over said, "Dear Mom, when I was in college, I used to drink a lot. It was kind of crazy. But now that I'm older, I prefer to use marijuana. It's less harmful to my body, I don't get hungover and, honestly, I feel safer around marijuana users. I hope this makes sense, but if not, let's talk. I love you." A follow-up ad for Father's Day showed a young man telling his father that he also likes to unwind after work, except with cannabis.[89] A billboard intended to catch the eyes of male voters was released in late June, also near the aforementioned stadium. The image showed a father with his arm around his teenaged son, beside the text, "Please, card my son. Regulate the sale of marijuana and help me keep it out of his hands."[90]

The support of conservative Republicans and Libertarians was as important to the Colorado Amendment 64 campaign as that of Democrats and liberals. Washington, a solid blue state, left the I-502 campaign with a more cohesive voter base, but the swing state of Colorado, birthplace of the Libertarian party, is decidedly purple. The Libertarian Party of Colorado emphatically endorsed Amendment 64 in May, for example, while the Colorado Democratic Party offered support but stopped short of an endorsement.[91] The Republican Liberty Caucus of Colorado also endorsed the amendment because prohibition is "inconsistent with Republican values," which call for more "personal responsibility" and less "federal overreach."[92] It was later a bragging point when conservative former Republican representative Tom Tancredo threw his weight behind the campaign.[93] Tancredo endorsed Amendment 64 in a *Colorado Springs Gazette* column in which he pointed to prohibition as a wasteful government program, and wrote, "I am endorsing Amendment 64 not despite my conservative beliefs, but because of them." According to Vicente, this was the moment the campaign earned "crossover appeal." Tancredo was a polarizing figure but was well known enough to raise awareness of the campaign, and that's what they most wanted.

Libertarian presidential candidate Gary Johnson restated his endorsement of the amendment in mid-June—he had already expressed support when signatures were gathered—and held a press conference inside a Denver dispensary. But while a presidential candidate's support brought valuable and sustained national media attention to Amendment 64, Johnson's appearances also served his own campaign. He hoped to obtain votes in the key swing state from cannabis enthusiasts who were upset about

Obama's crackdown on the industry. (Some even wondered if there were enough of these voters to cost Obama Colorado in the tight presidential race.) Johnson stood out because he was the only candidate at the time who addressed both the legalization initiatives and cannabis prohibition head on; Obama avoided the topic, and Romney openly opposed all cannabis use.

In the weeks leading up to the election, each campaign had very different mountains before them, but their boots were laced for the hike. While Colorado's Campaign to Regulate Marijuana Like Alcohol had to stay vigilant as the opposition put up a well-organized and -funded fight, New Approach Washington would, for the most part, allow the opposition to self-destruct.

The Washington Association of Sheriffs and Police Chiefs, the Washington Association for Substance Abuse and Violence Prevention, and the Snohomish County drug task force commander Pat Slack opposed the initiative, but didn't band together or fund-raise.[94] The only organized or funded—and those words are used loosely—opposition to the I-502 campaign came from within the cannabis community. Holcomb was prepared for the infighting by virtue of having dealt with the Seattle-area cannabis community for so many years, most recently with the Big Bill. A group called No on I-502 included Steve Sarich. Recalling his attitude toward the the Big Bill, Sarich told *USA Today* that I-502 was "a Trojan horse."[95] "There's a new plan for prohibition in this country," he continued. "The government knows they're losing the battle, with more medical-marijuana states . . . so their new strategy, a deviously brilliant one, is 'You can have your pot—but we're going to arrest you now for drugged driving.'" No on I-502's complaints were similar to another group's, Sensible Washington, which had issues with strict driving restrictions and the proposed age limit for cannabis use (they objected that those under twenty-one remained criminalized, which was a valid argument, but voters were unlikely to allow cannabis for anyone younger).[96] Those against I-502 showed up at a press conference, holding signs with messages like "Per se is bad policy" or "Legalize not penalize."[97] One person even came in a Grim Reaper costume. It is possible that this behavior kept more sensible opposition at bay and helped New Approach Washington.

At Seattle Hempfest that August, tens, if not hundreds, of thousands of cannabis lovers gathered in Myrtle Edwards Park to consume cannabis, listen to music, and visit vendors. Organizers of the event remained neutral because of these divisions within the community. Yet at the event, New Approach Washington volunteers fielded unprovoked debates, boos, and middle fingers. In an op-ed that month, the *Seattle Times* scolded Hempfesters to "get real" because the new law, should it pass, "will have to be acceptable to a majority of people—and not just a majority of revelers at Hempfest or voters in liberal Seattle."[98]

Despite these disagreements, statewide support for Initiative 502 remained well over 50 percent, with some polls showing as high as 57.[99] In the conservative eastern part of Washington, however, support usually hovered around 40 percent.[100] The campaign did benefit from the endorsement of the area's largest paper, the *Spokesman-Review*, but Holcomb knew that it would take more to persuade the traditionalists, so she sent Rick Steves on a tour of nine cities that October. When charming an older, more conservative audience in Spokane a couple of weeks before the vote, Steves earned loud applause when he said, according to the *Seattle Times*, "I'm a hardworking, churchgoing, child-raising, taxpaying citizen," and "If I want to go home and smoke a joint and stare at the fireplace for two hours, that's my civil liberty."[101] A trio of TV ads featuring three powerful figures aired in the same month as Steves's convincing tour: former chief federal prosecutor John McKay, former U.S. attorney Katrina Pflaumer, and former Seattle FBI special agent in charge Charlie Mandigo.[102] The ads emphasized that legalizing and regulating

cannabis would allow law enforcement to target violent criminals, raise revenue for the state, and reduce youth access because
"drug dealers don't check IDs." One final release from Public
Policy Polling three days before the election showed Initiative
502 at a strong 53 percent.[103]

Colorado's Amendment 64, on the other hand, had vigorous opposition and had to improvise. The campaign's calendar in these
final months was often upended because of the group No on 64's
events. If the yes team caught wind that No on 64 was planning
to host an appearance with faith leaders, they would beat them
to the punch and introduce faith leaders in support. This back
and forth motivated Tvert. "When I first started I was just 'Oh my
gosh, this issue is so important and I care so much about it, I need
to work on it,'" he said. "But then it just becomes a given and it's
really now you're captivated by the game and the opposition."

Weld County District Attorney Ken Buck had begun to orga-
nize Smart Colorado, also known as No on 64, in the summer of
2012.[104] The group's website banner included a lineup of smiling
kids near the text "Wrong for Colorado!" Through small gather-
ings across the state, the group targeted suburban mothers and
business owners with the message that cannabis, a gateway drug,
would increase access for children and be bad for both youth and
business.

More than one-third of the nearly $700,000 raised for Smart
Colorado came from an out-of-state nonprofit.[105] Save Our Society
from Drugs, based in Florida, was started by major Republican
donors Mel and Betty Sembler, longtime opponents of cannabis
law reform. The two also run the nonprofit Drug Free America
Foundation, which arranges workplace drug testing procedures
for businesses through a federal contract.[106] The foundation began as Straight Inc., the inpatient drug rehabilitation centers
from coast to coast that people learned were responsible for many
abuses between the late 1980s and early 1990s. In 1990, the *Los*

Angeles Times reported that, according to records, California investigators confirmed that participants of the program they shut down, primarily youth, were "subjected to unusual punishment, infliction of pain, humiliation, intimidation, ridicule, coercion, threats, mental abuse . . . and interference with daily living functions such as eating, sleeping and toileting."[107]

By that fall, some of the most prominent cannabis prohibitionists in the country were fighting, either directly or indirectly, against Amendment 64. The tangible reality of legalization jolted them into action, and their message influenced the campaign. In September 2012, Governor Hickenlooper added his opposition for the two reasons pushed by Smart Colorado.[108] He said, "Colorado is known for many great things—marijuana should not be one of them. Amendment 64 has the potential to increase the number of children using drugs and would detract from efforts to make Colorado the healthiest state in the nation. It sends the wrong message to kids that drugs are OK." Momentum built for the anti–Amendment 64 crowd as two former Colorado governors, Bill Ritter and Bill Owens, went out of their way to express their disapproval of cannabis legalization because "it's really bad for our kids."[109] Tvert, who had until now refrained from calling out Hickenlooper, forcefully reacted to this opposition.[110] "Hickenlooper's statement today ranks as one of the most hypocritical statements in the history of politics," he wrote in a statement. "After building a personal fortune by selling alcohol to Coloradans, he is now basing his opposition to this measure on concerns about the health of his citizens and the message being sent to children. We certainly hope he is aware that alcohol actually kills people. Marijuana use does not."

Tensions ran high for the Amendment 64 campaign that month. It turned out that the Colorado Ballot Information Booklet, also known as the Blue Book, was missing language in the pro-64 argument.[111] The legislative council had taken out three sentences and neglected to put them back in: "The use of marijuana by adults may be less harmful than the use of alcohol or tobacco, both of which are already legal for adults to use and are regulated by the state. Furthermore, marijuana may be beneficial for individuals with certain debilitating conditions. The consequences of burdening adults with a criminal record for the possession of small amounts of marijuana are too severe, and there are better uses for state resources than prosecuting such low-level crimes." As a result, curious voters saw an unbalanced perspective. The Amendment 64 campaign was quick to publicize this error. Even the *Denver Post*, which had refrained from supporting the campaign, wrote an op-ed voicing frustration with the Blue Book.[112] But the largest paper in the state eventually opposed Amendment 64. In a piece published October 14, the *Post*, which supported legalization in general, cited concerns about federal intervention and insisted one state should not lead the way.[113] This was an unexpected position coming out of libertarian Colorado, especially considering that the *Seattle Times* had insisted that states needed to lead on the issue.

Even more dissonant was the opposition of Denver mayor Michael Hancock, who said cannabis would be bad for business, despite the multimillion-dollar industry medical cannabis brought to the city and state. Hancock's sentiments were shared by, to name just a few, the Downtown Denver Partnership, Visit Denver, and the Denver Metro Chamber of Commerce.[114] Hancock warned, according to the local CBS station, "Passing Amendment 64 will be detrimental to Denver's business, and our efforts to recruit businesses to our city as well as retain businesses in our city."[115]

The campaign was undeterred and stuck with the method that Steve Fox described as "something for them, something for us." The opposition could say nothing without a challenge. Betty Aldworth, who later joined the Amendment 64 campaign as campaign advocacy director, was at the mayor's press conference, prepared with a rebuttal to the bad-for-business argument; she would make sure that the yes side remained part of the news coverage. That day, the campaign released a statement to say that the state's largest union, the United Food and Commercial Workers Local 7, endorsed the amendment.[116] Why? Job creation and economic growth for Coloradans. The campaign finally released its pinnacle advertisement in October, moving from the SAFER message toward a more holistic one. This wasn't because the alcohol comparisons weren't working, Tvert said, but because he believed people first needed to hear the SAFER message before they would listen further about the benefits of legalization. The ad showed dollar signs pouring out of the state until a female narrator said, "Let's vote for the good guys and against the bad guys. Let's have marijuana tax money go to our schools, rather than criminals in Mexico. Vote for Colorado. Vote yes on Amendment 64."

By Election Day, each campaign had already faced its opponents, but one of the most powerful had remained eerily silent. Eric Holder had not yet spoken out against either initiative, as he had vehemently with California in 2010, despite a group of former DEA officials again publicly urging him to do so.[117] Holder's condemnation could scare off any tentative voters and offer ammunition to those, especially in Colorado, who referenced the mess of federal intervention as a rationale for a no vote. One theory for Holder's silence during the campaign was that, in a swing state like Colorado, excessive federal intervention into a state matter could sour voters to Obama and hand the state to Romney.

By November 6, 2012, New Approach Washington brought in nearly $6 million, with large contributions of $2 million from Peter Lewis and more than $1.6 million from Drug Policy Action.[118] Additionally, the campaign had received contributions of nearly $200,000 from ACLU of Washington and $100,000 from a local elderly philanthropist named Harriet Bullitt who believed that voters should have the choice to end cannabis prohibition. The

No on 502 campaign had raised under $7,000, most of it from members. In Colorado, the Campaign to Regulate Marijuana Like Alcohol had raised $2.5 million, with $1.2 million from MPP. Smart Colorado, otherwise known as No on 64, had raised less than $700,000, with its largest donation of $285,000 from Save Our Society from Drugs. These numbers, as much as any other variable during the campaigns, told the story of the evolving societal attitude toward cannabis.

Although the two campaigns were tailored to the voters of their states, they also offered the nation a range of reasons to support the end of cannabis prohibition. Americans put off by the earnest New Approach Washington could get a kick out of the audacious style of the Campaign to Regulate Marijuana Like Alcohol. Those who didn't believe that cannabis was safer than alcohol could get behind the new public health approach. Not one, but two, states had drawn a new map—and polls showed voters more than willing to follow the unfamiliar routes. (Oregon also had a legalization initiative on the 2012 ballot, but, with wide-open language and a limited campaign budget, it wouldn't pass.)

At Casselman's Bar and Venue in Denver the night of the election, the crowd of Amendment 64 supporters began to celebrate the moment they arrived. As more precincts counted their votes, the numbers climbed for Amendment 64 until the results revealed that, for the first time in more than seventy-five years, a state had ended cannabis prohibition. Mason Tvert, Steve Fox, Brian Vicente, Betty Aldworth, and the head of MPP Rob Kampia all strutted onstage like they were about to accept an Oscar. Aldworth used her moment to focus on the statewide collaboration necessary for their triumph. "I appreciate every bit of congratulations that you all have given to me tonight. But, it's not about me. It's not about the folks up here on the stage. It is about you! . . . Every single person in Colorado who called their

Grandma or called their high school classmates. Every person who shared a video online or whatever, waved a sign or went to the polls today. Those of you who have been doing this work for so many months with us, it is about you."[119]

While everyone soaked up the evening, Tvert could not shut off. The moment he realized Colorado voters would pass Amendment 64, he sat down at his laptop and wrote a press release because he knew the world was watching and "it was the opportunity to get the message across." His phone rang nonstop. He did pause, though, to thank his parents, who had traveled from Arizona.

The day before the election Vicente learned that his younger brother had been diagnosed with leukemia. That night he had a "heavy heart." But on stage, he felt a collective joy as he looked at hundreds of people he'd worked with for decades, and he was happy to stand alongside Tvert and Fox, with whom he had been in "the trenches."

Steve Fox went into election night "cautiously optimistic." Even when early results showed the campaign ahead, he was nervous that they could still get crushed in more rural areas of the state. Once he realized they had won, he stepped back, watched others celebrate, and absorbed the scene before him. With an unexpected 55 percent of Coloradans voting yes on Amendment 64, he felt that America wouldn't "turn the clock back on this." Tvert had his first interview of the next day before sunrise and Fox offered to make the media rounds with him. The two stayed up all night reminiscing on their last eight years together and how they couldn't believe they'd accomplished what they had set out to do from the beginning.

The mood inside Seattle's Hotel Ändra was more emotional than rowdy. At one point, a longtime Seattle Hempfest volunteer sat on steps and cried because she was so overwhelmed. When I-502 earned more than 63 percent of the vote in King County, where Seattle is located, Holcomb knew Initiative 502 had won. By the time she made her speech, her son Dashiell was drifting to sleep on her husband's shoulder. He woke up when she called out to him, and then he smiled and held out his balloon. Holcomb called her husband and son her "two ninja warriors."

Holcomb's husband took the podium. He'd spent the evening praising his wife's work, and now his eyes watered. "Alison has a tendency to work a lot and very hard. And she's a workaholic. She's a grinder. You put her to task and she's going to take it down, she's going to get you that victory. And we talked about whether it was worth it as a family to do this thing. And then we talked about what it means to be a parent and what it means to set an example for a child," he said, that "you can work to make a difference in the world." Holcomb's husband said that now he could tell his son, "Dashiell, Mama changed the world. Not by herself, but by standing up for something."

Cannabis advocates were delighted to announce after Election Day 2012 that more Colorado residents voted for cannabis legalization than voted for the reelection of Barack Obama. They valued this as an indication of buttressed leverage against an intransigent federal government and a reminder of how unpopular President Obama's unrelenting stance on cannabis had become. In Colorado, more than 1.3 million people voted for Amendment 64; in Washington, 1.7 million voted for Initiative 502. Although California's Proposition 19 failed in 2010, it received 4.6 million votes. In just those three elections, nearly 8 million Americans cast their vote to end cannabis prohibition.

7

A NEW LEAF

More than three-quarters of a century has passed since America last transitioned out of a prohibition. The similarities between alcohol and cannabis prohibition are staggering.[1] Both had racist roots. Both empowered criminals, in one case bootleggers and mobsters and in the other the cartels. Neighboring countries—Canada for liquor and Mexico for cannabis—supplied Americans' enduring demand for an outlawed substance. With the same bravado police used to dramatically smash barrels of alcohol, the DEA now hacks down rows of lush green plants. Both prohibitions went after consumers more often than producers or distributors, meting out the punishment to the least culpable. States one by one bowed out of enforcement of the Volstead Act and left the feds to raid speakeasies or arrest drinkers; similarly, since the 1970s, states have one by one decriminalized (or, in some cases, legalized) cannabis. In both cases, a struggling economy led to a willingness to tax and regulate a new job- and revenue-generating industry, even if it involved an illegal substance. Now and then, efforts at prohibition were driven by the naïve notion that a society can be forced to be drug- or drink-free.

Of course, federal alcohol prohibition lasted only thirteen years, compared to more than seventy-five years for cannabis. So the end of cannabis prohibition will unfold more slowly—and with more complications than can be foreseen. But it is, without doubt, ending.

In Colorado and Washington, months would pass before rules were finalized, licenses were distributed, and cannabis stores opened to the general adult public, but the votes had an immediate influence. Days after the election, Colorado's Boulder County district attorney Stan Garnett announced that his office would drop unresolved possession cases for adults twenty-one and older found with no more than one ounce of cannabis; the county police chief followed suit.[2] In Denver, seventy pending cases were reviewed for dismissal.[3] In an attempt to grasp at a disappearing past, Ken Buck, the Weld County DA who led the No on 64 effort, said in a statement that he would not dismiss any cases, adding, "But more importantly, our office prosecutes low-level possession cases to get drug users help with their addictions. That practice will continue until state law changes." (The governor had not yet signed the initiative into law.)

On the Friday following the passage of I-502, Dan Satterberg, the prosecutor for King County, Washington's most populous, dismissed 175 pending misdemeanor possession cases.[4] As in Boulder, the King County sheriff followed the order. Until this moment, the magnitude of the election results hadn't sunk in for Holcomb, who was bottlenecked with media calls, coming down with something, and running only on adrenaline. Once Satterberg dismissed the cases, she recalls, "It finally started to feel like it's done, it's been done, the blow has been struck." As a former criminal defense attorney who represented those charged with possession, she said, "I had this amazing and overwhelming sense that this just had a really concrete impact on a lot of people's lives."

The Seattle Police Department revealed the cultural shift that accompanied its new policy when it published a cheeky blog post three days after the vote titled, "Marijwhatnow? A Guide to Legal Marijuana Use in Seattle."[5] The post covered some general news, such as how police would still pursue those who broke the new state law by, for example, driving under the influence. But at the very end of the post an embedded video clip showed a scene from *The Lord of the Rings* in which Bilbo puffs from a long pipe, blows a smoke ring, and looks at a beautiful sunset while talking to Gandalf about "the finest weed in the Southfarthing." About one month later, on the day when the law was to take effect at midnight, knowing some people planned a celebratory smoke at Seattle Center, another SPD blog post let revelers know that they would not be cited that evening because "the department's going to give you a generous grace period to help you adjust to this brave, new, and maybe kinda stoned world we live in."[6]

Signs of the times surfaced around Colorado, too. In mid-February 2013 the state capitol building reeked of cannabis, for no particular reason.[7] John Morse, the state senate president, took the opportunity to joke, according to local ABC 7 News, "Do you smell marijuana in here, or is it just me?" And he later said, "If the Sergeants would please douse all the doobies in the area." The same month, the *Denver Post* ran an advice piece, like a Hints from Heloise tip sheet for cannabis, that covered aspects of Colorado's new gardening opportunity: proper equipment, costs, strains, containers, watering schedule, and harvesting.[8] Home cultivation was the only way to obtain cannabis for general use until regulations for the new industry were established by the end of 2013. The Coloradans who wanted to exercise their right to plant a cannabis garden, and then realized the task was more complex than placing a seed in the ground, could now look to their regional paper for guidance.

Soon enough in both states, a handful of boundary pushers emerged. In Colorado, entrepreneurs eager to earn the distinction of "first" opened up Amsterdam-style businesses, with names like Club 64, White Horse Inn, Studio A64 aka Club 710, and the Front Tea and Arts.[9] These were private clubs where people paid in the ballpark of $20 for entry or membership. Some showed local art or hosted nightly events, like poetry readings. In Washington, two existing bars decided to allow cannabis consumption in private rooms.[10] The idea was that until a licensed industry was established, these venues would provide a private place for residents to consume their cannabis; all of the clubs were BYOBud. Some of these early birds didn't survive, and few others were willing to push their luck with the feds so early in the movement's boldest experiment yet.

By the first weeks of 2013, associations and coalitions had formed to secure their place in the new industry. The former executive director of the Washington Beer & Wine Distributors Association, for example, helped form the Northwest Producers and Processors Association.[11] Longtime underground cannabis botanists now had to share the playing field with vintners and brewmasters. According to the Seattle weekly newspaper *The Stranger*, Mayor Mike McGinn summed up the experience of watching this transition toward a legitimate market during a National Cannabis Industry Association event at the Washington Athletic Club in January: "It's fascinating that this is the new normal."[12]

The wonder of cannabis legalization gave way to the yearlong challenge to transform the new laws into working programs. Then Governor Christine Gregoire allowed I-502 to become law on December 6, 2012. On December 10, Governor Hickenlooper signed Amendment 64 into law and the state's constitution.[13] "Voters were loud and clear on Election Day," Hickenlooper said in a statement before announcing the creation of a task force to determine regulations for every possible corner of the new industry. The twenty-four-member task force was divided into subgroups: Consumer Safety and Social Issues, Criminal Law Issues, Local Authority and Control, Regulatory Framework, Tax/Funding and Civil Law Issues.[14] Their goal between mid-December and late February 2013 was to debate various topics and compile recommendations into a report for the Joint Select Committee (yes, jokes abounded) in the legislature. This was only the beginning: the legislature drafted bills, which the governor signed, and then the department of revenue created rules for much of the remainder of the year.[15]

One subcommittee chair quipped that the task force meetings—often standing-room only, some six hours long—were "like a fistfight in a phone booth," according to a *Denver Post* reporter tweeting directly from the meetings.[16] Representatives from the senate and house, law enforcement, the medical field, and the cannabis industry had an equal place at the table. At one meeting, the governor's chief legal counsel recommended limiting potency and, at another, someone showed a bottle of 190-proof Everclear to make the point that accurate labels were more necessary than a potency cap. When discussing cannabis-infused gummy worms or cheesecake, the conversation veered into dietary matters such as who was capable of eating a whole cheesecake. At one point, the conversations turned so intricate that someone suggested "sub-subcommittees," an *Associated Press* reporter tweeted from the meetings. At the final meeting, in response to Hickenlooper's jab at stoners when the law passed that Coloradans shouldn't "break out the Cheetos or Goldfish too quickly," someone brought Cheetos and Goldfish for the task force to eat. (Even after beating back nearly a century of prohibition, this organized movement was held by some to the old stereotypes.)

Washington did things a little differently. In forums across the state, people gave their two cents to the Liquor Control Board (LCB), which took their thoughts into consideration while drafting regulations throughout 2013. The second forum was held on January 24 in Seattle's City Hall and attracted hundreds of attendees.[17] Sharon Foster, chair of the state LCB, said, "Wow, there's one heck of a lot of interest in I-502, that's for sure." One of the first speakers, a farmer, boiled one of the foremost concerns down to "Don't forget the little guys." In other words, give everyone a fair shot at the new industry, not just the rich, and remember the pioneers who took great risks for decades to make this moment possible.[18] While a turnout could be expected in Seattle, the crowds were just as large at a later forum in the more conservative eastern city of Spokane.[19] "It is just this beautiful demonstration of democracy in action," Holcomb said of the meetings, "where you have people that have been very skeptical of the government . . . now coming forward and saying 'Okay, I'm willing to participate in this process and I want to be part of the rulemaking. I want to be part of creating this new regulatory system.' And they're engaging with the Liquor Control Board members. And the board members and the staff are engaging right back, listening to what they have to say, and having these conversations. So the energy that is moving this forward is unbelievable."

After months of PowerPoints, opinions, quarrels, snivels, and laughs, each state had hundreds of rules that would shape the retail outlets (and growing and processing facilities) set to open in early 2014. Steve Fox, of the Amendment 64 campaign, remained involved during Colorado's rulemaking and said that he was pleased with the groundbreaking process. "If my biggest complaint is that everyone who buys marijuana is going to have to receive it in some sort of childproof container, then we've come a long way since worrying about people being sent to jail for marijuana," he said.

Amendment 64 and Initiative 502 did not alter their states' medical cannabis laws, and only time will tell how these existing industries will affect the new ones. Colorado could easily partition its medical and general use cannabis industries because of the regulated system for medical cannabis already in place. In Washington, on the other hand, the federal crackdown crushed the Big Bill's attempt to structure the medical cannabis program, leaving the state in somewhat of a pickle once Initiative 502 passed. Washington's challenge is to quickly clean up its medical cannabis system—which has no registry, unregulated co-ops, quasi-legal dispensaries, and some of the highest possession and home-growing limits in the country—in order to keep a tight grip on cannabis in the state.

Both cases, however, raise the question of the future of medical cannabis. In the years ahead, will cannabis exist as both a medicine and a nightcap? How will medical cannabis distinguish itself from the cannabis sold in the new stores down the street? What will make medical cannabis "medical"? After all, medical cannabis is simply carefully grown cannabis used for a therapeutic purpose.

One eventual scenario for both states is that the medical portion of the cannabis community will shrink as those who do not need cannabis for serious medical conditions opt out because they want to buy their ounce without anyone asking too many questions. The number of medical cannabis dispensaries will also dwindle as the number of cannabis retail outlets increases. The medical dispensaries that do remain will likely serve older or truly ill patients who want TLC with their THC (or CBD). Another theory is that some people will remain in the medical programs because general use cannabis involves high taxes, age restrictions, and, in the case of Washington, no permission to home-grow. Once these businesses are up and running the interplay will become clear.

Lester Grinspoon, associate professor emeritus of psychiatry at Harvard Medical School and author of two books about cannabis, doesn't believe that medical dispensaries will survive alongside legal retail outlets in the long run because they will be selling the same product. Instead, he envisions cannabis retail stores that serve both groups and carry specialized products for various therapeutic uses. According to Dr. Grinspoon, the other source to fill that niche for medical users could be pharmaceutical companies that are able to create products equal in efficiency to the plant, offering some patients a targeted alternative to whole plant medicine. The question is when such a product will be on the market (still, only THC pills are available to U.S. patients). As long as there is no equivalent pharmaceutical product, demand for whole plant medical cannabis will likely continue.

It remains to be seen whether medical cannabis will be rescheduled or even federally regulated. There are models for national medical cannabis. In Israel, the Ministry of Health has distributed more than ten thousand licenses to registered patients, and also licensed a handful of farms to supply those patients.[20] In one nursing home in Na'an, half of the patients use medical cannabis. The head nurse told the *Inter Press Service*, "Though we know how to extend life, the pain is great. In geriatrics, the future doesn't matter any longer. What matters is the now—how to add quality of life to longevity." Or the United States could draw lessons from Canada, where the government has grown and supplied cannabis for patients since 2002, but announced in 2012 that it would privatize production through contracts.[21] The Czech Republic passed a medical cannabis law in 2013 and began to distribute cannabis from pharmacies to patients.[22] In Amsterdam, some individuals forgo the coffee shops for pharmacies and medical cannabis.[23] Despite the refrain that medical cannabis is a lie crafted by advocates of legalization, Amsterdam offers compelling evidence that, even though the majority of cannabis consumers are non-medical users, general use will not eliminate medical use in the United States.

The most unusual and complicated outcome of the Washington and Colorado laws—even by global standards—is that the United States is left with four distinct stances on cannabis within its borders. Seventeen states have decriminalized simple cannabis possession and use.[24] Twenty states and Washington, D.C., have legalized cannabis for medical use alone. Colorado and Washington have legalized and regulated cannabis for general use by adults twenty-one and over. And finally, the federal government maintains that cannabis possession for any purpose is a crime in every state.

After the landmark 2012 legalization vote, there was widespread uncertainty as to how the federal government would react. This is unexplored territory—not just in the United States, but worldwide. One thing is clear: the federal government cannot force states to recriminalize cannabis or even demand that state officials enforce federal law;[25] if the feds want their laws enforced, they have to do it themselves. Many of the clashes that exist with medical cannabis—concerning housing, employment, hospitals, and banking—will still arise as long as federal policy remains unchanged. One great fear was that the federal government would try to prevent the states from implementing a regulatory structure for the manufacture and sale of cannabis; this would mean a lengthy legal battle over whether a state-regulated industry impedes the federal government's ability to enforce its own laws; in such a case, the federal government would have a supremacy advantage. But there is no consensus on whether the new laws create such a conflict, and the process of sorting it out could take years. (In the event of a successful legal challenge to state-regulated production and retail, Colorado home cultivation, possession, and use would likely remain in place because it would be more difficult for the federal government to argue that these aspects of the law create a conflict. Washington, with neither home cultivation nor cannabis stores, would remain more susceptible to the underground marketplace.) All that Coloradans and Washingtonians could do post-passage was to draft impeccable regulations, hope, and wait.

During a 2009 press conference, Gil Kerlikowske, then director of the Office of National Drug Control Policy (or drug czar), said, "As regards to legalization, it's not in the president's vocabulary and it's not in mine."[26] But the luxury of easily dismissing legalization had evaporated by 2012. Voters in two states forced the federal government to acknowledge a marked societal movement. In reply to a We the People petition posted in January 2013, Kerlikowske said, "It is clear that we're in the midst of a serious national conversation about marijuana."[27] But he wrote little more and pasted in Obama's response to a question asked by Barbara Walters in a December 2012 post-election interview: "Do you think that marijuana should be legalized?"[28]

"Well, I wouldn't go that far," Obama said. "But what I think is that, at this point, Washington and Colorado, you've seen the voters speak on this issue. And as it is, the federal government has a lot to do when it comes to criminal prosecutions. It does not make sense from a prioritization point of view for us to focus on recreational drug users in a state that has already said that under state law that's legal. . . . this is a tough problem because Congress has not yet changed the law. I head up the executive branch; we're supposed to be carrying out laws. And so what we're going to need to have is a conversation about how do you reconcile a federal law that still says marijuana is a federal offense and state laws that say that it's legal."

Advocates and the media scrambled to decode Obama's words. He seemed willing to entertain a conversation, to "reconcile" the federal and state clash that has endured for years, and to realize that voters had voiced their desires. While his statement later in the interview that the administration had "bigger fish to fry" than cannabis users was irrelevant (over 95 percent of drug enforcement occurs at the state and local levels), Obama's use of "at this point" led some advocates to compare this opinion to his evolving stance on gay marriage.[29]

Still, the possibility of a negative federal response weighed on many minds when the votes rolled in on election night, casting a shadow on the victory. A U.S. attorney for the western district of Washington State released the following statement the morning after the vote (a nearly identical one was released in Colorado the same day): "The Department of Justice's enforcement of the Controlled Substances Act remains unchanged. In enacting the Controlled Substances Act, Congress determined that marijuana is a Schedule I controlled substance. The Department is reviewing the ballot initiative here and in other states and has no additional comment at this time."[30] The same day, Colorado governor John Hickenlooper, who had opposed Amendment 64, said that he expected some form of federal intervention but would work to abide by the new law.[31] In a statement, Hickenlooper said on the night of the vote, "The voters have spoken and we have to respect their will. This will be a complicated process, but we intend to follow through. That said, federal law still says marijuana is an illegal drug." Within days of Amendment 64's passage, Hickenlooper pressed attorney general Eric Holder during a call for clarity on the potential federal response.

Other Colorado politicians wasted no time in seeking resolutions, aware that momentum for cannabis law reform would continue to build and conflicts with federal law and law enforcement would therefore increase. Days after Amendment 64 passed, Colorado representative Diana DeGette expressed her desire to amend the federal Controlled Substances Act to indicate that, while rules for other substances were to remain intact, the act does not preempt state cannabis laws.[32] One week after the election, DeGette introduced the Respect States' and Citizens' Rights Act. The bill had a number of co-sponsors from across the country, including U.S. representatives Earl Blumenauer from Oregon, Steve Cohen from Tennessee, and Sam Farr from California.[33] The same day, U.S. Representative Jared Polis of Colorado wrote a letter, signed by sixteen legislators from coast to coast, to Attorney General Holder to emphasize that "it would be a mistake for the federal government to focus enforcement action on individuals whose actions are in compliance with state law."[34]

Incoming Washington governor Jay Inslee seemed more optimistic and proactive than Hickenlooper. At a press conference
one week following the vote, he said, "I think it'll serve the nation well to allow the state of Washington and Colorado to serve
as incubators of a new policy," going so far as to add that he
believed there were signs of "an honest consideration going on
in the [Obama] administration."[35] When Inslee and his attorney
general, Bob Ferguson, met with Holder in D.C. in January 2013,
they made it known that the state was forging ahead. Ferguson
didn't want the situation to escalate into a lawsuit, he said to
Holder, but should legal action be taken by the DOJ against the
state, he and his team were ready to defend state law.[36] (This
is in direct contrast to Colorado attorney general John Suthers,
who took the opportunity of Amendment 64's passage to reiterate in a statement that the state's legalization was "very bad public policy.")[37] In mid-February, Governor Inslee followed up with
a five-page letter to reassure Holder just how controlled the state
market would be.[38] "Clearly, the world is watching the states of
Colorado and Washington as their initiatives are implemented,"
wrote Inslee. "We intend to do it right."

Advocates were encouraged that neither state felt the need
to abruptly halt its process after phone calls and meetings with
Holder, during which he expressed that one major concern was
how the states would avoid cannabis diversion across state lines.[39]
He later added that he was also focused on the new laws' ability
to keep cannabis out of the hands of children.[40] Perhaps most
remarkably, there was no imminent lawsuit for months after the
initiatives were signed into law—a far departure from Holder's
firm threat to California before Election Day 2010.

One national opposition group is rooting for federal intervention. In mid-January 2013, Project SAM (Smart Approaches
to Marijuana) launched at the Denver Press Club.[41] While
it is a new group with a new name, the message is otherwise

carbon-copied from years prior, and the members are known opponents of cannabis. Christian Thurstone, a Denver doctor who focuses on adolescent addiction, had been an opponent of Amendment 64. Kevin Sabet, a former Office of National Drug Control Policy senior adviser to Kerlikowske, is a vocal presence in Colorado, Washington, and nationwide; he frequently appeared in the media to oppose the legalization initiatives and he debated everyone from Mason Tvert to Alison Holcomb to DPA's Ethan Nadelmann. The only new voice was Patrick Kennedy, former Rhode Island representative. Kennedy had previously expressed support for state medical cannabis laws and, until 2007, attempted to protect them from federal intervention; he voted for five straight years for the Hinchey-Rohrabacher amendment, which would have withheld funds for that purpose from the DOJ (it didn't pass).[12] By 2013, Kennedy changed his mind and told the Washington Post that "marijuana destroys the brain" and that it is "a very dangerous drug."[43] That February, Kennedy wrote a letter to Holder to urge him to enforce the Controlled Substances Act in the two offending states.[44]

Project SAM aims to provide an alternative to what it claims has become a conversation of extremes. (This is a stale sound bite repackaged—Kerlikowske, Sabet's former boss, had already presented this false dichotomy many times before and said he supported a "third way.")[45] On the SAM website, it says, "'Incarceration or legalization?' 'Lock 'em up, or let 'em loose?' These phrases have dominated the discussion about marijuana over the past decade. As a result, marijuana-legalization advocates—not scientists, doctors, people in recovery, disadvantaged communities or young people affected by marijuana use and its policies—have been at the forefront of changing marijuana laws in the United States."[46] Project SAM also offers a "third way" that acknowledges that some old policies have failed, but insists that legalization is not the answer.[47]

The debate is anything but extreme. And the laws in Colorado and Washington are so different and restrictive that "let 'em loose" is hardly applicable. Project SAM insists that legalization advocates dominate, to the exclusion of many, the conversation around cannabis. SAM must have missed the broad coalitions—which include the labor unions, Children's Alliance, NAACP, law enforcement, and bipartisan groups of legislators—that came to life between 2010 and 2012. Legalization happened precisely because so many diverse parties sat at the table.

As for SAM's wish list of "third way" solutions, all of them—from increased medical cannabis research to avoiding "Big Marijuana" to increased education about the health risks of cannabis use—have already been addressed by the legalization movement.[48] Project SAM's proposed policy for cannabis possession arrests—its answer to legalization that doesn't address anything beyond simple possession—is heavy-handed and intrusive: "That possession or use of a small amount of marijuana be a civil offense subject to a mandatory health screening and marijuana-education program as appropriate. Referrals to treatment and/ or social-support services should be made if needed. The individual could even be monitored for 6–12 months in a probation program designed to prevent further drug use." The differences between a user and an abuser seem lost on Project SAM.

These last-gasp solutions appeal to former George W. Bush speechwriter and current *Newsweek/Daily Beast* contributing editor David Frum, who wrote in 2012, "Marijuana smoking is a sign of trouble, a warning to heed, a behavior to regret and deplore." Frum, who eventually joined the Project SAM team and dismissed medical cannabis as a "laughable fiction," believes it to be the duty of the upper crust to forgo cannabis so that "those who feel they have the least to lose" will not be faced with temptation.[49] He later elaborated in another piece, "When we write social rules, we always need to consider: Who are we writing rules for? Some people can cope with complexity. Others need clarity. Some people will snap back from an early mistake. Others will never recover. 'Just say no' is an easy rule to follow." Frum's conclusion? "There's a trade-off, yes, and it takes the form of denying less vulnerable people easy access to a pleasure they believe they can safely use. But they are likely deluding themselves about how well they are managing their drug use."[50]

Despite SAM's best efforts, the national response to Colorado and Washington has been overwhelmingly positive. In Washington, D.C., a series of legislative gestures served as powerful symbols of change. Several bills were introduced in Congress throughout 2013 to address issues that ranged from banking options and taxes for the cannabis industry to an affirmative defense in cases of federal cannabis arrests.[51] Colorado representative Jared Polis introduced the Ending Federal Marijuana Prohibition Act of 2013 to decriminalize cannabis federally.[52] Oregon representative Earl Blumenauer introduced the States' Medical Marijuana Patient Protection Act to reschedule cannabis to Schedule III or lower.[53] In April 2013, Representative Steve Cohen of Tennessee introduced an act to create a National Commission on Federal Marijuana Policy that would evaluate how to reconcile federal and state cannabis laws, take stock of the human and financial costs of prohibition, and also explore the option of rescheduling cannabis.[54] Cohen confronted Holder directly at a hearing to say "it's been an injustice for forty years in this country, to take people's liberty for something that was similar to alcohol." He added, "This is the time to remedy this prohibition, and I would hope you would do so."[55] None of these bills stood much chance of passage, but collectively they spoke volumes.

The congressional support did not end there. U.S. Senate Judiciary Committee Chairman Patrick Leahy of Vermont made it clear that he would not let stand the federal and state legal discrepancy that had existed for decades. During a Q&A at the

Georgetown University Law Center, Leahy said, "I am concerned
that just because marijuana is illegal, the possession of it, under federal law, that we're just going to ignore what states do
and send law enforcement in there to enforce the federal law,"
he said. "I hate to see a great deal of law enforcement resources
spent on things like the possession and use of marijuana when
we have murder cases, armed robbery cases, things like that that
go unsolved." In response to another question, he said, "We have
spent tens of billions, hundreds of billions of dollars on this so
called 'war on drugs.' Well, we've lost."[56]

House minority leader Nancy Pelosi strengthened the affinity
between Congress and the cannabis movement when she told the
Denver Post in March that the new law "has to be respected. . . .
If you're going to have recreational marijuana, somebody is in
business to do that. And they have to have tax treatment in order
for them to function as a business. So how the state of Colorado
interacts with the federal government on the taxation issues is
something they have to work out."[57] Congress is slowly beginning to represent the will of American voters.

Soon after the 2012 election, bills were introduced in state
legislatures across the country, adding to the chorus of support.
Seventeen states proposed medical cannabis bills, while nine
states proposed decriminalization bills and nine others proposed cannabis legalization. Even conservative southern states
buzzed with activity. Republican Senate Minority Leader Mitch
McConnell supported Kentucky senator Rand Paul's bill to legalize hemp production in the state (like a hippie in a health food
store, Paul introduced the bill while wearing a hemp-made shirt).[58]
Kentucky was the country's hemp heartland in pre-prohibition
days; the return of hemp to the state would be a homecoming.

States that were not yet ready to address full cannabis legalization
contributed to the ongoing debate in other ways. The U.S. Conference of Mayors passed a resolution in June 2013 "in support of

states setting their own marijuana policies without federal interference"; they asked that federal resources not be spent on challenging state cannabis laws and programs and that the federal government reclassify cannabis, among other suggestions.[59] To curb the racially skewed and unwarranted arrests that result from controversial stop-and-frisk procedures, New York governor Andrew Cuomo urged his state, with the highest number of cannabis possession arrests in the country, to introduce legislation to clarify its decriminalization law. Under the original law, minor cannabis possession is decriminalized—unless it is in public. He wanted to decriminalize less than 15 grams in public view and require that cannabis be lit or actively consumed—not just removed from one's pocket during a frisk—to count as public and warrant a misdemeanor arrest.[60] This effort, should it succeed, has the potential to drastically reduce the tens of thousands of cannabis possession arrests in New York City, where the majority of such arrests occur in the state.

As political support for cannabis law reform strengthened, so did social progress. In April 2013, more than one hundred celebrities, including Nicki Minaj, Susan Sarandon, and Scarlett Johansson, signed a letter to Obama in favor of U.S. drug policy reform.[61] Bill Keller, former executive editor of the *New York Times*, wrote in a May 2013 op-ed for the paper, "The marijuana debate has entered a new stage. Today the most interesting and important question is no longer *whether* marijuana will be legalized—eventually, bit by bit, it will be—but *how*."[62] The *New York Times* Style section published an article three months prior on cannabis etiquette at parties, such as how to gauge attendee comfort and where to partake to avoid upsetting those who don't like the idea or the smoke: "The etiquette of pot smoking in social settings is largely uncodified. Yet the world needs an Emily Post to hack a pathway through this fuggy thicket, particularly given pot's increased presence in the mainstream."[63] Cannabis certainly has gone mainstream if the Gray Lady is concerned with "pot" parties; its readership includes those who need to know how to celebrate Passover in Paris or who blithely jet to Bangkok for a "36 Hours" getaway.

Holcomb said she knew that there was potential for building momentum after the election, but the pace has surprised even her. "I'm feeling—I hate saying that—but I'm feeling so incredibly optimistic," she said. "During the campaign I kept having this sense and I kept telling people, I said, 'You know, this is just going to be the arrow with diamond tip that starts to break the glass' . . . And that's what I believed. But that is what appears to be happening and it's awesome. It feels like there are all of these people throughout the nation and all over the world that were just waiting for someone to go, they just wanted someone to go first and show that it was okay."

The United States' approach over the past century has failed, and nobody can argue that the country is prematurely ending a promising policy to go hastily in a new direction. The concept of legalization and regulation has gained enough support that two states have set sail, with more than half the country applauding their efforts. There is no way to predict the exact results of these experiments and others in states that follow, but successes should encourage the federal government to create policies that reflect Americans' progressing desires.

The end of cannabis prohibition will mark the beginning of the end of the war on drugs—which has been, at its core, a war on cannabis and cannabis users. Of the 1.53 million drug arrests made across the country in 2011, 49.5 percent (more than 750,000) were for cannabis and, of those, 87 percent (663,000) were for possession only.[64] The Center for Investigative Reporting found that cannabis accounted for nearly 89 percent of all U.S. Customs and Border Protection seizures along the U.S.-Mexico border between January 2005 and October 2011.[65] Once the human and financial costs of cannabis prohibition are removed from the picture—halting unnecessary arrests, preserving law enforcement hours and efforts, and saving billions—a rational and more manageable conversation about the remains of the drug war can emerge.

But first the federal government has to admit to its drug war habit. "We should stop using the war metaphor," Kerlikowske said in an interview with the *National Journal* in 2009.[66] "We should stop comparing this to a war and be much smarter about how we are dealing with it—and in a much more comprehensive way. I've ended the war on drugs." But while Obama promised a focus on treatment and prevention, the proposed 2014 White House National Drug Control Budget, an indicator for how an administration approaches the war on drugs, showed the same imbalance as presidencies past. Less than half of the $25.4 billion—42 percent—went toward demand reduction (treatment, education, and prevention).[67]

Ironically, the man who launched the war on drugs engaged in the least warfare. Only Nixon (and only in his early years) devoted the majority of his drug war budget—69 percent—to demand reduction; the remainder went to supply reduction, which includes domestic and international law enforcement and interdiction. Reagan flipped the equation between 1981 and 1989: by the time he left office, the budget was 69 percent supply reduction and only 31 percent demand reduction. Reagan called this his "hot pursuit" policy, boasting, "It's true that when we close off one place they can move somewhere else. But one thing is different now: We're going to be waiting for them. To paraphrase Joe Louis, they can run but they can't hide."[68] (His tactics only moved the cocaine pathway from south Florida to the Mexican border.)

Under George H.W. Bush, the ratio improved a bit to 65 percent supply reduction and 35 percent demand reduction.[69] Bill Clinton promised more focus on treatment but had reduced demand reduction over the course of his presidency back to 70/30 by 2001.[70] George W. Bush also promised to focus more on treatment and at first brought demand reduction up to nearly 46 percent of the budget, but by the end of his term the ratio was 64/36.[71] Bush overreached in his insistence, as part of his misguided demand reduction efforts, that the war on drugs was part of the war on terror. When signing the Drug-Free Communities Act Reauthorization Bill on December 14, 2001, with the wounds from September 11 still bleeding, he said, "If you quit drugs, you join the fight against terror in America."[72] The Office of National Drug Control Policy (ONDCP) spent nearly $4 million on two Super Bowl ads in 2002.[73] In one, a youth said, "I helped murder families in Colombia." "It was just innocent fun," another shrugged. "I helped a bomber get a fake passport," a young boy confessed. "All the kids do it," another told viewers. "I helped blow up buildings," said one girl, and another chimed in, "My life, my body." The second ad ended with this kicker: "Where do terrorists get their money? If you buy drugs, some of it might come from you."

The new budget for 2014—58/42—is an improvement, but it still pours more resources into a futile approach. Even worse, the total budget has increased over time. Taking inflation into account, Nixon's original drug war budget of $112 million has increased approximately fortyfold to over $25 billion by 2014. In 2012, Lieutenant Colonel Michael F. Walther, retired director of the National Drug Intelligence Center of the Department of Justice, wrote a paper highlighting these data titled "Insanity: Four Decades of U.S. Counterdrug Strategy."[74] He likened this constant dumping of resources into a faulty policy to a cartoon by Dana Fradon in the July 24, 1978, issue of the New Yorker in which a crowned king proclaims, "Gentleman, the fact that all my horses and all my men couldn't put Humpty together again simply proves to me that I must have more horses and more men."[75]

Ever increasing arrests of users and dealers has not stopped using or dealing. And only 4 percent of Americans believe the war on drugs is working.[76] The combined forty-year outcome of this law enforcement–heavy strategy is 45 million arrests, $1 trillion spent, and America's international title of number one in incarceration.[77] The United States imprisons 2.2 million people; in second place is China with 1.6 million, and Russia is third with 688,600. Katrina vanden Heuvel, publisher of *The Nation* magazine, wrote in the *Washington Post*, "Americans aren't drug free—we're just the world's most incarcerated population. We make China look like Woodstock."[78]

Nearly 7 million, or one in every thirty-four, Americans are in the U.S. correctional systems; one in three black men will spend time in prison at some point in his life.[79] According to statistics from 2011, the latest data available, one in six state prisoners are in for a drug charge; in federal prison, that increases to one in two.[80] The federal prison population alone skyrocketed nearly 790 percent between 1980 (around the time Reagan re-declared the war on drugs) and 2013, and prisons are currently, on average, 40 percent over capacity. While many factors have likely contributed to the increasing federal prison population, mandatory minimums have played an unmistakable role, according to a congressional report titled "The Federal Prison Population Buildup."[81] The "historically unprecedented increase in the federal prison population" has paralleled "declining marginal returns," wrote the author, Nathan James, because a drug trafficker who is locked up is quickly replaced in the black market.

And they will continue to be replaced as long as demand is high, and demand will remain high as long as the United States continues to criminalize drug users far more often than it offers education and treatment.

While cannabis users who are arrested are not often sent to prison, there are still more than twenty thousand people incarcerated for mere possession.[82] According to a comprehensive 2013 report released by the ACLU, between 2001 and 2010 more than 8 million cannabis arrests were made in the United States (88 percent for possession), and the possession enforcement alone cost more than $3.6 billion in 2010. Across the country, blacks are nearly four times more likely than whites to be arrested for canna-bis possession, despite comparable rates of use; in some counties that number increases from four to thirty. Finally, 62 percent of those arrested are twenty-four or younger, which means their ar-rest records will follow them throughout adulthood. In response to this report, the *New York Times* editorial board issued in a June op-ed one of the paper's strongest statements to date about the effects of cannabis prohibition: "The costly, ill-advised 'war on marijuana' might fairly be described as a tool of racial oppression."

Again, when cannabis—which accounts for 80 percent of all illegal substance use in the United States—is removed from the drug war picture, the country can more effectively discuss and implement a new and more fitting public health policy for the remaining hard drugs.[83]

Before we can extensively rethink either cannabis policy or the broader drug war, however, we have to be unshackled from the international drug control treaties we promoted and pushed since 1912. The bedrock treaty is the Single Convention on Narcotic Drugs of 1961, which prompted Congress to enact the Controlled Substances Act. After Colorado and Washington legalized cannabis, the UN International Narcotics Control Board reminded the United States in its annual report that "this constitutes a significant challenge to the objective" of the treaty:

> 82. The Board underlines that the Single Convention on Narcotic Drugs of 1961 establishes, in its arti-cle 4 ("General obligations"), that the parties to the Convention shall take such legislative and administra-tive measures as may be necessary to give effect to and carry out the provisions of this Convention within their own territories and to *limit exclusively to medical and sci-*

*entific purposes the production, manufacture, export, im-
port, distribution of, trade in, use and possession of drugs.*

83. The Board stresses the importance of universal implementation of the international drug control treaties
by all States parties and urges the Government of the
United States to take necessary measures to ensure full
compliance with the international drug control treaties
in its entire territory.[84] [Emphasis added.]

Some countries have relaxed their cannabis policies and laws
enough to bring them just within the bounds of the treaty.[85] In
the Netherlands, for example, coffee shops are tolerated, and the
government turns a blind eye to the mass cultivation necessary
to supply these shops; legalizing and regulating that supply, as
Colorado and Washington have, would stand in violation of the
treaty. In Spain, more than three hundred cannabis cooperatives,
where members can privately grow or consume, exist with little
interference, though they are not technically legal. Other countries have taken the more traditional decriminalization approach
toward cannabis. In Paraguay, individuals may possess 10 grams
of cannabis, for example, while the limit is 5 grams in Mexico.

Colorado and Washington's cannabis laws are unprecedented
worldwide: both states legalized the entire loop, regulating from
seed to sale to use. In 2012, President José Mujica of Uruguay
indicated he also wanted to legalize and regulate cannabis through
its life cycle, which would make Uruguay the first country to do
so.[86] Holcomb, Vicente, and individuals with the Drug Policy
Alliance have made trips to Uruguay to share their experiences
in the United States and offer guidance on public education and
policy. Under the proposed plan, an Institute of Regulation and
Control of Cannabis would permit private companies to grow
cannabis, which would be dispensed from pharmacies throughout

the country of just over 3 million residents. Citizens over eighteen would be allowed to cultivate six plants, and clubs with between fifteen and forty-five members could grow ninety-nine plants. Mujica said in February 2013 to a Santiago, Chile, daily newspaper, *La Tercera*, "The repressive path that we have been taking for 50 years is failing." He added, "We have to fight to gain the market from drug trafficking. Therefore, if we legalize, we regulate. If you are a consumer, you identify yourself and I—the state—sell it to you. But if something is happening to you, I say 'come here, I will treat you.' I think that is much better than what we are doing today."[87]

The new laws in the United States have undoubtedly served as an icebreaker, particularly in Latin America. After decades of acquiescence, the area of the world that most supplies the American demand for drugs—and is the bloodiest battleground for the U.S.-driven war—has grown increasingly fed up.[88] Over the last decade, the United States has spent $20 billion to fight the drug war in the region; even today, four thousand troops are maintained there.[89] An early and momentous expression of discontent about the global drug war came out of Latin America in August 2011.[90] After a casino in Monterrey was set on fire—many believe by gangs of a cartel—and fifty-two people died, then Mexican president Felipe Calderón had a caustic response, according to *Time*: "If [the Americans] are determined and resigned to consume drugs, then they should seek market alternatives in order to cancel the criminals' stratospheric profits, or establish clear points of access [to drugs]. But this situation can't go on."

Mexican drug trafficking organizations (cartels) make at least $7 billion a year selling drugs to the United States.[91] That number represents one of the more conservative estimates; the DOJ puts their profits between $18 billion and $39 billion, but those figures are thought to be greatly exaggerated. Fifty-six-year-old billionaire Joaquín Guzmán Loera, or El Chapo, of the Sinaloa Cartel, made *Forbes*'s powerful people and billionaires lists in 2012.[92] With money comes power. As long as drug prohibitions endure, the cartel leaders can continue to use their profits and influence to further corruption, such as human trafficking and extortion.[93] Between 2008 and 2012, the United States devoted $1.9 billion to fight these organizations in Mexico, with little to show for its and Mexico's efforts except an escalation in hostilities. More than sixty thousand people were killed in Mexico between 2006 and 2012 in conflicts related to the drug war. Certainly, more criticism of this everlasting war would arise if those deaths took place on American soil.

The leaders of Colombia, where the majority of cocaine sold in the United States originates, and Guatemala, through which much of that cocaine travels, joined Calderón in his once-taboo dissent at the UN General Assembly in New York City in September 2012.[94] The three presidents released a joint declaration urging a revision of international drug policy. They wrote, "That despite the efforts of the international community over decades, the use of these substances continues to increase globally, generating substantial income for criminal organizations worldwide." Further, "That the United Nations should exercise it's [sic] leadership, as is it's [sic] mandate, in this effort and conduct deep reflection to analyze all available options, including *regulatory or market measures*, in order to establish a new paradigm that prevents the flow of resources to organized crime organizations" (emphasis added). (Just one year prior, President Juan Manuel Santos of Colombia had expressed hesitation after he said to the British daily *The Guardian* that he would agree to drug legalization and regulation if the international community came to a consensus, adding, "What I won't do is become the vanguard of that movement because then I will be crucified.")[95]

Guatemala's Otto Pérez Molina, the most vocal of the three, wrote a *Guardian* op-ed in 2012 stating, "The prohibition paradigm that inspires mainstream global drug policy today is based on a false premise: that the global drug markets can be eradicated.

We would not believe such a statement if it were applied to alcoholism or tobacco addiction, but somehow we assume it's right in the case of drugs. Why?" Molina continued, "Drug consumption, production and trafficking should be subject to global regulations, which means that consumption and production should be legalised but within certain limits and conditions."[96]

The failures of the drug war in the United States have empowered Latin American leaders to ask questions. "For decades, Latin American governments felt that 'there is little to nothing that we can truly do so long as the U.S. is opposed,'" said Ethan Nadelmann, head of the Drug Policy Alliance. "What's happened now is that, paradoxically, even as the U.S. government remains . . . one of the principal champions of the global war on drugs . . . the United States, not at the level of the federal government, but at the level of public opinion, civil society and state government, has now emerged as the global leader in marijuana reform. And so in a way, that is inspirational for people in Latin America. It's inspirational because they feel that when the federal government, our federal government, is trying to shove our drug war down their throat, they can look back and say 'your policies aren't even supported by your own people anymore.'"

In June 2013, the Organization of American States (OAS), to which every country in North America and South America belongs, released an unprecedented report titled "Scenarios for the Drug Problem in the Americas," which laid out four drug policy approaches for the next twelve years.[97] One possibility, never acknowledged at this level before, was the legalization and regulation of drugs, beginning with cannabis. While the report acknowledged this model could eventually, in theory, extend beyond cannabis, it held that other drugs were more likely to be decriminalized than legalized and regulated.

Just before the 43rd General Assembly of the OAS, following the release of this report, Human Rights Watch urged the

Americas to decriminalize drug use because "national drug control policies that impose criminal penalties for personal drug use undermine basic human rights," specifically the rights to privacy and health.[98] Further, the organization noted, human rights violations are seen as a result of the enforcement-heavy drug war, from the tens of thousands of deaths in Mexico to the racist application of drug laws in the United States.

The international drug war has long relied on many countries to row the boat in sync. Some now want to change their strokes. Despite federal policies, Americans have joined this call for change with the new laws in Colorado and Washington and an April 2013 Pew Research Center poll that showed a landmark 52 percent support for general cannabis legalization.[99]

Given that four different levels of legality on cannabis exist within the United States alone, who is to say that one international law will fit all? Perhaps a more flexible treaty will come to pass, and each country will be able to dictate, to some extent, its own national drug policy. While an international consensus would be best, countries that already acknowledge that the current approach has been unsuccessful should not be held back. Some may get on board for only the legalization and regulation of cannabis. Others might do so while implementing a Portugal-style model for hard drugs, taking cannabis out of the picture and then treating the use of other drugs—all decriminalized—as a public health issue. After just over a decade, the only country in the world to decriminalize all drugs has seen the removal of drug users from its criminal justice system alongside increased access to treatment for addicts. There has also been a decrease in drug-related deaths and diseases and youth drug use.[100] But this does not legalize or regulate drugs and therefore does not fully address the drug supply side—it only seeks to reduce demand by providing treatment to those who need it. While the legalization and regulation of drugs, as addressed in the OAS report, may be decades away or never realized (support for the legalization and regulation of non-cannabis drugs among individuals in United States and Canada, for example, remains below 11 percent), it is the only policy change that would directly topple drug trafficking organizations.[101]

In 2016, the UN General Assembly will hold a Special Session focused on the global drug problem.[102] Perhaps the conversation will be more realistic and relevant than the last Special Session on drugs, held in 1998, with the slogan "A Drug-Free World. We Can Do It."[103]

But it all begins with this new leaf.

CODA

In August 2013, there were three important developments regarding drug policy reform.

First, a ruling by a federal judge in New York found that stop-and-frisk procedures are unconstitutional.[104] Next, attorney general Eric Holder announced that the Obama administration would focus on criminal justice reform, beginning with drug-related "draconian mandatory minimum sentences." Holder said, "When applied indiscriminately, they do not serve public safety. They—and some of the enforcement priorities we have set—have had a destabilizing effect on particular communities, largely poor and of color."[105] Finally, the Department of Justice confirmed they had no plans to challenge personal use cannabis laws in Colorado and Washington.

In addition, deputy attorney general James M. Cole wrote a new memo to U.S. attorneys across the country that outlined guidelines that, if followed, would likely keep federal intervention at bay. These guidelines ranged from keeping minors and criminals away from the cannabis industry to ensuring cannabis stays within state borders.[106]

ACKNOWLEDGMENTS

Countless individuals were not directly involved in this book but have influenced—or still influence—our lives. Thank you for leading us here.

We thank friends, mentors, and former professors at the University of California, Irvine, Literary Journalism Department, the College of Saint Rose Communications Department, and the Columbia University Graduate School of Journalism.

To the late Judith Crist, who encouraged the journey and listened to the often rambling tales, thank you. You are never far from our thoughts.

Mike Sager, without your brief yet motivating advice ("Nike symbol"), we may not have crossed the country four times to find the story ("fill the bucket").

Thank you, Michael Shapiro, for seeing the pieces before us as the unfolding of a prohibition during a conversation in 2010 when, luckily, you had *Boardwalk Empire* on your mind.

And Paula Span, that first cannabis story, that foot in many doors from coast to coast, would not have been possible without your constant support. You've helped us continue onward.

To Cailin Brown, thank you for the gifts of perspective, laughter, and wine along the way, especially through the challenges.

At every pivotal moment, Amy Wilentz, you've been there with honesty and guidance. We are endlessly appreciative.

Our tireless agent, Laurie Abkemeier, we have been tremendously fortunate and grateful to work with you. Through your decades of experience and wisdom, you've prepared us for and helped us navigate the publishing world so well. "Thank you" hardly seems enough.

For ensuring this book got into the hands of readers, thank you to our patient editor, Azzurra Cox. Your foresight and masterful edits shaped the story. Thank you for your sense of humor and for seeing the diamond in the rough. And many heartfelt thanks to the rest of the talented and hardworking staff at The New Press who each played a crucial role in the completion of this book—Sarah Fan, Ben Woodward, Beverly Rivero—as well as copy editor Laura Starrett and jacket designer Christopher Moisan.

And from day one, thank you to everyone who let us into your homes and lives.

NOTES

INTRODUCTION

1. While we were in Seattle on election night and provide details from our experience, the descriptions of what happened inside Casselman's Bar and Venue come from interviews and the following YouTube videos: "Colorado Legalizes Marijuana with Prop 64 Part 1 of 2," November 7, 2012, YouTube, www.youtube.com/watch?v=yFeb5UtutNY, and "Colorado Legalizes Marijuana with Prop 64 Part 2 of 2," November 7, 2012, YouTube, www.youtube.com/watch?v=hoDSZE6Bzj0.

2. John Ingold, "Colorado Medical Marijuana Businesses Have Declined by 40 Percent," *Denver Post*, March 3, 2013.

3. Frank Newport, "Record-High 50% of Americans Favor Legalizing Marijuana Use," Gallup, October 17, 2011, www.gallup.com/poll/150149/record-high-americans-favor-legalizing-marijuana.aspx.

4. Rep. Earl Blumenauer and Rep. Jared Polis, "The Path Forward: Rethinking Federal Marijuana Policy," February 2013, 3, blumenauer.house.gov/images/stories/2013/The_Path_Forward.pdf.

5. Pew Research Center for the People & the Press, "Majority Now Supports Legalizing Marijuana," April 4, 2013, www.people-press.org/2013/04/04/majority-now-supports-legalizing-marijuana.

6. American Civil Liberties Union, "The War on Marijuana in Black and White: Billions of Dollars Wasted on Racially Biased Arrests," June 2013, www.aclu.org/files/assets/061413-mj-report-rfs-rel4.pdf.

7. Hearings Before the House of Representatives Committee on Ways and Means, *Taxation of Marihuana*, 75th Cong., 1st sess., April 27, 28, 29, 30, and May 4, 1937, HR 6385.

8. Blumenauer and Polis, "Path Forward," 8.

9. Pew Research Center for the People & the Press, "Majority Now Supports Legalizing Marijuana."

10. Drug Policy Alliance, Board of Directors and Honorary Board, www
.drugpolicy.org/staff-and-board/board-directors.

11. Open Congress, Ending Federal Marijuana Prohibition Act of 2011, HR
2306, www.opencongress.org/bill/112-h2306/show; House of Representatives,
112th Cong., 2d sess., July 17, 2012, HR 6134, thehill.com/images/stories/blogs
/flooraction/jan2012/hr6134.pdf; Barney Frank and Ron Paul Letter to Barack
Obama, November 13, 2012, http://www.votehemp.com/PDF/2011-14-12_Frank
_Paul_Letter_to_Obama_re_marijuana.pdf.

12. Jaime Garza, "BOE to Sponsor Legislation to Exempt Hospice Patients
from Sales Taxes on Medical Marijuana," State Board of Equalization, March 13,
2013, www.boe.ca.gov/news/2013/28-13-H.pdf.

13. Washington State Liquor Control Board, "Initiative 502 Fiscal Impact
Through Fiscal Year 2017," August 10, 2012, www.liq.wa.gov/publications
/Marijuana/I-502/502_fiscal_impact.pdf.

14. Amendment 64: Use and Regulation of Marijuana, www.colorado
.gov/cs/Satellite?blobcol=urldata&blobheader=application%2Fpdf&blobkey
=id&blobtable=MungoBlobs&blobwhere=1251834064719&ssbinary=true.

15. Executive Office of the President of the United States, Office of National
Drug Control Policy, "National Drug Control Budget, FY 2014 Funding Highlights," April 2013, www.whitehouse.gov/sites/default/files/ondcp/policy-and-re
search/fy_2014_drug_control_budget_highlights_3.pdf.

16. Federal Bureau of Investigation, "Crime in the United States 2011," www
.fbi.gov/about-us/cjis/ucr/crime-in-the-u.s/2011/crime-in-the-u.s.-2011/persons
-arrested/persons-arrested.

17. "White House National Drug Control Budget FY 2014 Funding Highlights," April 2013, www.whitehouse.gov/sites/default/files/ondcp/policy-and
-research/fy_2014_drug_control_budget_highlights_3.pdf.

18. Clare Ribando Seelke and Kristin M. Finklea, "U.S.-Mexican Security
Cooperation: The Mérida Initiative and Beyond," Congressional Research
Service Report, June 12, 2013, www.fas.org/sgp/crs/row/R41349.pdf.

19. "Legal Marijuana? New Domestic and International Initiatives Challenge
the Status Quo," Brookings Institution, October 3, 2012, www.brookings.edu/~
/media/events/2012/10/03%20legal%20marijuana/20121003_legal_marijuana.pdf.

20. American Civil Liberties Union, "War on Marijuana in Black and
White."

21. New York Civil Liberties Union, "NYPD to Lodge 5 Millionth Street
Stop Under Mayor Bloomberg Today," press release, March 14, 2013, www.nyclu
.org/news/nypd-lodge-5-millionth-street-stop-under-mayor-bloomberg-today.

22. New York Civil Liberties Union, Racial Justice, "Stop-and-Frisk Facts,"
www.nyclu.org/node/1598.

23. Harry Levine, Loren Siegel, and Gabriel Sayegh, "One Million Police
Hours Making 440,000 Marijuana Possession Arrests in New York City, 2002–
2012," Drug Policy Alliance, March 2013, www.drugpolicy.org/sites/default/files
/One_Million_Police_Hours.pdf.

24. "82% Say U.S. Not Winning War on Drugs," *Rasmussen Reports*, August 18, 2013; Associated Press, "AP Impact: After 40 Years, $1 Trillion, US War on Drugs Has Failed to Meet Any of Its Goals," March 13, 2010, Fox News, www.foxnews.com/world/2010/05/13/ap-impact-years-trillion-war-drugs-failed -meet-goals.

25. 2012 Elections Colorado, "Amendment 64—Legalize Marijuana Election Results," *Denver Post*, data.denverpost.com/election/results/amendment/2012/64 -legalize-marijuana; Washington Secretary of State Sam Reed, "November 6, 2012 General Election Results," vote.wa.gov/results/20121106/Measures-All.html.

1. A PLANT BY ANY OTHER NAME

1. U.S. Department of Agriculture Natural Resources Conservation Service, "Results for Scientific Name = Cannabis," plants.usda.gov/java/name Search?keywordquery=Cannabis&submit.x=12&submit.y=8.

2. Ethan B. Russo, "Taming THC: Potential Cannabis Synergy and Phytocannabinoid-Terpenoid Entourage Effects," *British Journal of Pharmacology* 163, no. 7 (August 2011): 1344–64, doi:10.1111/j.1476-5381.2011.01238.x.

3. Mohamed Ben Amar, "Cannabinoids in Medicine: A Review of Their Therapeutic Potential," *Journal of Ethnopharmacology* 105, no. 1–2 (April 2006): 1–25, doi:10.1016/j.jep.2006.02.001.

4. Mark Eddy, "Medical Marijuana: Review and Analysis of Federal and State Policies," Congressional Research Service Report, April 2, 2010, 1.

5. W.B. O'Shaughnessy, "On the Preparations of the Indian Hemp, or Gunjah—Cannabis Indica Their Effects on the Animal System in Health, and Their Utility in the Treatment of Tetanus and Other Convulsive Diseases," *Provincial Medical Journal and Retrospect of the Medical Sciences* 5, no. 123 (February 4, 1843): 363–69, www.ncbi.nlm.nih.gov/pmc/articles/PMC2490264/?page=1.

6. Eddy, "Medical Marijuana," 2–3. (Note: Some say 1941, others say 1942.)

7. "Conversation with Raphael Mechoulam," *Addiction* 102, no. 6, (June 2007): 887–93, doi:10.1111/j.1360-0443.2007.01795.x; Raphael Mechoulam, ed., *Cannabinoids as Therapeutics* (Basel: Birkhäuser, 2005), 47.

8. Yehiel Gaoni and Raphael Mechoulam, "Isolation, Structure and Partial Synthesis of an Active Constituent of Hashish," *Journal of the American Chemical Society* 86, no. 8 (1964): 1646–47, doi:10.1021/ja01062a046.

9. Blanchard Randall IV, "The Medical Use of Marijuana: Policy and Regulatory Issues," Congressional Research Service Report, December 13, 1991.

10. Roger G. Pertwee, "Emerging Strategies for Exploiting Cannabinoid Receptor Agonists as Medicines," *British Journal of Pharmacology* 156, no. 3 (February 2009): 397–411, doi:10.1111/j.1476-5381.2008.00048.x.

11. W.A. Devane, L. Hanus, A. Breuer, et al., "Isolation and Structure of a Brain Constituent That Binds to the Cannabinoid Receptor," *Science* 258, no. 5090 (December 18, 1992): 1946–49, doi:10.1126/science.1470919.

12. "Report to the Legislature and Governor of the State of California Presenting Findings Pursuant to SB847 Which Created the CMCR and

Provided State Funding," Center for Medicinal Cannabis Research, February 17, 2010, 5, www.cmcr.ucsd.edu/images/pdfs/CMCR_REPORT_FEB17.pdf.

13. Pertwee, "Emerging Strategies for Exploiting Cannabinoid Receptor Agonists as Medicines."

14. Daniele Piomelli, Andrea Giuffrida, Antonio Calignano, and Fernando Rodriguez de Fonseca, "The Endocannabinoid System as a Target for Therapeutic Drugs," *Trends in Pharmacological Sciences* 21, no. 6 (June 2000): 218–24, available at www.ahrn.net/library_upload/uploadfile/file2185.pdf.

15. C. Heather Ashton, "Pharmacology and Effects of Cannabis: A Brief Review," *British Journal of Psychiatry* 178, no. (2001): 101–6, doi:10.1192/bjp.178.2.101.

16. Michael C. Lee, Markus Ploner, Katja Wiech, et al., "Amygdala Activity Contributes to the Dissociative Effect of Cannabis on Pain Perception," *Pain* 154, no. 1 (January 2013): 124–34, doi:10.1016/j.pain.2012.09.017.

17. National Cancer Institute at the National Institutes of Health, "Cannabis and Cannabinoids: Laboratory/Animal/Preclinical Studies," March 21, 2013, www.cancer.gov/cancertopics/pdq/cam/cannabis/healthprofessional/page4.

18. Tikun Olam website: www.tikun-olam.info.

19. See GW Pharmaceuticals website about Sativex: www.gwpharm.com/sativex.aspx.

20. Roger G. Pertwee, "Targeting the Endocannabinoid System with Cannabinoid Receptor Agonists: Pharmacological Strategies and Therapeutic Possibilities," *Philosophical Transactions of the Royal Society B Biological Sciences* 367, no. 1607 (December 2012): 3353–63, doi: 10.1098/rstb.2011.0381.

21. Sanofi, "Rimonabant Accepted for Filing by the FDA," press release, June 23, 2005, www.sanofi.ca/l/ca/en/layout.jsp?cnt=02953686-0083-4E91-8A34-AF718ED151A1.

22. U.S. Department of Justice Drug Enforcement Administration Office of Diversion Control, List of Controlled Substances, www.deadiversion.usdoj.gov/schedules/index.html.

23. Centers for Disease Control and Prevention, "Vital Signs: Overdoses of Prescription Opiod Pain Relievers—United States, 1999–2008," *Morbidity and Mortality Weekly Report* 60, no. 43 (November 4, 2011): 1487–92, www.cdc.gov/mmwr/preview/mmwrhtml/mm6043a4.htm.

24. Gardiner Harris, "Researchers Find Study of Medical Marijuana Discouraged," *New York Times*, January 18, 2010.

25. Tia Taylor, "Supporting Research into the Therapeutic Role of Marijuana," American College of Physicians Position Paper, 2008.

26. Nicole Flatow, "Caltech Physicist: If All Science Were Run Like Marijuana Research, Creationists Would Control Paleontology," *Think Progress*, February 25, 2013, thinkprogress.org/justice/2013/02/25/1629721/caltech-physicist-if-all-science-were-run-like-marijuana-research-creationists-would-control-paleontology/; Melody Pupols, "An Update on MAPS Medical Marijuana Initiatives: Can Marijuana Ease Symptoms of PTSD for War

Veterans?," *MAPS Bulletin Report* 22, no. 3 (Winter 2012): 22–25, www.maps
.org/news-letters/v22n3/v22n3_22-25.pdf.

27. Center for Medicinal Cannabis Research, "Center for Medicinal Cannabis
Research Established at University of California," press release, August 29, 2000,
www.cmcr.ucsd.edu/images/pdfs/CMCR_PressRelease_Aug_2000.pdf; see also
Center for Medicinal Cannabis Research website, www.cmcr.ucsd.edu.

28. "Report to the Legislature and Governor of the State of California
Presenting Findings Pursuant to SB847 Which Created the CMCR and Provided
State Funding," Center for Medicinal Cannabis Research, February 17, 2010,
www.cmcr.ucsd.edu/images/pdfs/CMCR_REPORT_FEB17.pdf.

29. Igor Grant, J. Hampton Atkinson, Ben Gouaux, and Barth Wilsey,
"Medical Marijuana: Clearing Away the Smoke," *Open Neurology Journal* 6
(March 4, 2012), doi:10.2174/1874205X01206010018.

30. See the website for the 23rd Annual Symposium of the International
Cannabinoid Research Society, June 21–26, 2013, www.icrs2013.org.

31. Hearings Before the House of Representatives Subcommittee on Criminal
Justice, Drug Policy and Human Resources of the Committee on Government
Reform, *Marijuana and Medicine: The Need for a Science-Based Approach*, 108th
Cong., 2d sess, 2004, 14.

32. Janet E. Joy, Stanley J. Watson Jr., and John A. Benson Jr., eds., *Marijuana
and Medicine: Assessing the Science Base* (Washington, DC: National Academy
Press, 1999), 11.

33. *Marijuana and Medicine.*

34. Ibid., 81.

35. See PubMed Health for information about Ondansetron, www.ncbi.nlm
.nih.gov/pubmedhealth/PMHT0011501/?report=details#side effects, and for information about Aprepitant, www.ncbi.nlm.nih.gov/pubmedhealth/PMHT000
9092/?report=details#side_effects.

36. Raphael Mechoulam, "Cannabis—A Valuable Drug That Deserves
Better Treatment," *Mayo Clinic Proceedings* 87, no. 2 (February 2012): 107–9,
doi:10.1016/j.mayocp.2011.12.002.

2. HISTORY REPEATING

1. Mark Eddy, "Medical Marijuana: Review and Analysis of State and
Federal Policies," Congressional Research Service Report, December 29, 2005,
1; Renée Johnson, "Hemp as an Agricultural Commodity," Congressional
Research Service Report, December 22, 2010, 9.

2. Edmund Saul Dixon, *Flax and Hemp: Their Culture and Manipulation*
(New York: G. Routledge & Co., 1854), 116.

3. USDA, "Industrial Hemp in the United States: Status and Market
Potential," January 2000, www.ers.usda.gov/media/328262/ages001e_1_.pdf.

4. Dixon, *Flax and Hemp*, 116.

5. Tim Robinson, *William Roxburgh: The Founding Father of Indian Botany*
(Chichester: Royal Botanic Garden Edinburgh/Phillimore, 2008).

6. *Encyclopaedia Britannica, Or Dictionary of Arts, Sciences, and General Literature*, vol. 11 (Edinburgh: Adam and Charles Black, 1856), 312.

7. Mannfred A. Hollinger, *Introduction to Pharmacology* (Boca Raton, FL: CRC Press, 2003), 360.

8. Albert Ellery Bergh, ed., *The Writings of Thomas Jefferson* (Washington, DC: Thomas Jefferson Memorial Association, 1907), 367.

9. See Center for Substance Abuse Research overview page for marijuana, www.cesar.umd.edu/cesar/drugs/marijuana.asp.

10. Celinda Franco, "Federal Domestic Illegal Drug Enforcement Efforts: Are They Working?" Congressional Research Service Report, January 27, 2010, appendix, www.fas.org/sgp/crs/misc/R40732.pdf.

11. Dale H. Gieringer, "The Origins of Cannabis Prohibition in California," *Federal Legal Publications* (New York, 1999; substantially revised July 2012); Johnson, "Hemp as an Agricultural Commodity."

12. Paul M. Gahlinger, *Illegal Drugs: A Complete Guide to Their History, Chemistry, Use and Abuse* (New York: Penguin, 2004).

13. Franco, "Federal Domestic Illegal Drug Enforcement Efforts."

14. Hearings Before the House of Representatives Select Committee on Crime, 91st Cong., 1st sess., October 14 and 15, 1969, 49.

15. Mark Eddy, "Medical Marijuana: Review and Analysis of Federal and State Policies," Congressional Research Service Report, April 2, 2010, 2. See also the UN Office on Drugs and Crime website for information about the 1912 Hague International Opium Convention, www.unodc.org/unodc/en/frontpage /the-1912-hague-international-opium-convention.html, and later drug treaties; UN Office on Drugs and Crime, "Drug Control Under the League of Nations," 1920–1945," in *2008 World Drug Report* (Vienna: United Nations Office on Drugs and Crime, 2008), 192–96, www.unodc.org/documents/wdr/WDR_2008 /WDR2008_100years_drug_control_league.pdf.

16. Daniel Okrent, *Last Call: The Rise and Fall of Prohibition* (New York: Scribner, 2011), 46.

17. Joseph D. McNamara, "The American Junkie," Hoover Institution, Stanford University, April 30, 2004, sec. 2, www.hoover.org/publications/hoover -digest/article/6763.

18. Gieringer, "Origins of Cannabis Prohibition in California," 13; see also "Doctors of Ancient Mexico," *New York Times*, January 6, 1901.

19. Hearings Before the House of Representatives Committee on Ways and Means, *Taxation of Marihuana*, 75th Cong., 1st sess., April 27, 28, 29, 30, and May 4, 1937, 33.

20. See the Papers of Harry J. Anslinger for background on Harry Anslinger, U.S. Commissioner of Narcotics, 1930–1962, Harry S. Truman Library & Museum, www.trumanlibrary.org/hstpaper/anslinger.HTM.

21. *Taxation of Marihuana.*

22. Franco, "Federal Domestic Illegal Drug Enforcement Efforts," 31–32.

23. Emanuel Perlmutter, "Narcotics Laws Called Too Weak; U.S. Commissioner Asserts Stiffer Penalties Would Cut Addiction 60%," *New York Times*, December 4, 1957.

24. First Report by the Select Committee on Crime, *Marihuana*, 91st Cong., 2d sess., April 6, 1970, 87.

25. National Institute on Drug Abuse, *DrugFacts: Nationwide Trends*, December 2012, www.drugabuse.gov/publications/drugfacts/nationwide-trends.

26. Albert Rosenfeld, "Marijuana: Millions of Turned-on Users," *Life*, July 7, 1967.

27. *Marihuana*, 47.

28. Hearings Before the House of Representatives Subcommittee on Government Operations, *Problems Relating to the Control of Marihuana*, 90th Cong., 2d sess., 12–13, 36.

29. *Marihuana*, 13–17.

30. *Problems Relating to the Control of Marihuana*, 31.

31. Hearings Before the House of Representatives Select Committee on Crime, *Crime in America—Views on Marihuana*, 91st Cong., 1st sess., October 14 and 15, 1969, 67, 50.

32. "War on Drug Abuse Outlined by President," *Milwaukee Journal*, July 14, 1969.

33. *Marihuana*, 4.

34. Franco, "Federal Domestic Illegal Drug Enforcement Efforts," 31–33; Eddy, "Medical Marijuana," December 9, 2005, 3.

35. "Scenarios for the Drug Problem in the Americas," Organization of American States, 2013–2025, www.oas.org/documents/eng/press/Scenarios_Report.pdf.

36. Michael F. Walther, "Insanity: Four Decades of US Counterdrug Strategy," Carlisle Papers, Strategic Studies Institute, December 27, 2012, www.strategicstudiesinstitute.army.mil/pubs/display.cfm?pubid=1143; "Nixon Asks $155 Million in Drug War," *Palm Beach Post*, June 18, 1971.

37. *Crime in America—Views on Marihuana*, 34.

38. Richard Nixon, "Special Message to the Congress on Drug Abuse Prevention and Control," June 17, 1971, Public Papers of the President, American Presidency Project, University of California, Santa Barbara, www.presidency.ucsb.edu/ws/?pid=3048.

39. Chicago Daily News Service, "War on Drugs Headed to Defeat," *Miami News*, September 24, 1975.

40. Mark Eddy, "War on Drugs: Legislation in the 108th Congress and Related Developments," Congressional Research Service Report, October 1, 2003, 3.

41. *Problems Relating to the Control of Marihuana*, 70.

42. Hearings Before the House of Representatives Select Committee on Narcotics Abuse and Control, *Decriminalization of Marihuana Part I*, 95th Cong., 1st sess., March 14–16, 1977, 2–4.

43. Report of the House of Representatives Select Committee on Narcotics Abuse and Control, *Considerations For and Against the Reduction of Federal*

Penalties for Possession of Small Amounts of Marihuana for Personal Use, 95th Cong., 1st sess., 17.

44. Deborah Blum, "The Chemist's War," *Slate*, February 19, 2010, www.slate.com/articles/health_and_science/medical_examiner/2010/02/the_chemists_war.html.

45. Washington Post Service, "Illegal Quaalude Prescription Linked to Carter Drug Adviser," *Pittsburgh Press*, July 19, 1978.

46. Charles B. Seib, "The Curious Coverage of the Bourne Affair," *The Day*, August 7, 1978.

47. Ronald Shaffer, "Unnamed Witnesses Say Bourne Used Pot, Cocaine at Party," *St. Petersburg Times*, July 21, 1978.

48. Hearings Before the House of Representatives Select Committee on Narcotics Abuse and Control, *Domestic Cultivation of Marihuana*, 98th Cong., 1st sess., July 22 and 23, 1983, 159, 153, 151, 160.

49. "Statement of Ronald F. Lauve, Senior Associate Director, General Government Division, Before the Subcommittee on Crime, House Committee on the Judiciary on Military Cooperation with Civilian Law Enforcement Agencies," July 28, 1983, 1–3, archive.gao.gov/d40t12/122004.pdf.

50. For more information about the Comprehensive Crime Control Act of 1984, see the U.S. Department of Justice website, www.justice.gov/jmd/afp/02fundreport/02_2.html.

51. Eric Blumenson and Eva Nilsen, "The Drug War's Hidden Agenda," *The Nation*, March 9, 1998, 11–16, available at www.pbs.org/wgbh/pages/frontline/shows/snitch/readings/hidden.html.

52. Franco, "Federal Domestic Illegal Drug Enforcement Efforts," 35. For more information about the Anti-Drug Abuse Act of 1988, 100th Cong., 1987–88, see www.govtrack.us/congress/bills/100/hr5210#summary/libraryofcongress.

53. Jim Abrams, "Congress Passes Bill to Reduce Disparity in Crack, Powder Cocaine Sentencing," *Washington Post*, July 29, 2010.

54. Franco, "Federal Domestic Illegal Drug Enforcement Efforts," 35.

55. Michelle Alexander, *The New Jim Crow: Mass Incarceration in the Age of Colorblindness* (New York: The New Press, 2010), 47–55.

56. *Domestic Cultivation of Marihuana*, 212, 211, 215.

57. For more about the President's Drug Awareness Teen Titans issues, see superherouniverse.com/articles/teen_titans.htm.

58. "No Hope with Dope," *Saved by the Bell* episode, aired November 30, 1991, www.imdb.com/title/tt0695205.

59. For more information in the matter of the Marijuana Rescheduling Petition, the U.S. Department of Justice Drug Enforcement Administration Opinion by Administrative Law Judge Francis L. Young, see http://resources.iowamedicalmarijuana.org/imm/young.pdf.

60. For more information about Proposition P, see www.marijuanalibrary.org/Proposition_P_Nov_1991.html.

61. Gina Kolata, "Patients Going Underground to Buy Experimental Drugs," *New York Times*, November 4, 1991.

62. Robert C. Randall and Alice M. O'Leary, *Marijuana Rx: The Patient's Fight for Medicinal Pot* (New York: Thunder's Mouth Press, 1998), 416.

3. HALF-BAKED LAWS

1. Hearings Before the House of Representatives Subcommittee on Criminal Justice, Drug Policy and Human Resources of the Committee on Government Reform, *Marijuana and Medicine: The Need for a Science-Based Approach*, 108th Cong., 2d sess., April 1, 2004, 254.

2. Mark Eddy, "Medical Marijuana: Review and Analysis of Federal and State Policies," Congressional Research Service Report, April 2, 2010, 38.

3. Mark Eddy, "Medical Marijuana: Review and Analysis of Federal and State Policies," Congressional Research Service Report, December 29, 2005, 14, 15.

4. Ian Donnis, "The Politics of Pain," *Boston Phoenix*, January 6–12, 2006; Nancy Krause, "R.I. Rep. Thomas Slater Dead at 68," WPRI 12, August 10, 2009, www.wpri.com/dpp/news/local_wpri_providence_rep_thomas_slater_dies _from_lung_cancer_20090810_nck.

5. "Shumlin's Stance on Marijuana Earns Him Big Donations from Outside Vermont," *Vermont Today*, October 3, 2010; Nigel Jaquiss, "Grass Ceiling," *Willamette Week*, June 27, 2012, www.wweek.com/portland/article-19375-grass _ceiling.html; Oregon Secretary of State Elections Division, secure.sos.state .or.us/orestar/cneSearch.do?cneSearchButtonName=search&cneSearchFiler CommitteeId=15406.

6. For more about medical cannabis laws in the United States, current and upcoming, see Marijuana Policy Project, mpp.org; Drug Policy Alliance, drug policy.org; and the National Organization for the Reform of Marijuana Laws, norml.org.

7. Blanchard Randall IV, "Medical Use of Marijuana: Policy and Regulatory Issues," Congressional Research Service Report, March 1, 2002, 23.

8. C-SPAN House Session, July 29, 1999, www.c-spanvideo.org/videoLibrary /transcript/transcript.php?id=96060.

9. Kelley Vlahos, "Bob Barr, Unlikely Leader but Possible Third Party Warrior," *Fox News*, April 18, 2007, www.foxnews.com/story/0,2933,266627,00.html.

10. "Clinton Tried Marijuana as a Student, He Says," *New York Times*, March 30, 1992.

11. See the following three sources: Randall, "Medical Use of Marijuana," 27; Eddy, "Medical Marijuana," December 29, 2005, 10; American Civil Liberties Union, "Unanimous Federal Appeals Court Rejects Government's Attempt to Punish Doctors for Recommending Medical Marijuana," October 29, 2002, www.aclu.org/criminal-law-reform/unanimous-federal-appeals-court-rejects -governments-attempt-punish-doctors.

12. Niki D'Andrea, "Prop 203—the Arizona Medical Marijuana Act—Puts the Chronic in Chronic Pain," *Phoenix New Times*, October 21, 2010.

13. Connecticut Pharmacists Association, "Position on SB 5389: An Act Concerning the Palliative Use of Marijuana"; see also CPA Testimony Submitted

to the Judiciary Committee, Re: HB 5389: AAC, *The Palliative Use of Marijuana*, March 7, 2012, www.cga.ct.gov/2012/JUDdata/Tmy/2012HB-05389-R000307 -Marghie%20Giuliano-%20Connecticut%20Pharmacist%20Association %20-TMY.PDF.

14. "Editorial: Pharmacies Logical as Medical Pot 'Dispensaries,'" *Gloucester Daily Times*, December 14, 2012.

15. Proposition 215: Text of Proposed Law, vote96.sos.ca.gov/Vote96/html /BP/215text.htm.

16. *Marijuana Policy Report* 3, no. 2/3 (Summer/Fall 1997).

17. *Marijuana Policy Report* 4, no. 1 (Spring 1998): 5–6.

18. *Marijuana Policy Report* 3, no. 2/3 (Summer/Fall 1997): 11, 14.

19. *Marijuana Policy Report* 4, no. 1 (Spring 1998): 20.

20. *United States v. Oakland Cannabis Buyers' Cooperative*, 532 U.S. 483, 121 S.Ct. 1711 (2001), www.law.cornell.edu/supct/pdf/00-151P.ZO.

21. San Francisco Board of Supervisors Ordinance 275-05, November 2005, www.safeaccessnow.org/downloads/San_Francisco.pdf. See also R. Stickney, "Timeline: Medical Marijuana in San Diego," NBC San Diego, May 6, 2013; California Senate Bill 420, www.leginfo.ca.gov/pub/03-04/bill/sen/sb_0401-0450 /sb_420_bill_20031012_chaptered.html; "L.A.'s Medical Marijuana Mess," editorial, *Los Angeles Times*, July 26, 2012.

22. California Senate Bill 420.

23. There are differences between cannabis cooperatives and collectives, though both involve members. Cooperatives buy cannabis from some members and sell to other members. In a collective, everyone grows together and everyone owns a piece of the collective and pays or contributes however he or she can.

24. "Guidelines for the Security and Non-Diversion of Marijuana Grown for Medical Use," Department of Justice, State of California, August 2008, www .ag.ca.gov/cms_attachments/press/pdfs/n1601_medicalmarijuanaguidelines .pdf.

25. Marijuana Policy Project, "Model Medical Marijuana Bill," www.mpp.org /legislation/model-medical-marijuana-bill.html.

26. Public Law, Chapter 631, LD 1811, 124th Maine State Legislature, "An Act to Amend the Maine Medical Marijuana Act," 2010, www.mainelegislature .org/legis/bills/bills_124th/chappdfs/PUBLIC631.pdf.

27. Ibid.

28. Associated Press, "GOP Candidate Chris Christie Opposes N.J.'s Medical Marijuana Bill," *NJ.com*, March 19, 2009, www.nj.com/news/index.ssf/2009/03 /christie_criticizes_medical_ma.html.

29. Susan K. Livio, "Rutgers Declines Growing Medical Marijuana to Not Risk Federal Funding," *NJ.com*, July 24, 2010, www.nj.com/news/index.ssf/2010 /07/rutgers_declines_growing_medic.html.

30. New Jersey Medical Marijuana Program Rules, www.state.nj.us/health /medicalmarijuana/documents/mmp_rules.pdf.

31. "Radical" Russ Belville, "New Jersey Proposals for Medical Marijuana Rules Far Too Restrictive," NORML, October 6, 2010, stash.norml.org/new -jersey-proposals-for-medical-marijuana-rules-far-too-restrictive.

32. Senate Bill 5073 ("The Big Bill"), Washington State Legislature, apps .leg.wa.gov/documents/billdocs/2011-12/Pdf/Bills/Senate%20Bills/5073.pdf; Certification of Enrollment, Engrossed Second Substitute Senate Bill 5073, 62nd Washington State Legislature, 2011 Regular Session, April 21, 2011, apps.leg.wa.gov/documents/billdocs/201112/Pdf/Bills/Senate%20Passed%20 Legislature/5073-S2.PL.pdf.

33. Susan K. Livio, "Message from State Reveals E-mail Addresses, Names of N.J. Medical Marijuana Patients," NJ.com, December 19, 2012, www.nj.com /news/index.ssf/2012/12/message_from_state_reveals_e-m.html.

34. For our discussion of the state-to-state patchwork, we consulted the following state laws, program websites, and articles: Delaware Medical Marijuana Act, delcode.delaware.gov/title16/c049a/index.shtml; Chapter 420f: Palliative Use of Marijuana, www.cga.ct.gov/current/pub/chap 420f.htm; Drug Policy Alliance, "Access to Medical Marijuana for Patients with Post Traumatic Stress Disorder (PTSD) in New Mexico Is Protected," press release, May 1, 2013, www .drugpolicy.org/news/2013/05/access-medical-marijuana-patients-post-traumatic -stress-disorder-ptsd-new-mexico-protec#sthash.rmSOhBOA.dpuf; Maine Use of Medical Marijuana program, www.maine.gov/dhhs/dlrs/mmm; State of Rhode Island Department of Health Medical Marijuana program, www.health.ri.gov /healthcare/medicalmarijuana; Massachusetts Department of Health Implementation of an Act for the Humanitarian Medical Use of Marijuana, www .mass.gov/eohhs/docs/dph/regs/105cmr725.pdf; Michigan Department of Licensing and Regulatory Affairs, Michigan Medical Marihuana Program, courts.mi .gov/Administration/SCAO/Documents/Family-Probate/AGOpinion-Medical MarijuanaAct.pdf; Senate Bill No. 326, Montana, votesmart.org/static/billtext /24012.pdf; Oregon Medical Marijuana Program, public.health.oregon.gov/Dis easesConditions/ChronicDisease/medicalmarijuanaprogram/Pages/index.aspx; Arizona Department of Health Services, Arizona Medical Marijuana Program, www.azdhs.gov/medicalmarijuana/faqs/index.php?pg=qualifying-patients; Alaska Medical Marijuana, norml.org/legal/item/alaska-medical-marijuana; Washington State Legislature, Medical Cannabis (formerly medical marijuana), apps .leg.wa.gov/rcw/default.aspx?cite=69.51a&full=true#69.51A.045; State of New Jersey Department of Health Medicinal Marijuana Program, www.state.nj.us /health/medicalmarijuana; District of Columbia Medical Marijuana, norml.org /legal/item/district-of-columbia-medical-marijuana; New Mexico Medical Cannabis Program, www.nmhealth.org/idb; Hawaii Department of Public Safety, Medical Marijuana Physician's Guidelines and Patient Information, dps.hawaii .gov/about/divisions/law-enforcement-division/ned; Vermont Criminal Information Center, Medical Marijuana Registry, vcic.vermont.gov; Mike DiBonis, "Liquor Regulators May Help Oversee D.C. Medical Marijuana Program," Washington Post, August 7, 2010; State of Connecticut, Department of Consumer

Protection, Medical Marijuana Regulation, www.ct.gov/DCP/site/default.asp; Mary Jo Layton, "New Jersey's Lone Marijuana Dispensary Overwhelmed with Requests," *NorthJersey.com*, February 4, 2013, www.northjersey.com/montclair /New_Jerseys_lone_marijuana_dispensary_overwhelmed_with_requests.html ?page=all; "Panel Approves Rules for Medical Marijuana," *WCVB Boston*, May 8, 2013, www.wcvb.com/health/panel-considers-rules-for-medical-marijuana /-/9848730/20061392/-/item/0/-/bue2x6z/-/index.html.

35. Maria Luisia Tucker, "Looks Like Medical Marijuana Is a No Go in New Mexico," *AlterNet*, February 6, 2006, www.alternet.org/story/32271/looks_like _medical_marijuana_is_a_no_go_in_new_mexico; New Mexico Department of Health Medical Cannabis Program, nmhealth.org/mcp.

4. GREEN DIGGERS

1. Chris Walsh, "Exclusive: US Medical Marijuana Sales to Hit $1.5B in 2013, Cannabis Revenues Could Quadruple by 2018," *Medical Marijuana Business Daily*, March 21, 2013.

2. Court documents involving Valerie and Mike Corral and their Santa Cruz Wo/Men's Alliance for Medical Marijuana, www.santacruzvsashcroft.com /pleadings_corral.htm.

3. Department of Community Health, Director's Office, Michigan Medical Marijuana, www7.dleg.state.mi.us/orr/Files/AdminCode/104_45_Admin Code.pdf.

4. Andy Balaskovitz, "All Eyes on McQueen," *Lansing City Pulse*, March 13, 2013.

5. Jonathan Oosting, "Michigan Supreme Court: Dispensaries Selling Medical Pot Can Be Shut Down as Public Nuisance," *MLive.com*, February 8, 2013, www .mlive.com/news/index.ssf/2013/02/michigan_supreme_court_dispens.html.

6. "Feds, Police Raid Las Vegas Medical Marijuana Shops," *Las Vegas Sun*, September 8, 2010.

7. "Owner Reacts to Drug Raids," *KLAS-TV Las Vegas*, September 9, 2010, www.8newsnow.com/story/13128165/owner-reacts-to-drug-raids.

8. Valerie Miller, "Seven Arrested in Raids of Las Vegas Marijuana Outfits," *Las Vegas Review-Journal*, April 15, 2011; Paul Takahashi, "5-Year-Old Boy Removed from Home after Drug Raid," *Las Vegas Sun*, April 15, 2011.

9. "Another Housing Bubble Brewing in Nevada?" *Realtor Mag*, January 25, 2013; Cristina Silva, Associated Press, "Nevada's Boom and Bust Leaves 167,000 Empty Houses," *USA Today*, March 27, 2011.

10. Mike Blasky, "Police Battle Marijuana Grow Houses in Las Vegas Area," *Las Vegas Review-Journal*, September 5, 2011.

11. "Marijuana Grow House Discovered in W. Las Vegas," *Guardian Express*, January 10, 2013; William D'Urso, "Metro Thinks Marijuana Grow Houses Might Be Connected," *News 3 KSNV Las Vegas*, January 13, 2013, www.mynews3.com/content/news/story/grow-houses-marijuana-Metro-drugs /H97zAKsEWkKZrx1JUmYjNA.cspx.

12. State of Washington, Senate Bill 5073 ("The Big Bill"), apps.leg.wa.gov /documents/billdocs/2011-12/Pdf/Bills/Senate%20Bills/5073.pdf.

13. Tim Martin, "Latest Bid to Recall Attorney General Bill Schuette Again Involves Medical Marijuana Advocate," *MLive.com*, September 5, 2012, www .mlive.com/politics/index.ssf/2012/09/bill_schuette_recall_attempt.html.

14. Tim Martin, "Medical Marijuana Dispensaries Would Be Legalized Under Proposal from Michigan Lawmaker," *MLive.com*, February 14, 2013, www .mlive.com/politics/index.ssf/2013/02/medical_marijuana_centers_mich.html.

15. Francis McCabe, "Nevada's Pot Distribution Law Called Unconstitutional," *Las Vegas Review-Journal*, March 2, 2012.

16. Molly Waldron, "ACLU Weighs In on Nevada Medical Marijuana Law," *Channel 13 Action News*, March 22, 2013, www.ktnv.com/news/local/199637221 .html.

17. For more information about the Oregon Medical Marijuana Act, see www.oregon.gov/osp/des/docs/med_mj_patient_info.pdf.

18. John Hoeffel, "California: A Medical Marijuana Success Story: West Hollywood Enforces a Strict Ordinance and Eliminates the Drama that Plagues L.A.," *Los Angeles Times*, November 6, 2009; "An Ordinance of the City of West Hollywood Governing the Operation of Medical Marijuana Dispensaries," www.safeaccessnow.org/downloads/West_Hollywood.pdf.

19. The Greater Los Angeles Collective Alliance, "GLACA Protocols," glaca.net/j15/index.php?option=com_content&view=article&id=3&Itemid=3.

20. Nicholas Goldberg, "Medical Marijuana: Measure D Still the Best Choice," *Los Angeles Times*, May 15, 2013.

21. Josh Harkinson, "How Industrial Pot Growers Ravage the Land: A Google Earth Tour," *Mother Jones*, February 6, 2013.

22. Allen St. Pierre, "Where Is America's Cannabis Capital?" NORML blog, December 22, 2009, blog.norml.org/2009/12/22/where-is-americas-cannabis-capital.

23. John Ingold, "Colorado Medical-Marijuana Businesses Have Declined by 40 Percent," *Denver Post*, March 3, 2013.

24. Colorado Senate Bill 10-109, www.colorado.gov/cs/Satellite?blobcol=url data&blobheadername1=Content-Disposition&blobheadername2=Content -Type&blobheadervalue1=inline%3B+filename%3D%22Senate+Bill+109.pdf %22&blobheadervalue2=application%2Fpdf&blobkey=id&blobtable=Mungo Blobs&blobwhere=1251807305716&ssbinary=true.

25. Colorado House Bill 10-1284, www.colorado.gov/cs/Satellite?blobcol=url data&blobheadername1=Content-Disposition&blobheadername2=Content -Type&blobheadervalue1=inline%3B+filename%3D%22House+Bill+1284.pdf %22&blobheadervalue2=application%2Fpdf&blobkey=id&blobtable=MungoB lobs&blobwhere=1251807310652&ssbinary=true.

26. Colorado Department of Revenue Laws and Regulations, www.colorado .gov/cs/Satellite/Rev-MMJ/CBON/1251592984795.

27. Eric Gorski, "Medical Marijuana Dispensaries: High-Tech Tracking System Unfulfilled," *Denver Post*, March 24, 2013.

28. John Ingold, "Colorado Medical-Marijuana Rules Rewrite Seeks Efficiency, Simplicity," *Denver Post*, January, 28, 2013.

29. Ingold, "Colorado Medical-Marijuana Businesses Have Declined by 40 Percent."

30. OrganaLabs cannabis-infused products, www.organalabs.com/product list.htm.

31. Associated Press, "Northeast Patients Group Pot Dispensary Now Known as Wellness Connection of Maine," *Bangor Daily News*, December 19, 2011; David Downs and Michael Montgomery, "Berkeley Pot Dispensary Biggest Casualty of Crackdown," *California Watch*, April 30, 2012, californiawatch.org /dailyreport/berkeley-pot-dispensary-biggest-casualty-crackdown-15994.

32. Arizona Department of Health Services, Arizona Medical Marijuana Program, www.azdhs.gov/medicalmarijuana.

33. Arizona Department of Health Services, Arizona Medical Marijuana Program FAQs, www.azdhs.gov/medicalmarijuana/faqs/index.php?pg=dispensaries.

34. Connecticut General Assembly, Chapter 420f: Palliative Use of Marijuana, www.cga.ct.gov/current/pub/chap_420f.htm.

35. Charles Crumm, "Medical Marijuana: Michigan Takes in Nearly $3 for Every $1 Spent to Administer It," *Oakland Press*, February 6, 2013.

36. Arizona Department of Health Services, Arizona Medical Marijuana Program, Renewal Information, www.azdhs.gov/medicalmarijuana/renewals.

5. THE CLASH

1. American Civil Liberties Union, "Are You Living in a Constitution Free Zone?" December 15, 2006, www.aclu.org/national-security_technology-and -liberty/are-you-living-constitution-free-zone.

2. Safer Alternatives Maine Medical Marijuana Dispensary, www.safealter nativesmaine.org.

3. Julia Bayly, "Northern Maine Marijuana Dispensary Close to Resolving Zoning Problems," *Bangor Daily News*, January 5, 2013.

4. Todd Garvey, "Medical Marijuana: The Supremacy Clause, Federalism, and the Interplay Between State and Federal Laws," Congressional Research Service Report, November 9, 2012.

5. Nushin Rashidian and Alyson Martin, "Medical Marijuana Raises Tough Questions in Nursing Homes," *New Old Age* blog, *New York Times*, October 27, 2012, newoldage.blogs.nytimes.com/2010/10/27/medical-marijuana-raises-tough -questions-in-nursing-homes/.

6. Kris Hermes, "Medical Marijuana Patient Norman Smith Passes, But Not Without a Fight," Americans for Safe Access, August 9, 2012, safeaccess now.org/blog/blog/2012/08/09/medical-marijuana-patient-norman-smith-passes -but-not-without-a-fight.

7. Letter from Cedars-Sinai Medical Center Comprehensive Transplant Center to Norman Smith, "RE: Transplant Delisting," February 1, 2011, americansforsafeaccess.org/downloads/Smith_Transplant_Denial.pdf.

8. Anna Gorman, "Medical Marijuana Jeopardizes Liver Transplant," *Los Angeles Times*, December 3, 2011.

9. Stephen C. Webster, "Hospital Denies Woman's Kidney Transplant Due to Medical Marijuana Use," *Raw Story*, June 11, 2012, www.rawstory.com/rs/2012/06/11/hospital-denies-womans-kidney-transplant-due-to-medical-marijuana-use.

10. Gorman, "Medical Marijuana Jeopardizes Liver Transplant."

11. Randa Hamadeh, Abbas Ardehali, Richard M. Locksley, and Mary K. York, "Fatal Aspergillosis Associated with Smoking Contaminated Marijuana, in a Marrow Transplant Recipient," *Chest* 94, no. 2 (August 1988): 432–33, doi:10.1378/chest.94.2.432.

12. Hermes, "Medical Marijuana Patient Norman Smith Passes."

13. Susan Sharon, "Medical Marijuana 101: You Can't Smoke That on Campus," *Morning Edition*, National Public Radio, May 24, 2012, www.npr.org/blogs/health/2012/05/24/153525631/medical-marijuana-101-you-cant-smoke-that-on-campus.

14. Todd Garvey and Brian T. Yeh, "State Legalization of Recreational Marijuana: Selected Legal Issues," *Congressional Research Service Report*, April 5, 2013.

15. Chris Roberts, "Medical Marijuana Users Can Get Booted from Public Housing at Any Time," *The Snitch* blog, *SF Weekly*, December 5, 2012, blogs.sf weekly.com/thesnitch/2012/12/medical_marijuana_users_can_lo.php.

16. Matthew Stone, "MaineHousing to Hold Off on Enforcing Medical Marijuana Ban," *Bangor Daily News*, October 16, 2012.

17. *Joseph Casias v. Wal-Mart Stores, Inc.; Wal-Mart Stores East, L.P.; and Troy Estill*, F. 3d 428 (6th Cir. 2012), www.ca6.uscourts.gov/opinions.pdf/12a0343p-06.pdf.

18. American Civil Liberties Union, "ACLU Sues Wal-Mart on Behalf of Cancer Patient Fired for Legally Using Medical Marijuana," press release, June 29, 2010, www.aclu.org/criminal-law-reform/aclu-sues-wal-mart-behalf-cancer-patient-fired-legally-using-medical-marijuana.

19. *Joseph Casias v. Wal-Mart Stores, Inc., and Troy Estill*, 764 F. Supp.2d 914 (Dist. Court, Mich. 2011), www.mpp.org/assets/pdfs/library/Joseph-Casias-decision.pdf.

20. Robert L. Petzel, VHA Directive 2010-035, July 22, 2010, www.advanced holistichealth.org/PDF_Files/VHAdirectiveJuly22.pdf; Dan Frosch, "V.A. Easing Rules for Users of Medical Marijuana," *New York Times*, July 23, 2010.

21. Americans for Safe Access, "Legal Info," americansforsafeaccess.org/section.php?id=100.

22. Arthur Herbert, "Open Letter to All Federal Firearms Licensees," U.S. Department of Justice Bureau of Alcohol, Tobacco, Firearms and Explosives, September 21, 2011, www.nssf.org/share/PDF/ATFOpenLetter092111.pdf.

23. Office of the Attorney General, "Attorney General Bill Lockyer Calls for Meeting with Federal Authorities About Unprecedented Medical Marijuana Raids," press release, State of California Department of Justice, September 6, 2001, oag.ca.gov/news/press-releases/attorney-general-bill-lockyer-calls-meeting-federal-authorities-about.

24. John Ritter, "Pot Raid Angers State, Patients," *USA Today*, September 16, 2002.

25. Ibid.

26. American Civil Liberties Union, "Civil Asset Forfeiture," www.aclu.org /criminal-law-reform/civil-asset-forfeiture.

27. David C. Maurer, "Justice Assets Forfeiture Fund: Transparency of Balances and Controls over Equitable Sharing Should Be Improved," U.S. Government Accountability Office, July 2012, www.gao.gov/assets/600/592349.pdf.

28. Gale Holland, "Here's Why Medical Pot Isn't Going Away," *Los Angeles Times*, March 8, 2013.

29. Bill Rosendahl, "Coming out of the (Cannabis) Closet," *Huffington Post*, May 21, 2013, www.huffingtonpost.com/bill-rosendahl/coming-out-of-the -cannabis-closet_b_3315723.html.

30. "Barack Obama on Marijuana Decriminalization (2004)," YouTube, January 31, 2008, www.youtube.com/watch?v=wQr9ezr8UeA.

31. "Senator Barack Obama on Medical Marijuana—Aug. 21, 2007," YouTube, August 21, 2007, www.youtube.com/watch?v=GUze-oYsswI.

32. "Barack Obama and Medical Marijuana (interview Q&A)," YouTube, April 21, 2008, www.youtube.com/watch?v=LvUziSfMwAw.

33. "US Attorney General Eric Holder: Ending Medical Marijuana Raids Now . . . ," YouTube, February 26, 2009, www.youtube.com/watch?v=kjZeW2 fcQHM.

34. David W. Ogden, "Memorandum for Selected United States Attorneys," *Justice Blog*, U.S. Department of Justice, October 19, 2009, http://blogs.justice .gov/main/archives/192.

35. David Johnston and Neil A. Lewis, "Obama Administration to Stop Raids on Medical Marijuana Dispensers," *New York Times*, March 18, 2009.

36. Ogden, "Memorandum for Selected United States Attorneys."

37. Ibid.

38. Montana Department of Public Health and Human Services, "History of Qualifying Patients, Providers, and Doctors January 2005–June 2012," www .dphhs.mt.gov/marijuanaprogram/mmphistoricaldata.pdf.

39. Diane Cochran, "Medical Marijuana Card OK'd after 8 minutes, 6 questions," *Billings Gazette*, August 21, 2010.

40. Colorado Department of Public Health and Environment, "Medical Marijuana Statistics: Archives," www.colorado.gov/cs/Satellite/CDPHE-CHEIS /CBON/1251593017044.

41. "Chris Williams Discusses Raid on Medical Marijuana Grow Operation," YouTube, March 14, 2011, www.youtube.com/watch?v=PeKfhcB6PeM.

42. Matt Hagengruber, "Marijuana Raids Built on Years of Investigations," *Billings Gazette*, March 15, 2011; Eve Byron, "Jury Finds Chris Williams Guilty on All Eight Counts in Medical Marijuana Case," *Helena Independent Record*, September 27, 2012; Matt Hagengruber and Angela Brandt, "Federal Raids: Raids Target Medical Marijuana Business," *Billings Gazette*, March 14, 2011.

43. "Chris Williams Discusses Raid," YouTube.

44. Byron, "Jury Finds Chris Williams Guilty."

45. "Chris Williams Discusses Raid," YouTube.

46. Rebecca Richman Cohen, "The Fight Over Medical Marijuana," *New York Times*, November 7, 2012; History of Federal Firearms Laws in the United States, Appendix C, www.justice.gov/archive/opd/AppendixC.htm.

47. Byron, "Jury Finds Chris Williams Guilty."

48. Eve Byron, "From Marine to Deadhead: Chris Williams Is a Complex Man," *Helena Independent Record*, October 28, 2012.

49. Eve Byron, "Most of Chris Williams' Marijuana Convictions to Be Dropped," *Helena Independent Record*, December 19, 2012.

50. John Adams, "RAW Video: Schweitzer Brands GOP Bills," *The Lowdown*, April 13, 2011, mtlowdown.blogspot.com/2011/04/raw-video-schweitzer-brands -gop-bills.html.

51. 26 USC § 280E—Expenditures in Connection with the Illegal Sale of Drugs, www.law.cornell.edu/uscode/text/26/280E.

52. Carolyn Jones, "Oakland Pot Dispensary Gets $2.5 Million IRS Bill," *San Francisco Chronicle*, October 4, 2011; Preliminary Questions for January 31, 2013 Hearing on Oral Argument, *City of Oakland v. Eric Holder, Melinda Haag* (N.D. Cal. 2013) (No. C 12-3566), law.justia.com/cases/federal/district-courts/california /candce/3:2012cv05245/259744/46; Complaint, *City of Oakland v. Eric Holder, Melinda Haag* (N.D. Cal. 2012) (No. C 12-5245), www.oaklandcityattorney.org /PDFS/Fed%20med%20cannabis%20complaint%20Oct.%2010%202012.pdf.

53. Letter from U.S. Attorney Melinda Haag to Oakland City Attorney John Russo, February 1, 2011, www.cannabistherapyinstitute.com/legal/feds/doj .haag.memo.pdf.

54. "City of Oakland Budget Facts: Mayor Jean Quan's Proposed Policy Budget for FY 2011–13," www2.oaklandnet.com/Government/o/CityAdministration/d /BudgetOffice/index.htm.

55. James M. Cole, "Memorandum for United States Attorneys," U.S. Department of Justice, June 29, 2011, extras.mnginteractive.com/live/media /site36/2011/0701/20110701_113435_pot_memo_one.pdf.

56. Ibid.

57. The nine states are Maine, Vermont, Rhode Island, Montana, Washington, Oregon, California, Arizona, and Colorado. "What's the Co$t? The Federal War on Patients," Americans for Safe Access, June 2013, americans forsafeaccess.org/downloads/WhatsTheCost.pdf.

58. Letter from U.S. Attorney Melinda Haag to Oakland City Attorney John Russo, February 1, 2011.

59. *City of Oakland v. Eric Holder, Melinda Haag.*

60. Andrew S. Ross, "U.S. Attorney: Why I'm Busting Harborside Health Center," *Bottom Line* blog, *San Francisco Chronicle*, July 11, 2012, blog.sfgate.com /bottomline/2012/07/11/u-s-attorney-why-im-busting-harborside-health-center.

61. Jon Brooks, "Interview with U.S. Attorney Haag on Pot Operations," *KQED News*, March 15, 2012, blogs.kqed.org/newsfix/2012/03/15/interview-w -us-attorney-haag-on-pot-operations-if-its-close-to-children-thats-a-line-were -going-to-draw.

62. David Downs and Michael Montgomery, "Berkeley Pot Dispensary Biggest Casualty of Crackdown," *California Watch*, April 30, 2012, californiawatch.org /dailyreport/berkeley-pot-dispensary-biggest-casualty-crackdown-15994.

63. Jon Brooks, "Interview: Mayor Tom Bates Laments Closing of Berkeley Patients Group Marijuana Dispensary," *KQED News*, March 15, 2012, blogs .kqed.org/newsfix/2012/03/15/interview-mayor-tom-bates-laments-closing-of -berkeley-patients-group-marijuana-dispensary.

64. Letter from Colorado U.S. Attorney John F. Walsh to dispensaries near schools, March 23, 2012, extras.mnginteractive.com/live/media/site36/2012/0323 /20120323_052432_dispensary-ltr-redacted.pdf.

65. Federal Deposit Insurance Corporation, "FDIC Law, Regulations, Related Acts," www.fdic.gov/regulations/laws/rules/8000-1600.html.

66. John Ingold, "Last Bank Shuts Doors on Colorado Pot Dispensaries," *Denver Post*, October 1, 2011.

67. The Board of Supervisors of the County of Mendocino Ordinance No. 4291 Amending Chapter 9.31 of Title 9 of the Mendocino County Code entitled "Medical Marijuana Cultivation Regulation," February 14, 2012, www .mendocinosheriff.com/mm/Ord4291.pdf.

68. Sarah Moughty, "California County to End Marijuana Permitting Program," *Frontline*, February 15, 2012, www.pbs.org/wgbh/pages/frontline /social-issues/the-pot-republic-social-issues/california-county-to-end-marijuana -permitting-program.

69. The Board of Supervisors of the County of Mendocino Ordinance No. 4291 Amending Chapter 9.31 of Title 9 of the Mendocino County Code entitled "Medical Marijuana Cultivation Regulation."

70. Mendocino County Sheriff's Office, "9.31 Medical Marijuana Regulations," www.mendocinosheriff.com/mm/931SheriffsSummary.pdf; Mendocino County Motion to Quash, December 21, 2012, americansforsafeaccess.org/downloads /Mendocino_MTQ.pdf.

71. Tiffany Revelle, "County Strikes Deal with Feds over Medical Marijuana Records," *Ukiah Daily Journal*, April 10, 2013.

72. Letter from U.S. Attorneys Jenny A. Durkan and Michael C. Ormsby to former governor Christine Gregoire, U.S. Department of Justice, April 14, 2011, reason.com/assets/db/13050453232855.pdf.

73. See the Delaware Medical Marijuana Program website, dhss.delaware. gov/dph/hsp/medmarhome.html; "Delaware Legalizes Medical Marijuana," Reuters, May 13, 2011; Chad Livengood and Doug Denison, "Medical Marijuana Law Busted," *Delaware Online*, February 12, 2012, www.delawareonline.com /article/20120212/NEWS/202120349/Medical-marijuana-law-busted.

74. Statehouse Bureau Staff, "Gov. Christie to Delay Implementing N.J.'s Medical Marijuana Law," *NJ.com*, June 16, 2011, www.nj.com/news/index.ssf /2011/06/christie_to_delay_implementing.html.

75. *State of Arizona et al. v. United States of America et al.*, U.S. District Court of Arizona, Motion to Dismiss, August 1, 2011, 2:11-cv-01072-SRB, www.mpp .org/assets/pdfs/blog/Feds_Motion_to_Dismiss.pdf.

76. Letter from Arizona U.S. Attorney Ann Scheel to Governor Jan Brewer, February 16, 2012, http://www.keytlaw.com/arizonamedicalmarijuanalaw/scheel-letter-120216.pdf

77. Americans for Safe Access, "What's the Co$t? The Federal War on Patients."

78. Chris Roberts, "Jobs, Revenue Lost in Pot Dispensary Crackdown," *San Francisco Chronicle*, November 25, 2011.

79. Jaime Garza, "BOE to Sponsor Legislation to Exempt Hospice Patients from Sales Taxes on Medical Marijuana," State Board of Equalization, March 13, 2013, www.boe.ca.gov/news/2013/28-13-H.pdf.

80. Michael Cooper, "2 Governors Asking U.S. to Ease Rules on Marijuana to Allow for Its Medical Use," *New York Times*, November 30, 2011.

81. Mason-Dixon Polling & Research, Marijuana Policy Project National Survey Question, May 2012, www.mpp.org/assets/pdfs/download-materials/MPP-M-D-Poll-5-12.pdf.

82. Jesselyn McCurdy, "ACLU Urges YES Vote on Rohrabacher-Hinchey-McClintock-Farr Amendment to H.R. 5326," American Civil Liberties Union, May 9, 2012, www.aclu.org/files/assets/aclu_vote_recommendation_for_hinchey_rohr_cjs_amend_5-9-12.pdf.

83. "Jimmy Kimmel Confronts Barack Obama on Medical Marijuana Raids—Whitehouse Correspondents Dinner," YouTube, May 4, 2012, www.youtube.com/watch?v=o_qX3G-0yXA.

84. Jacob Sullum, "Bummer: Barack Obama Turns Out to Be Just Another Drug Warrior," *Reason*, October 2011.

85. Tim Dickinson, "Obama's War on Pot," *Rolling Stone*, March 1, 2012.

86. Tim Craig, "Medical Marijuana Dispensary Prepares to Open in D.C.," *Washington Post*, December 31, 2012.

6. PHOENIX

1. John Hoeffel, "Proposition 19: High-Profile Issue, Low-Profile Campaign," *Los Angeles Times*, October 18, 2010.

2. Harry G. Levine, Jon B. Gettman, and Loren Siegel, "Arresting Blacks for Marijuana in California: Possession Arrests, 2006–08." Drug Policy Alliance, LA, October 2010, www.scribd.com/doc/39846781/Arresting-Blacks-for-Marijuana-in-California-Possession-Arrests-2006-08.

3. Text of Proposition 19 submitted to California attorney general's office, July 27, 2009, ag.ca.gov/cms_attachments/initiatives/pdfs/i821_initiative_09-0024_amdt_1-s.pdf.

4. Secretary of State Official Voter Information Guide for November 2, 2010, California general election, entry for Proposition 19, voterguide.sos.ca.gov/past/2010/general/propositions/19.

5. Oaksterdam University, www.oaksterdamuniversity.com.

6. Dan Simon, "Oakland, California, Passes Landmark Marijuana Tax," CNN, July 22, 2009, edition.cnn.com/2009/POLITICS/07/22/california.pot

.tax; League of Women Voters of California Education Fund, Fiscal Impact for Oakland's Measure V in California's 2010 general election, www.smartvoter.org /2010/11/02/ca/alm/meas/V.

7. National Conference of State Legislatures, "Initiative Petition Signature Requirements," April 7, 2010, cdn.ca9.uscourts.gov/datastore/library/2013/02/26 /Angle_Legislatures.pdf.

8. Text of Proposition 19 submitted to California attorney general's office.

9. Stu Woo, "Legal-Pot Backers Split on Timing," *Wall Street Journal*, October 3, 2009.

10. Daniel Okrent, *Last Call: The Rise and Fall of Prohibition* (New York: Scribner, 2010), 328.

11. Assembly Bill 390, California Legislature, February 23, 2009, www.leginfo .ca.gov/pub/09-10/bill/asm/ab_0351-0400/ab_390_bill_20090223_introduced.pdf.

12. Assemblymember Tom Ammiano, "Majority of Californians Now Support Marijuana Legalization," press release, May 4, 2009, www.asmdc.org /members/a17/press-releases/majority-of-californians-now-support-marijuana -legalization; State Board of Equalization Staff Legislative Bill Analysis for AB 390, www.boe.ca.gov/legdiv/pdf/ab0390-1dw.pdf.

13. Mark DiCamillo and Mervin Field, "Release 2306," *Field Poll*, April 30, 2009, media.sacbee.com/smedia/2009/04/29/15/0429rls.source.prod_affiliate.4.pdf.

14. Stoners Against the Prop. 19 Tax Cannabis Initiative, votetaxcannabis 2010.blogspot.com/p/response-to-chris-conrads-missive.html.

15. Letter from U.S. Attorney Melinda Haag to Oakland City Attorney John Russo, February 1, 2011, www.cannabistherapyinstitute.com/legal/feds/doj .haag.memo.pdf.

16. East Bay Alliance for a Sustainable Economy, "The State of Work in the East Bay and Oakland," 2010, www.workingeastbay.org/downloads/State%20of %20Work%20in%20the%20East%20Bay%20and%20Oakland%202012.pdf.

17. Malia Wollan, "Oakland's Plan to Cash in on Marijuana Farms Hits Federal Roadblock," *New York Times*, March 2, 2011.

18. Okrent, *Last Call*, 146.

19. Oaksterdam University, Jeff Jones faculty profile, www.oaksterdamuniversity .com/faculty.html#jjones.

20. Ibid.

21. V. Dion Haynes, "Judge Orders Cannabis Club Closed," *Chicago Tribune*, October 15, 1998.

22. Nate Silver, "The Broadus Effect? Social Desirability Bias and California Proposition 19," *FiveThirtyEight*, July 26, 2010, www.fivethirtyeight.com/2010/07 /broadus-effect-social-desirability-bias.html.

23. Daniel J. Hopkins, "No More Wilder Effect, Never a Whitman Effect: When and Why Polls Mislead about Black and Female Candidates," *Journal of Politics* 71, no. 3 (July 2009): 769–81, doi:10.1017/S0022381609090707.

24. David Downs, "SF Dems Give Key Endorsements to Prop 19," *East Bay Express*, August 12, 2010; Los Angeles Democratic Party, "Endorsements for 2010 General Election," www.lacdp.org/endorsements/endorsements-11210

-statewide-local-elections; Sarah Lovering, "Celebrities Join MPP in Promoting Prop 19," Marijuana Policy Project, blog.mpp.org/tax-and-regulate/celebrities -join-mpp-in-promoting-prop-19/10252010; Secretary of State Official Voter Information Guide for November 2, 2010, California general election, entry for Proposition 19; SEIU, "SEIU California's Positions on the 2010 General Election Ballot Initiatives," draft.seiuca.org/politics/Rebuild_California__SEIU _Voter_Guide.aspx; ACLU, "California ACLU Affiliates Endorse Proposition 19's Move Toward a Rational Marijuana Policy," press release, July 22, 2010, www.aclunc.org/news/press_releases/california_aclu_affiliates_endorse _proposition_19's_move_toward_a_rational_marijuana_policy.shtml; Tom Angell, "National Black Police Association Endorses Marijuana Legalization," press release, Law Enforcement Against Prohibition, August 19, 2010, cops saylegalize.blogspot.com/2010/08/national-black-police-association.html; Subha Ravindhran, "Latino Police Officers Group Endorses Prop. 19," ABC 7 KABC-TV Los Angeles, October 27, 2010, abclocal.go.com/kabc/story?section =news/politics/local_elections&id=7750096; Mark Hinkle, "California Prop 19: Legalized Pot Coming to the California Ballot in November," Libertarian Party, July 3, 2010, www.lp.org/blogs/mark-hinkle/california-prop-19-legalized -pot-coming-to-the-california-ballot-in-november; "Medical Marijuana Patient Advocates Issue Voter Guides for November Elections," press release, Americans for Safe Access, October 26, 2010, safeaccessnow.org/punbb/view topic.php?id=6027.

25. "Proposition 19: The Battle Over Legalizing Marijuana," Los Angeles Times, November 23, 2010, projects.latimes.com/prop19/.

26. Reddit, "Reddit's Official Statement on Prop 19 Ads," reddit blog, August 27, 2010, www.reddit.com/r/blog/comments/d67uj/reddits_official _statement_on_prop_19_ads/.

27. "Proposition 19: The Battle Over Legalizing Marijuana."

28. California Chamber of Commerce, "Questions and Answers About Proposition 19's Impact on the Workplace," www.calchamber.com/pressreleases /documents/qaprop19.pdf.

29. Secretary of State Official Voter Information Guide for November 2, 2010, California general election, entry for Proposition 19.

30. Text of Proposition 19 submitted to California Attorney General's office.

31. Ibid.

32. See League of California Cities, "Learn About Cities," www.cacities.org /Resources/Learn-About-Cities; Secretary of State, "California County Codes," www.sos.ca.gov/business/notary/forms/notary-county-codes.pdf; Beau Kilmer, Jonathan P. Caulkins, Rosalie Liccardo Pacula, Robert J. MacCoun, and Peter H. Reuter, Altered State? Assessing How Marijuana Legalization in California Could Influence Marijuana Consumption and Public Budgets (Santa Monica, CA: Rand, 2010), 48, www.rand.org/content/dam/rand/pubs/occasional_papers/2010 /RAND_OP315.pdf.

33. "Proposition 19: Vote No," editorial, San Francisco Chronicle, September 16, 2010.

34. "Snuff Out Pot Measure," editorial, *Los Angeles Times*, September 24, 2010.

35. Jesse McKinley, "California Reduces Its Penalty for Marijuana," *New York Times*, October 1, 2010.

36. "Holder: Feds Would Enforce Drug Laws if California Legalizes Pot," CNN, October 16, 2010, www.cnn.com/2010/POLITICS/10/15/holder.marijuana/index.html.

37. Nate Silver, "Is Proposition 19 Going Up in Smoke?" *Five Thirty Eight* blog, *New York Times*, October 21, 2010, fivethirtyeight.blogs.nytimes.com/2010/10/21/is-proposition-19-going-up-in-smoke.

38. Peter Hecht, "New Proposition 19 Ad Declares 'War on Marijuana Has Failed,'" *Sacramento Bee*, October 25, 2010.

39. Drug Policy Alliance, "Drug Policy Alliance in California," November 2011, www.drugpolicy.org/sites/default/files/DPA%20in%20California_Nov%202011.pdf.

40. Coalition for Cannabis Policy Reform, "Official Statement of the Yes on Proposition 19 Campaign in Response to Election Results," Facebook, November 2, 2010, www.facebook.com/notes/yes-on-19-control-tax-cannabis-2010/official-statement-of-the-yes-on-proposition-19-campaign-in-response-to-election/172227559455415.

41. Release #2356, *Field Poll*, September 26, 2010, www.field.com/fieldpollonline/subscribers/Rls2356.pdf.

42. Release #2287, *Field Poll*, September 18, 2008, www.field.com/fieldpollonline/subscribers/Rls2287.pdf; Jon Walker, "It Would Be Hard to Get Higher: Prop 19 Has Unprecedented Awareness Among Young CA Voters," *FireDogLake*, September 29, 2010, elections.firedoglake.com/2010/09/29/it-would-be-hard-to-get-higher-prop-19-has-unprecedented-awareness-among-young-ca-voters.

43. Michael D. Shear, "A Petitioning System Goes to Pot, and More," *New York Times*, September 26, 2011; Brendan Sasso, "Petition to Legalize Pot Is First to Hit White House Threshold; ET Proposal Close," *The Hill*, September 22, 2011, thehill.com/blogs/hillicon-valley/technology/183411-marijuana-legalization-first-online-petition-to-require-white-house-response.

44. Frank Newport, "Record-High 50% of Americans Favor Legalizing Marijuana Use," Gallup, October 17, 2011, www.gallup.com/poll/150149/record-high-americans-favor-legalizing-marijuana.aspx.

45. Levi Pulkkinen, "Ex–U.S. Attorney: Time to Change Pot Laws," *Seattle Post-Intelligencer*, November 16, 2009.

46. National Institute on Alcohol Abuse and Alcoholism, "Early Drinking Linked to Higher Lifetime Alcoholism Risk," press release, July 3, 2006, www.niaaa.nih.gov/news-events/news-releases/early-drinking-linked-higher-lifetime-alcoholism-risk; National Institute on Drug Abuse, "Marijuana: Facts Parents Need to Know," March 2011, www.drugabuse.gov/sites/default/files/parents_marijuana_brochure.pdf.

47. Sherry L. Murphy, Jiaquan Xu, and Kenneth D. Kochanek, "Deaths: Final Data for 2010," *National Vital Statistics Report* 61, no. 4 (May 8, 2013), www.cdc.gov/nchs/data/nvsr/nvsr61/nvsr61_04.pdf.

48. University of Colorado Boulder, "CU Student Group Honoring Gordie Bailey with 'Week of Remembrance'" Sept. 12–17," press release, September 11, 2008, www.colorado.edu/news/releases/2008/09/11/cu-student-group-honoring-gordie-bailey-week-remembrance-sept-12-17; Department of Public Relations, Colorado State University, "Colorado State University's Greek Community Implements Alcohol Awareness Programs and Reforms for Greek Life," press release, September 2, 2005, www.news.colostate.edu/Release/1351.

49. "SAFER: 5 Years of Marijuana Reform with Attitude," YouTube, May 17, 2010, www.youtube.com/watch?v=Uhpq6mcDkp0.

50. "Group Fires Up Initiative to Legalize Pot Statewide," *ABC 7 News*, December 28, 2005, www.thedenverchannel.com/news/group-fires-up-initiative-to-legalize-pot-statewide.

51. "Battered Woman Billboard Draws Criticism," *ABC 7 News*, October 14, 2005, www.thedenverchannel.com/news/battered-woman-billboard-draws-criticism.

52. Michael McCollum, "Marijuana Backers Remove Woman's Billboard Photo," *Denver Post*, October 20, 2005.

53. "SAFER: 5 Years of Marijuana Reform with Attitude," YouTube.

54. Christopher N. Osher, "Denver Pot Issue passes by Thin Margin," *Denver Post*, November 2, 2005

55. Stephanie Simon, "Denver Is First City to Legalize Small Amount of Pot," *Los Angeles Times*, November 3, 2005.

56. Yes on 44 billboard, www.picable.com/Concepts/Violence/Marijuana-No-Hangovers-No-Violence-No-Carbs.2948333.

57. "SAFER: 5 Years of Marijuana Reform with Attitude," YouTube.

58. Joel Warner, "Mason Tvert and Brian Vicente's Plan to Legalize Colorado Pot in 2012," *Latest Word* blog, *Denver Westword*, November 25, 2009, blogs.westword.com/latestword/2009/11/mason_tvert_and_brian_vicentes.php.

59. Ibid.

60. Mark Baldassare, Dean Bonner, Sonja Petek, and Nicole Willcoxon, "Statewide Survey: Californians and Their Government," Public Policy Institute of California, December 2010, www.ppic.org/content/pubs/survey/S_1210MBS.pdf.

61. Franjo Grotenhermen, Gero Leson, Günter Berghaus, et al., "Developing Science-Based Per Se Limits for Driving Under the Influence of Cannabis (DUIC)," *DUIC Report*, September 2005, www.canorml.org/healthfacts/DUIC report.2005.pdf.

62. Renée Johnson, "Hemp as an Agricultural Commodity," Congressional Research Service Report, December 22, 2010; Hemp Industries Association, "As Momentum Builds for Policy Change, U.S. Market for Products Made from Industrial Hemp Continues to Thrive," press release, February 25, 2013, www.thehia.org/PR/PDF/2013-02-25-hia_$500_million_annual_sales.pdf.

63. Text of Initiative 502, sos.wa.gov/_assets/elections/initiatives/i502.pdf; Text of Amendment 64, www.leg.state.co.us/LCS/Initiative%20Referendum/1112 initrefr.nsf/c63bddd6b9678de787257799006bd391/cfa3bae60c8b4949872579

c7006fa7ee/$FILE/Amendment%2064%20-%20Use%20&%20Regulation%20of
%20Marijuana.pdf.

64. Clare Pramuk, "Fiscal Impact Statement for Amendment 64," Colorado
Legislative Council Staff, September 18, 2012, www.colorado.gov/cs/Satellite
?blobcol=urldata&blobheader=application%2Fpdf&blobkey=id&blobtable
=MungoBlobs&blobwhere=1251821710778&ssbinary=true; Washington Office of
Financial Management, "Fiscal Impact Statement for Initiative 502," August 10,
2012, www.ofm.wa.gov/initiatives/2012/502_fiscal_impact.pdf.

65. Jonathan P. Caulkins, Angela Hawken, Beau Kilmer, and Mark Kleiman,
"A Voter's Guide to Legalizing Marijuana," *American Interest*, November/
December 2012.

66. Christopher Stiffler, "Amendment 64 Would Produce $60 Million in
New Revenue and Savings for Colorado," Colorado Center on Law and Policy,
August 16, 2012, www.cclponline.org/postfiles/amendment_64_analysis_final.pdf.

67. Washington Office of Financial Management, "Fiscal Impact Statement
for Initiative 502."

68. Ibid.

69. Eli Stokols, "Petition Drive Begins to Legalize Marijuana in Colorado,"
KDVR Fox 31, July 7, 2011, www.regulatemarijuana.org/news/video-kdvr-fox-31
-petition-drive-begins-legalize-marijuana-colorado.

70. Campaign to Regulate Marijuana Like Alcohol, "Petition Drive Central,"
www.regulatemarijuana.org/s/petition-drive-central.

71. Nina Sparano, "Retired Cop and Former Judge Support Marijuana
Initiative," *KDVR Fox 31*, August 3, 2011, www.regulatemarijuana.org/news
/video-kdvr-fox-31-retired-cop-and-former-judge-support-marijuana-initiative.

72. ACLU of Colorado, "ACLU Joins Campaign to Regulate Marijuana Like
Alcohol," September 14, 2011, aclu-co.org/news/aclu-joins-campaign-to-regulate
-marijuana-like-alcohol.

73. Tom Jensen, "Colorado Miscellaneous," Public Policy Polling, August 11,
2011, publicpolicypolling.blogspot.com/2011/08/colorado-miscellaneous.html.

74. Campaign to Regulate Marijuana Like Alcohol, "Having a 'Marijuana'
Conversation," www.regulatemarijuana.org/s/having-marijuana-conversation.

75. Campaign to Regulate Marijuana Like Alcohol, "The Initiative Has
Qualified for the November Ballot!" February 27, 2012, www.regulatemarijuana
.org/news/initiative-has-qualified-november-ballot.

76. Gene Johnson, "Activists: New Legal Pot Push Calibrated to Voters,"
KOMO News, June 22, 2011, www.komonews.com/news/local/124377394.html
?tab=video&c=y.

77. "Legalize Marijuana in Washington State," editorial, *Seattle Times*,
June 22, 2011.

78. Joel Connelly, "State Dems: Legalize Marijuana," *Seattle Post-Intelligencer*,
September 18, 2011.

79. Curtis Cartier, "New Approach Washington, Pot-Legalization Effort,
Get Huge Cash Infusion—Rival Effort Promises to Fight with New Initiative,"
Seattle Weekly, November 2, 2011.

80. "King 5 Poll: The Key Support for Legalizing Marijuana? Baby Boomers," *King 5 News*, November 23, 2011, makupfront.tumblr.com/post/13219159166 /king-5-poll-the-key-support-for-legalizing-marijuana.

81. Jim Camden, "Lawmakers to Consider Pot Initiative," *Spokesman-Review*, January 27, 2012.

82. See Kirk Johnson, "Marijuana Push in Colorado Likens It to Alcohol," *New York Times*, January 26, 2012; Alex Dobuzinskis, "Pot Legalization Efforts Forge Ahead in Key States," Reuters, January 31, 2012, www.reuters.com /article/2012/01/31/us-usa-marijuana-legalization-idUSTRE80U1Q220120131.

83. See Jake Ellison, "Seattle Mayor: Legalize Marijuana So We Can Stop Crime," *KPIU 88.5*, February 21, 2012, www.kplu.org/post/seattle-mayor -legalize-marijuana-so-we-can-stop-crime; M.L. King County Labor Council, "Resolutions for 2012 Election," January 20, 2012, www.mlkclc.org/docs /Resolutions%202012.pdf; Jonathan Martin, "Sixteen State Lawmakers Endorse Marijuana-Legalization Initiative," *Seattle Times*, May 2, 2012; Nina Shapiro, "Black Pastors Endorse I-502 Despite Controversy in African American Community," *Seattle Weekly*, June 14, 2012; Alison Holcomb, "NAACP Alaska, Oregon and Washington State-Area Conference Endorses Initiative 502 to Legalize, Tax, and Regulate Marijuana for Adults," press release, New Approach Washington, August 24, 2012, www.newapproachwa.org/sites/newapproach wa.org/files/I-502%20Press%20Release%C2%A0%E2%80%93%20NAACP %20AOW%20S-AC%20-%20Logo.pdf; "Women's Rights Organization Endorses Washington's Marijuana-Legalization Initiative," *Bainbridge Island Review*, August 28, 2012.

84. American Civil Liberties Union of Washington State, "What Is Your County Spending on Marijuana Law Enforcement?" www.aclu-wa.org/what -your-county-spending-marijuana-law-enforcement.

85. Jonathan Martin, "Children's Alliance Backs Pot Measure on Ballot," *Seattle Times*, September 10, 2012.

86. Talk It Up, www.talkitupcolorado.org/about.

87. Campaign to Regulate Marijuana Like Alcohol, "Campaign Billboard Stirs Conversation—Take Action to Keep It Going!" April 6, 2012, www .regulatemarijuana.org/news/campaign-billboard-stirs-conversation-%E2%80 %93-take-action-keep-it-going.

88. Campaign to Regulate Marijuana Like Alcohol, "Campaign Runs First TV as, 'Dear Mom,' Just in Time for Mother's Day," May 10, 2012, www.regulate marijuana.org/news/campaign-runs-first-tv-ad-dear-mom-just-time-mothers -day-1.

89. Campaign to Regulate Marijuana Like Alcohol, "'Dear Dad' Web Video Launched Just in Time for Father's Day," June 15, 2012, www.regulatemarijuana .org/news/watch-dear-dad-web-video-launched-just-time-fathers-day.

90. Campaign to Regulate Marijuana Like Alcohol, "Moms and Dads for Marijuana Regulation Post YES on 64 Billboard," June 28, 2012, www .regulatemarijuana.org/news/moms-and-dads-marijuana-regulation-post-yes-64 -billboard.

91. Libertarian Party of Colorado, "Amendment 64—Campaign to Regulate Marijuana Like Alcohol," lpcolorado.org/amendment-64-campaign-to-regulate -marijuana-like-alcohol.

92. Republican Liberty Caucus of Colorado, "Statement of Support for Amendment 64," October 2, 2012, rlccolorado.com/2012/10/02/statement-of -support-for-amendment-64/.

93. Campaign to Regulate Marijuana Like Alcohol, "Tom Tancredo: Marijuana Prohibition Has Failed Us," reprinted from *Colorado Springs Gazette*, September 21, 2012, www.regulatemarijuana.org/tancredo.

94. Jonathan Martin, "Little Organized Opposition to Marijuana-Legalization Initiative," *Seattle Times*, October 4, 2012.

95. "States Consider Moving Beyond Medical Marijuana," *USA Today*, October 24, 2012.

96. Sensible Washington, "Deconstructing I-502: Opposition In Summary," October 10, 2012, sensiblewashington.org/blog/2012/deconstructing-i-502-part -8-opposition-in-summary/.

97. Maggie Clark, "A Marijuana Revolt?" *Stateline* blog, Pew Charitable Trusts, September 7, 2012, www.pewstates.org/projects/stateline/headlines/a -marijuana-revolt-85899415933.

98. "Get Real About Initiative to Legalize Marijuana," editorial, *Seattle Times*, August 20, 2012.

99. Joel Connelly, "Gay Marriage, Marijuana Well Ahead in Poll," *Seattle Post-Intelligencer*, October 5, 2012.

100. Jonathan Martin, "Marijuana Initiative 502 a Tough Sell in Eastern Washington," *Seattle Times*, October 24, 2012.

101. Ibid.

102. New Approach Washington, "Television Ads," www.newapproachwa.org /page/television-ads.

103. Public Policy Polling, "WA-Gov a Toss Up, Obama and Gay Marriage Well Ahead," November 3, 2012, www.publicpolicypolling.com/pdf/2011/PPP _Release_WA_1103.pdf.

104. "Ken Buck Leading Smart Colorado, Group Opposed to Marijuana Legalizing Initiative Amendment 64," *Huffington Post*, June 12, 2012, www .huffingtonpost.com/2012/06/11/ken-buck-smart-co-marijuana_n_1590035.html.

105. John Ingold, "Parts of Colorado's Pot Legalization Strategy Exported to Other States," *Denver Post*, December 29, 2012.

106. Lee Fang, "GOP Mogul Behind Drug Rehab 'Torture' Centers Is Bankrolling Opposition to Pot Legalization in Colorado," *The Nation*, September 18, 2012. www.thenation.com/blog/170007/gop-mogul-behind-drug -rehab-torture-centers-bankrolling-opposition-pot-legalization-colo.

107. Carla Rivera, "Parents Protest Straight's Fate: Substance Abuse: Dozens Demonstrate Anger at State's Denial of License for Controversial Youth Treatment Program," *Los Angeles Times*, November 2, 1990.

108. "Gov. Hickenlooper Opposes Amendment 64," September 12, 2012, www.colorado.gov/cs/Satellite?c=Page&childpagename=GovHickenlooper%2FCBONLayout&cid=1251630730489&pagename=CBONWrapper.

109. "No On 64: Governors Bill Ritter and Bill Owens," YouTube, October 16, 2012, www.youtube.com/watch?v=bD5Cv4b0W04.

110. Campaign to Regulate Marijuana Like Alcohol, "Campaign to Regulate Marijuana Like Alcohol Responds to Gov. Hickenlooper's Statement in Opposition to Amendment 64," Septmeber 12, 2012, www.regulatemarijuana.org/s/campaign-regulate-marijuana-alcohol-responds-gov-hickenloopers-statement-opposition-amendment-64.

111. Michael Roberts, "Marijuana: Amendment 64 Camp Prefers Deal to Suing over Blue Book Language," *Latest Word* blog, *Denver Westword*, September 11, 2012, blogs.westword.com/latestword/2012/09/marijuana_amendment_64_blue_book_deal.php.

112. "Editorial: Panel Erred in Blue Book Edits," *Denver Post*, September 11, 2012.

113. "Editorial: Amendment 64 Is the Wrong Way to Legalize Marijuana," *Denver Post*, October 14, 2012.

114. John Ingold, "Colorado Business, Labor Leaders Differ Over Marijuana Legalization," *Denver Post*, October 16, 2012.

115. "Pot Legalization Proponents, Opponents Gather at Convention Center," *CBS 4 Denver*, October 15, 2012, denver.cbslocal.com/2012/10/15/pot-legalization-proponents-opponents-gather-at-convention-center.

116. Campaign to Regulate Marijuana Like Alcohol, "UFCW Local 7—Colorado's Largest Union—Joins Statewide Organizations in Endorsing Amendment 64," October 15, 2012, www.regulatemarijuana.org/news/ufcw-local-7-%E2%80%93%C2%A0colorados-largest-union-%E2%80%93%C2%A0joins-statewide-organizations-endorsing-amendment-64.

117. Alex Dobuzinskis, "Eric Holder Urged to Oppose Marijuana Ballots by Ex-DEA Heads," *Huffington Post*, September 7, 2012, www.huffingtonpost.com/2012/09/07/eric-holder-marijuana_n_1866384.html.

118. See "Pot Legalization Campaign Has Bullitt's Backing," *Wenatchee World*, November 2, 2011; John Ingold, "Marijuana Legalization's Aftermath: State Must Set Regulations," *Denver Post*, November 9, 2012; Ingold, "Parts of Colorado's Pot Legalization Strategy Exported to Other States."

119. "Colorado Legalizes Marijuana with Prop 64 Part 1 of 2," November 7, 2012, YouTube, www.youtube.com/watch?v=yFeb5UtutNY; "Colorado Legalizes Marijuana with Prop 64 Part 2 of 2," November 7, 2012, YouTube, www.youtube.com/watch?v=hoDSZE6Bzj0.

7. A NEW LEAF

1. Daniel Okrent, *Last Call: The Rise and Fall of Prohibition* (New York: Scribner, 2010), 252, 242;

2. William Breathes, "Marijuana: Boulder DA Drops Pot, Paraphernalia

Cases Due to Amendment 64's Passage," *Latest Word* blog, *Denver Westword*, November 14, 2012, blogs.westword.com/latestword/2012/11/marijuana_boulder _district_attorney_dropping_pot_cases_amendment_64.php; Valerie Richardson; "Pot Smokers' Outlook Still Hazy After Colorado Legalization Vote," *Washington Times*, November 27, 2012.

3. Kurtis Lee and Yesenia Robles, "Denver Joins Boulder in Dropping Prosecution of Limited Pot Possession," *Denver Post*, November 15, 2012.

4. Levi Pulkkinen, "Satterberg Dismisses All Misemeanor Marijuana Cases," *Seattle Post-Intelligencer*, November 9, 2012.

5. Jonah Spangenthal-Lee, "Marijwhatnow? A Guide to Legal Marijuana Use in Seattle," SPD Blotter, November 9, 2012, spdblotter.seattle.gov/2012/11 /09/marijwhatnow-a-guide-to-legal-marijuana-use-in-seattle.

6. Jonah Spangenthal-Lee, "Officers Shall Not Take Any Enforcement Action—Other Than to Issue a Verbal Warning—for a Violation of I-502," SPD Blotter, December 5, 2012, spdblotter.seattle.gov/2012/12/05/officers-shall -not-take-any-enforcement-action-other-than-to-issue-a-verbal-warning-for-a -violation-of-i-502.

7. Anica Padilla, "Strong Smell of Marijuana Reported Inside Colorado Capitol Wednesday Morning," *ABC 7 News*, February 13, 2013, www.the denverchannel.com/news/local-news/strong-smell-of-marijuana-reported-inside -colorado-capitol-wednesday-morning.

8. Vicky Uhland, "Marijuana: The Truth About Growing Your Own Pot," *Denver Post*, February 22, 2013.

9. The following sources relate to cannabis clubs in Colorado soon after Amendment 64 passed: Jim Spellman, "Pot Activists Divided Over New Cannabis Club," CNN, January 2, 2013, www.cnn.com/2013/01/01/us/colorado-marijuana-club/index.html; Bryce Crawford, "Colorado Springs Pot Delivery Stretches the Law," *Colorado Springs Independent*, January 30, 2013; John Ingold, "Colorado's First Marijuana Den Shut Down in Landlord Dispute," *Denver Post*, January 1, 2013; William Breathes, "Pot Clubs/Cannabis Cafes Drawing Crowds," *Latest Word* blog, *Denver Westword*, January 16, 2013, blogs.westword .com/latestword/2013/01/pot_clubs_cannabis_cafes_colorado.php.

10. Bob Young, "Inslee Pushes Liquor Board to Stop Spread of 'Pot Bars,'" *Seattle Times*, March 31, 2013.

11. Jonathan Martin, "Groups Seek to Influence New Rules for Growing, Selling Pot," *Seattle Times*, January 6, 2013.

12. Dominic Holden, "The Messy Reality of Legal Pot," *The Stranger*, January 30, 2013.

13. "Gov. Hickenlooper Signs Amendment 64 Proclamation, Creates Task Force to Recommend Needed Legislative Actions," press release, December 10, 2012, www.colorado.gov/cs/Satellite/GovHickenlooper/CBON/1251634887823.

14. Amendment 64 Implementation Task Force Regulatory Framework Working Group, "Minutes of Meeting," January 3, 2013, www.colorado.gov/cs /Satellite?blobcol=urldata&blobheader=application%2Fpdf&blobkey=id&blob table=MungoBlobs&blobwhere=1251848595205&ssbinary=true.

15. 2013 Joint Select Committee on the Implementation of A64 Task Force Recommendations, www.colorado.gov/cs/Satellite?c=Page&childpagename =CGA-LegislativeCouncil%2FCLCLayout&cid=1251640377831&pagename =CLCWrapper.

16. Tweets from the Twitter accounts of John Ingold (@john_ingold), *Denver Post* reporter, and Kristen Wyatt (@APkristenwyatt), Associated Press reporter, beginning in mid-December 2012 through late February 2013.

17. Hana Kim, "Hundreds Pack City Hall with Questions, Advice Over New Pot Law," *KHBQ Fox 13*, January 24, 2013, q13fox.com/2013/01/24/hundeds-pack -seattle-city-hall-with-questions-over-new-pot-law/.

18. "Cannabis Legalization: I-502 Open Forum 2—Seattle Washington, 01 /24/2013 PT 1 of 2," YouTube, February 16, 2013, www.youtube.com/watch?v =Ow3vKRmCNjw.

19. Associated Press, "450 Attend Marijuana Forum in Spokane," *Seattle Times*, February 13, 2013.

20. Pierre Klochendler, "Some Take Cannabis Illicitly, Israelis Take It Seriously," Inter Press Service News Agency, December 15, 2012, www.ipsnews .net/2012/12/some-take-cannabis-illicitly-israelis-take-it-seriously.

21. Health Canada Medical Use of Marihuana: http://www.hc-sc.gc.ca/dhp -mpo/marihuana/index-eng.php.

22. Agence France-Presse, "Czech Pharmacies Begin Selling Medical Marijuana," *Raw Story*, April 2, 2013, www.rawstory.com/rs/2013/04/02/czech -pharmacies-begin-selling-medical-marijuana.

23. Information about Bedrocan, www.bedrocan.nl/english/home.html.

24. Earl Bluemenauer and Jared Polis, "The Path Forward: Rethinking Federal Marijuana Policy," 2013, polis.house.gov/uploadedfiles/the_path_forward.pdf.

25. Todd Garvey and Brian T. Yeh, "State Legalization of Recreational Marijuana: Selected Legal Issues," Congressional Research Service Report, April 5, 2013, www.fas.org/sgp/crs/misc/R43034.pdf .

26. "LEAP Stumps the Drug Czar," YouTube, June 24, 2009, www.youtube .com/watch?v=gMwszvAgQeg.

27. "Support a Law Protecting States' Rights to Legalize, Regulate and Tax Marijuana like Alcohol," White House We the People petition, petitions .whitehouse.gov/petition/support-law-protecting-states-rights-legalize-regulate -and-tax-marijuana-alcohol/QBDs6Gkk?utm_source=wh.gov&utm_medium =shorturl&utm_campaign=shorturl.

28. Ibid.

29. Rachel Weiner, "Obama: I've Got 'Bigger Fish to Fry' Than Smokers," *Washington Post*, December 14, 2012.

30. Jonathan Martin, "Justice Department: Federal Marijuana Law 'Unchanged by Legalization,'" *Seattle Times*, November 7, 2012; Charles Ashby, "State Confronts Haze of Questions After Voters Make Marijuana Legal," *Daily Sentinel* (Grand Junction, CO), November 8, 2012.

31. Sadie Gurman, "Coloradoans Say Yes to Recreational Use of Marijuana," *Denver Post*, November 6, 2012.

32. Kurtis Lee, "DeGette Files Bill to Require Feds to Respect Marijuana Law," *Denver Post*, November 16, 2012.

33. Michael Roberts, "Marijuana: Eighteen Legislators Ask Feds to Respect Colorado's Amendment 64," *Latest Word* blog, *Denver Westword*, November 19, 2012, blogs.westword.com/latestword/2012/11/marijuana_amendment_64_letter_federal_government_respect_pot_laws.php.

34. Congressman Jared Polis, "Polis, Colleagues Urge Feds to Respect State Marijuana Laws," press release, November 16, 2012, polis.house.gov/news/documentsingle.aspx?DocumentID=312490.

35. Josh Felt, "Inslee on Pot," *Seattle Met*, November 14, 2012.

36. "State to Feds: We'll Be Ready If You Sue Over Legalized Pot," *Spin Control* blog, *Spokesman-Review* (Spokane, WA), January, 22, 2013, www.spokesman.com/blogs/spincontrol/2013/jan/22/state-feds-well-be-ready-if-you-sue-over-legalized-pot/.

37. John W. Suthers, "Attorney General Statement on Passage of Amendment 64, November 7, 2012," press release, November 7, 2012, www.coloradoattorneygeneral.gov/press/news/2012/11/07/attorney_general_releases_statement_passage_amendment_64.

38. Bob Young, "Inslee Assures Feds on Pot: We'll Do It Right," *Today File* blog, *Seattle Times*, February 14, 2013, blogs.seattletimes.com/today/2013/02/inslee-assures-feds-on-pot-well-do-it-right/.

39. Bob Young, "Inslee Encouraged by Marijuana Talk with Attorney General Holder," *Seattle Times*, January 22, 2013.

40. Frederic J. Frommer, "Holder: Marijuana's Effect on Children a Factor," *Denver Post*, April 18, 2013.

41. Sam Levin, "Marijuana: Project SAM, Anti-Legalization Group, Launches Colorado Chapter, Mason Tvert Attacks," *Latest Word* blog, *Denver Westword*, January 10, 2013, blogs.westword.com/latestword/2013/01/marjiuana_project_sam_colorado_chapter_mason_tvert.php.

42. Mike Riggs, "Patrick Kennedy's Anti-Pot Crusade Conflicts with His Own Congressional Record," *Reason*, February 13, 2013.

43. "Patrick Kennedy on Marijuana: 'Destroys the Brain and Expedites Psychosis,'" *Reliable Source* blog, *Washington Post*, January 8, 2013, www.washingtonpost.com/blogs/reliable-source/post/patrick-kennedy-on-marijuana-destroys-the-brain-and-expedites-psychosis/2013/01/08/795a20ae-59e3-11e2-88d0-c4cf65c3ad15_blog.html.

44. Project SAM letter to Attorney General Eric Holder, February 7, 2013, learnaboutsam.com/wp-content/uploads/2013/02/feb-kennedy-letter-doj.pdf.

45. "Statement of the Government of the United States of America World Federation Against Drugs," 3rd World Forum, delivered by R. Gil Kerlikowske, director of U.S. National Drug Control Policy, May 21, 2012, www.whitehouse.gov/ondcp/news-releases-remarks/principles-of-modern-drug-policy-directors-remarks-at-the-world-federation-against-drugs.

46. Project SAM, learnaboutsam.com/a-real-conversation-about-pot/.

47. Ibid.

48. Project SAM views on marijuana and tobacco, learnaboutsam.com/mari
juana-is-like-tobacco; Project SAM view on legal reforms, learnaboutsam.com
/legal-reform-3/.

49. David Frum, "David Frum on the Perils of Legalizing Pot," *Daily Beast,*
December 17, 2012, www.thedailybeast.com/newsweek/2012/12/16/david-frum
-on-the-perils-of-legalizing-pot.html.

50. David Frum, "Be Afraid of Big Marijuana," CNN Opinion, September 10, 2013, www.cnn.com/2013/09/10/opinion/frum-big-marijuana-cv/; David
Frum, "Marijuana Use Is Too Risky a Choice," CNN, January 7, 2013, www.cnn
.com/2013/01/07/opinion/frum-marijuana-risk/index.html.

51. Todd Garvey and Brian T. Yeh, "State Legalization of Recreational Marijuana: Selected Legal Issues," Congressional Research Service Report, April 5,
2013, www.fas.org/sgp/crs/misc/R43034.pdf. For more information about cannabis-
related legislation in the House of Representatives, please see H.R. 710: Truth in
Trials Act, www.govtrack.us/congress/bills/113/hr710; H.R. 501: Marijuana Tax
Equity Act of 2013, www.govtrack.us/congress/bills/113/hr501; H.R. 964: Respect
States' and Citizens' Rights Act of 2013, www.govtrack.us/congress/bills/113
/hr964; H.R. 1523: Respect State Marijuana Laws Act of 2013, www.govtrack
.us/congress/bills/113/hr1523/text; H.R. 1635: National Commission on Federal
Marijuana Policy Act of 2013, www.govtrack.us/congress/bills/113/hr1635.

52. H.R. 499: Ending Federal Marijuana Prohibition Act of 2013, www
.govtrack.us/congress/bills/113/hr499.

53. Representative Earl Blumenauer, "Blumenauer Introduces States'
Medical Marijuana Patient Protection Act," press release, February 25, 2013,
blumenauer.house.gov/index.php?option=com_content&task=view&id=2177
&Itemid=73.

54. Congressman Steve Cohen, "Cohen Introduces Bill to Create National
Commission on Federal Marijuana Policy," press release, April 18, 2013, cohen
.house.gov/press-release/cohen-introduces-bill-create-national-commission
-federal-marijuana-policy.

55. Jake Ellison, "Pot and Politics: Meet the Anti-Prohibition Warrior from
Tennessee," *The Pot* blog, *Seattle Post-Intelligencer,* May 19, 2013, blog.seattlepi
.com/marijuana/2013/05/19/pot-politics-meet-the-anti-prohibition-warrior-from
-tennessee.

56. "Senator Leahy Address," Georgetown Law, January 16, 2013, apps.law
.georgetown.edu/webcasts/eventDetail.cfm?eventID=1914.

57. Electra Draper, "House Minority Leader Nancy Pelosi Talks Budget,
Guns, Pot in Denver," *Denver Post,* March 11, 2013.

58. Trip Gabriel, "Hemp Growing Finds Allies of a New Stripe in Kentucky,"
New York Times, February 12, 2013.

59. U.S. Conference of Mayors, Resolution Number 32, 2013, americansfor
safeaccess.org/downloads/Resolution_US_Mayors_Conference_2013.pdf.

60. New York State Assembly Bill A6716A, assembly.state.ny.us/leg/?default
_fld=&bn=A06716&term=2013&Summary=Y&Memo=Y&Text=Y.

61. Associated Press, "100 Entertainers Ask Obama to Change Drug, Jail Policy," Fox News, April 9, 2013, www.foxnews.com/entertainment/2013/04/09 /100-entertainers-ask-obama-to-change-drug-jail-policy.

62. Bill Keller, "How to Legalize Pot," New York Times, May 19, 2013.

63. Henry Alford, "Sending Out Smoke Signals," New York Times, February 22, 2013.

64. Criminal Justice Information Services Division, "Crime in the United States, 2011," Federal Bureau of Investigation, U.S. Department of Justice, www.fbi.gov/about-us/cjis/ucr/crime-in-the-u.s/2011/crime-in-the-u.s.-2011 /persons-arrested/persons-arrested.

65. Kelly Chen, "A Quick Guide to Our Map of Drugs Seized Near the Border," Center for Investigative Reporting, June 20, 2013, cironline.org/blog/ post/quick-guide-our-map-drugs-seized-near-border-4741.

66. "Q&A: Gil Kerlikowske 'I've Ended the War on Drugs,'" National Journal, May 28, 2009, www.nationaljournal.com/njonline/-i-ve-ended-the-war-on-drugs --20090528.

67. "White House National Drug Control Budget FY 2014 Funding Highlights," April 2013, www.whitehouse.gov/sites/default/files/ondcp/policy -and-research/fy_2014_drug_control_budget_highlights_3.pdf.

68. Ronald Reagan: "Radio Address to the Nation on Federal Drug Policy," American Presidency Project, University of California, Santa Barbara, October 2, 1982, www.presidency.ucsb.edu/ws/?pid=43085.

69. "National Drug Control Strategy FY 2001 Budget Summary," Office of National Drug Control Policy, February 2000, www.ncjrs.gov/ondcppubs /publications/policy/budget00/budget2000.pdf.

70. Joseph B. Treaster, "Clinton Continues Old Drug Policies," New York Times, April 12, 1993; "National Drug Control Strategy FY 2001 Budget Summary."

71. "National Drug Control Strategy FY 2009 Budget Summary," Office of National Drug Control Policy, February 2008, www.whitehouse.gov/sites/default /files/ondcp/policy-and-research/fy09budget_0.pdf.

72. "President Signs Drug-Free Communities Reauthorization Bill," CNN, December 14, 2001, transcripts.cnn.com/TRANSCRIPTS/0112/14/se.01.html.

73. Allison North Jones, "Strong Views on Ads Linking Drug Use to Terrorism," New York Times, April 2, 2002.

74. Michael F. Walther, "Insanity: Four Decades of U.S. Counterdrug Strategy," Carlisle Papers, Strategic Studies Institute, December 27, 2012, www .strategicstudiesinstitute.army.mil/pubs/display.cfm?pubid=1143.

75. New Yorker cartoon, www.condenaststore.com/-sp/Gentlemen-the-fact -that-all-my-horses-and-all-my-men-couldn-t-put-Humpty-New-Yorker-Cartoon -Prints_i8640841_.htm.

76. "82% Say U.S. Is Not Winning War on Drugs," Rasmussen Reports, August 18, 2013, www.rasmussenreports.com/public_content/lifestyle/general _lifestyle/november_2012/7_think_u_s_is_winning_war_on_drugs.

77. See "Drug War Today," *The House I Live In*, www.thehouseilivein.org /get-involved/drug-war-today; Associated Press, "AP Impact: After 40 Years, $1 Trillion, US War on Drugs Has Failed to Meet Any of Its Goals," Fox News, March 13, 2010, www.foxnews.com/world/2010/05/13/ap-impact-years-trillion -war-drugs-failed-meet-goals; International Centre for Prison Studies, "Entire World—Prison Population Totals," www.prisonstudies.org/info/worldbrief/wpb _stats.php?area=all&category=wb_poptotal.

78. Katrina vanden Heuvel, "Time to End the War on Drugs," *Washington Post*, November 20, 2012.

79. Lauren E. Glaze and Erika Parks, "Correctional Populations in the United States, 2011," Bureau of Justice Statistics, November 2012, bjs.gov/content/pub /pdf/cpus11.pdf.

80. E. Ann Carson and William J. Sabol, "Prisoners in 2011," Bureau of Justice Statistics, December 2012, www.bjs.gov/content/pub/pdf/p11.pdf.

81. Nathan James, "The Federal Prison Population Buildup: Overview, Policy Changes, Issues, and Options," Congressional Research Service Report, January 22, 2013, www.fas.org/sgp/crs/misc/R42937.pdf.

82. American Civil Liberties Union, "The War on Marijuana in Black and White: Billions of Dollars Wasted on Racially Biased Arrests," June 2013, www .aclu.org/files/assets/061413 mj report rfs rel4.pdf.

83. National Institute on Drug Abuse, "DrugFacts: Nationwide Trends," www.drugabuse.gov/publications/drugfacts/nationwide-trends.

84. International Narcotics Control Board, "Annual Report, 2012," www .incb.org/documents/Publications/AnnualReports/AR2012/AR_2012_E_ Chapter_II.pdf.

85. Ari Rosmarin and Niamh Eastwood, *A Quiet Revolution: Drug Decriminalisation Policies in Practice Across the Globe* (London: Release, 2012), www.opensocietyfoundations.org/sites/default/files/release-quiet-revolution -drug-decriminalisation-policies-20120709.pdf.

86. Global Initiative for Drug Policy Reform, "Uruguay," Beckley Foundation, reformdrugpolicy.com/beckley-main-content/new-approaches/future-directions -for-drug-policy-reform/latin-america/uruguay.

87. Drug Policy Alliance, "José 'Pepe' Mujica: 'Someone Has to Clear the Cuckoos from Marijuana,'" February 2, 2013, www.drugpolicy.org/resource/jos %C3%A9-pepe-mujica-someone-has-clear-cuckoos-marijuana.

88. Mark P. Sullivan, "Latin America and the Caribbean: Key Issues for the 113th Congress," Congressional Research Service Report, February 8, 2013, www.fas.org/sgp/crs/row/R42956.pdf.

89. Dario Lopez, Garance Burke, Frank Bajak et al., "U.S. Military Expands Its Drug War in Latin America," *USA Today*, February 3, 2013.

90. Tim Padgett, "Mexico's Narco-Epiphany: Is Calderón Suggesting the U.S. Legalize Drugs?" *Time*, August 30, 2011.

91. "Legal Marijuana? New Domestic and International Initiatives Challenge the Status Quo," Brookings Institution, October 3, 2012, www.brookings.edu

/~/media/events/2012/10/03%20legal%20marijuana/20121003_legal_marijuana
.pdf; Patrick Radden Keefe, "Cocaine Incorporated," *New York Times Magazine*,
June 15, 2012.

92. On Loera, see *Forbes*'s Powerful People: December 2012 profile, www
.forbes.com/profile/joaquin-guzman-loera.

93. Clare Ribando Seelke and Kristin M. Finklea, "U.S.-Mexican Security
Cooperation: The Mérida Initiative and Beyond," Congressional Research
Service Report, June 12, 2013, www.fas.org/sgp/crs/row/R41349.pdf.

94. George Murkin, "Latin American Leaders Call on the UN to Explore
Alternatives to the War on Drugs," Count the Costs, August 8, 2012, www.count
thecosts.org/blog/latin-american-leaders-call-un-explore-alternatives-war-drugs.

95. Jamie Doward, "Colombian President Calls for Global Rethink on
Drugs," *The Guardian*, November 12, 2011.

96. Otto Pérez Molina, "We Have to Find New Solutions to Latin America's
Drug Nightmare," *The Guardian*, April 7, 2012.

97. Scenario Team Appointed by the Organization of American States,
Scenarios for the Drug Problem in the Americas, 2013–2025 (Washington, DC:
Organization of American States, 2013), www.druglawreform.info/images/stories
/documents/OAS-Report_Scenarios-for-the-drug-problem-in-the-Americas.pdf.

98. Human Rights Watch, "Americas: Decriminalize Personal Use of Drugs,"
June 4, 2013, www.hrw.org/news/2013/06/04/americas-decriminalize-personal
-use-drugs.

99. Pew Research Center for the People & the Press, "Majority Now Supports
Legalizing Marijuana," April 4, 2013, www.people-press.org/2013/04/04/majority
-now-supports-legalizing-marijuana/.

100. Wiebke Hollersen, "'This Is Working': Portugal, 12 Years after Decrimi-
nalizing Drugs," *Spiegel Online*, March 27, 2013, www.spiegel.de/international
/europe/evaluating-drug-decriminalization-in-portugal-12-years-later-a-891060
-2.html.

101. Mario Canseco, "Most Americans and Canadians Are Ready to Legalize
Marijuana," Angus Reid Public Opinion, November 29, 2012, www.angus-reid
.com/polls/47901/most-americans-and-canadians-are-ready-to-legalize-marijuana.

102. "Illicit Drugs Represent Roadblock to Rule of Law and Democracy, Says
UN Official," UN News Centre, March 11, 2013, www.un.org/apps/news/story
.asp?NewsID=44333.

103. UN General Assembly, Twentieth Special Session, "World Drug
Problem," June 8–10, 1998, www.un.org/ga/20special.

104. Joseph Goldstein, "Judge Rejects New York's Stop-and-Frisk Policy," *New
York Times*, August 12, 2013.

105. "Attorney General Eric Holder Delivers Remarks at the Annual Meeting
of the American Bar Association's House of Delegates," San Francisco, August 12,
2013, www.justice.gov/iso/opa/ag/speeches/2013/ag-speech-130812.html.

106. James M. Cole, "Memorandum for All United States Attorneys," August 29, 2013, www.justice.gov/iso/opa/resources/3052013829132756857467.pdf.